PERSIAN LITERATURE

PERSIAN LITERATURE

CLAUD FIELD

SHUBHI PUBLICATIONS

GURGAON — INDIA

Published by

SHUBHI PUBLICATIONS

LG-5, Grand Mall, M.G. Road,
Gurgaon-122 002. (Haryana) - India
Phone : 95-124-4081199 / 4088499 / 4375199

First Indian Edition - 2007

Printed in India at

EFFICIENT OFFSET PRINTERS

215, Shahzadabagh Indl. Complex,
Phase-II, Delhi-110 035. (India)

CONTENTS

1

ANCIENT RELIGION AND LITERATURE OF PERSIA

THE discovery of the Zend-Avesta, or collection of ancient religious texts of Persia, is one of the most striking romances of literature. In the year 1754 a young Frenchman, Anquetil du Perron, when visiting Leroux-Deshauterayes, a famous Orientalist of that time, saw on his table four sheets of manuscript, written in a strange character. They had been given to Deshauterayes by his uncle, Ètienne Fourmont, who had received them from the Bodleian Library at Oxford. It was a copy of part of an Indian manuscript, which, though facsimiles of it had been sent to all the Orientalists of Europe, remained as undecipherable as the cuneiform characters of Assyria and the hieroglyphs of Egypt were at the same period. This proved the turning-point in Anquetil's life, and he started for India as soon as possible, determined to solve the problem.

After a nine months' voyage he arrived at Pondicherry, whence he proceeded to Surat, the chief seat of the fire-worshippers, or Parsees. On arriving there, he proceeded with the greatest diligence to inquire after the ancient Zend works. By his connection with the French factory, then established at Surat, he was able, after much difficulty and a liberal expenditure of money, to prevail upon two learned Parsee priests, acquainted with Zend and Pehlevi, to teach him those languages, which no European had ever learnt before him. He returned to Europe in 1761, with a hundred and eighty manuscripts, and in 1771 published his work called "Zend-Avesta" in three volumes.

This publication was received by the Orientalists and scholars of England with a shout of derision. The foremost among these was Sir William Jones, who, in his "Lettre à Monsieur Anquetil du Perron," declared that Zoroaster could not have written such foolishness, and that it was doubtless the rhapsody of some modern Parsee. " The whole college of Parsees," he said, " would assure us in vain, for we would not believe it, that the most unskilful charlatan would write the nonsense of which your two volumes are full. Either Zoroaster was wanting in common-sense or he did not write the book which you attribute to him. If he had not common-sense,

On this chapter *cf.* J. B. Fraser, "Account of Persia." I

he should be left in obscurity '; if he did not write this book, it was impudent to publish it under his name. Thus you have either insulted the taste of the public in publishing nonsense, or you have deceived it in passing off a forgery as a genuine document. In each case you deserve its contempt."

Anquetil did not reply, but the controversy continued during his lifetime and after his death. The whole educated public of England was ranged on the side of Sir William Jones, and for more than sixty years firmly believed that the Zend-Avesta was an apocryphal work of comparatively recent date. His attack, however, had found but few supporters in Germany. The Zend-Avesta was translated into German soon after its publication, and theologians used it for throwing light on those parts of the Bible which relate to Persia.

In the early part of the nineteenth century the journey of Rask, the learned Danish Orientalist, to India for the purpose of philological inquiry and the collection of Zend and Pehlevi manuscripts, which he then procured, furnished material for a unanimous verdict among scholars as to the undoubted antiquity both of Zend and Pehlevi, and as to each having been in its time a spoken language. Anquetil's claim was fully vindicated.

The Zend-Avesta, which was brought to light in this remarkable way, consists of twenty-one *nosks,* or books, of which only one, the Vendidad (the ecclesiastical law of the Parsees), is preserved entire, while of the others only a few fragments exist. The name " Zend-Avesta " itself does not occur until about one thousand five hundred years after it is supposed to have been published, when it is mentioned in the geographical work of Masoudi. The work itself was carefully concealed by the Parsees until Anquetil du Perron drew it from its obscurity and presented it to the European world.

The Zend-Avesta is composed in a language of which there is no other specimen, as the Zend differs in many respects from all other dialects ever used in Persia. Although written in characters not unlike the Pehlevi, its structure closely resembles that of the Sanskrit. It has forty-eight letters, corresponding in their powers with those of Indian extraction, including twelve vowels; while the Pehlevi has only nineteen characters and no vowels. A very great number of the words are pure Sanskrit, and altogether it appears to be a dialect of that radical language.

The Parsees attribute many wonderful influences to the Zend-Avesta, and claim that it contains the principles of all arts and sciences, although they are concealed under symbols and mysteries. The Vendidad consists of a series of questions proposed to Ahura-Mazda, the god of the ancient Persians, by Zoroaster, with the corresponding replies. The whole is devoid of any pretension to literary merit, a deficiency which vouches in some degree for the fact of its being the work of an early age. The circumstance that it is often referred to with high respect in the other books of the Zend-Avesta, while it proves that they are of a later date, affords also an additional testimony in favour of the antiquity of the former.

The Zend-Avesta, generally speaking, consists of a series of liturgic services for various occasions, rather than of matter which would lead us to regard it as an original work on religion, and, as the Abbé Foucher well remarks, " bears exactly the same relation to the books of Zoroaster that our missals and breviaries do to the

Bible." The Abbé refers even the most ancient portion of it to a period long posterior to the genuine works of Zoroaster–the period of the restoration of the ancient Persian religion under the Sassanides.

In Pehlevi there are extant translations of four of the books of Zoroaster—the Vendidad, the Vespered, the Yesht, and Khurdavesta. There are, besides, three more books in the same language—the Arda Viraf, a description of the Parsee paradise and hell, curiously anticipating Dante ; the Bundehesh, an account of the Creation ; and a romance, Akhez Jadoo, a still later production.

During the last century two other books on the same subject were published, the Dabistan and the Desatir. The former professes to be a compilation as well from Pehlevi manuscripts as from verbal information received from Zoroastrians, made during the seventeenth century by Muhammad Muhsin Fani, a native of Kashmir. It contains a history of twelve different religions, commencing with that founded by Hoshang, who introduced the worship of fire. Sir John Malcolm, the historian of Persia, derives all that is known of the Paishdadian dynasties, as well as those supposed to precede them, from this source; but he admits that the author betrays a suspiciously strong disposition to connect the ancient history of the Persians with that of the Hindus, adding that such doubts are increased by the character of the author, who, though professing Muhammadanism at heart, sympathized with the doctrines of the Brahmins.

The Desatir, the work to which the Dabistan frequently alludes, was said to be a compilation of treatises by fifteen successive prophets, the last of whom, Sassan, who flourished in the reign of the Emperor Khusru Parvez, translated the original text into Persian. The work is filled with rhapsodies in praise of the Creator, the sun, moon, and planets. Though so great a scholar as Sir William Jones believed in its authenticity, further examination proved it to be a late forgery, and therefore it need not be discussed further.

The doctrines, both theological and philosophical, of Zoroaster were familiarly known to ancient writers; for though not particularly described, his works are frequently referred to. But great uncertainty prevails as to the age in which he lived. Some, believing that there was more than one individual of this name, maintain that the appellation was assumed by a series of lawgivers; but that it was borne by at least two persons is asserted by several scholars, and the Abbé Foucher, on the authority of Pliny, supports this idea, as the only one which can explain the conflicting facts that have been related regarding him. He supposes the first zoroaster to have been a native of Rhé, or Rhages, in Media; that he established his religion in Bactriana, under Cyaxares I.; built a great fire-temple in Balkh, called Azer Gushtasp; and was put to death, with all his inferior priests, during an incursion of the Scythians about the year 630 B.C.

The second Zoroaster, according to the Abbé, appeared in the reign of Darius. He conceives him to have been a disciple of Daniel, or of some other Jewish prophet, and that he may have been one of the twenty-four apostates seen in a vision by Ezekiel as adoring the rising sun. Anquetil du Perron, on the other hand, maintains that there was never more than one Zoroaster, or Zerdusht, and he was a native of Urumiah, and that he flourished in the sixth century before Christ and in the reign of Darius Hystaspes. He supposes him to have been born about the year 589 B.C., and to have been engaged in "consulting Ahura-Mazda "—that is, in maturing his religious code—between the thirtieth and fortieth year of his age. After this he lived thirty-seven years, when he was put to death by the Scythians, as is related by the Persian historians, in 512 B.C. According to Du Perron, Zoroaster retired to compile his Zend-Avesta in the Elburz Mountains, whence he carried it to Darius at Balkh, and the monarch caused the work to be transcribed on twelve thousand well-prepared cow-hides, and transported them to Istakhar as the only fit receptacle of so valuable a deposit.The story of his Jewish origin he treats as a slander of the Muhammadans. Du Perron further supposes that the first Zoroaster alluded to by Pliny, and referred by him, as well as by other Greek and Latin authors, to a very remote age, was no other than the Hoomo of the Zend-Avesta, the Hom of the Parsees, a personage who figures largely in the sacred books of the latter, and who first proposed his tenets as a national creed to the Paishdadian King, Jamshid. The second Zoroaster, placed by the Christian and Muham madan historians under the reign of Cambyses, he refers to the year 558 B.C.

The religion of ancient Persia, according to Du Perron, is divisible into two periods. The first commences in the time of Jamshid, when Hom, the tutelar genius of the law, who lived in the time of that monarch's father, presented it to the young King ; but that Prince was so much alarmed by the strict observances and ceremonies required, that he remonstrated, and would only agree to adopt its moral principles in the government of his realm on condition that during his reign misery and death should disappear from the world. This compromise was agreed to, and the law continued on this imperfect footing until the appearance of the true Zoroaster. Some adhered to the worship of fire as a symbol of the Deity, others adored the stars or idols.

To revive the original purity of the law, to perfect its doctrines and enforce its observances, were the objects for which Zoroaster, according to his own declaration, was especially sent. He collected and arranged the dogmas which constituted the fundamental part of the creed, adding such precepts as he obtained from Ahura-Mazda and a ritual fully as severe as that of any religious code upon record. What the nature of this theological system was we can only judge from the scanty documents that have escaped the wreck of successive revolutions; and how far even these are authentic is a question which is much disputed.

The Avesta of Zoroaster, according to Du Perron, sets out by declaring the existence of a great first principle which it calls Zerwan, an expression which is understood to denote time—time without beginning and without end. This incomprehensible Being is author of the two great active powers of the universe—Ahura-Mazda, the principle of all good, and Ahriman, the principle of all evil. And the question why light and darkness and good and evil were mingled together by a beneficent and omnipotent Creator was as much discussed by the ancient Persians as by modern metaphysicians.

Another matter of dispute was the manner in which the creative energy was exerted. Was the universe formed by means of emanations from the Deity Himself or by modifications of pre-existing matter ? Du Perron supposes Zoroaster to have denied the latter conjecture, for the Avesta declares that Ahura-Mazda rose from the pure elements of fire and water—the fire self-originated, brilliant, dazzling ; the water pure, soft, beneficent, and of a golden hue. The word "Ahura-Mazda" signifies "great King," and his epithets are "luminous," "brilliant." He is perfectly pure, intelligent, just, powerful, active, and beneficent ; the centre and author of the perfections of all Nature ; the first creative agent produced by the self-existent.

Ahriman is directly the opposite of this. His name and epithets imply essential wickedness ; he is a being occupied in perverting and corrupting everything good. He is said to be "enveloped in crime," " the source of misery and evil." In the Zend-Avesta, Ahura-Mazda gives the following metaphorical picture of his rival : "He is alone, wicked, impure, accursed. He has long knees, a long tongue, and is devoid of good." He is called a King, however, and stated to be " without end." He is, in short, the coexistent and almost coequal opponent of Ahura-Mazda, independent of him and alone capable of resisting him. The latter can neither destroy him nor prevent his constant efforts to annihilate or persecute the, beings produced by the power of good, and to banish justice and virtue from the earth. It is no easy matter to comprehend the explanations given of the nature of Ahriman, nor the arguments used to relieve the Eternal from the charge of having willed the creation of a being so malevolent. At one time he is described as being so essentially wicked that, were it possible to deprive him of life, his component parts would unite themselves to their original elements—earth to earth, water to water, air to air, and so on ; in consequence of which all would be infected, without producing any advantage. But in another place he is represented as a power originally good, who, like Lucifer, fell from that high estate through rebellion and disobedience. Du Perron concludes that Zoroaster meant to assign priority of existence to Ahriman ; that, full of conceit of his own perfections and blinded as to the extent of his power, when he beheld in Ahura-Mazda a being of equal might, jealousy rendered him furious, and he rushed into evil, seeking the destruction of everything calculated to exalt his rival's glory. Ahura-Mazda, as he sprang into existence, saw his malicious adversary, and made vain attempts to annihilate him., No sooner had he called into being a pure world, when, as if the impulses of good and evil were simultaneous, Ahriman immediately opposed to it a world of impurity.

The instrument employed by the Almighty in giving an origin to these opposite principles, as well as in every subsequent creative act, was His Word. This sacred and mysterious agent, which in the Zend- Avesta is frequently mentioned under the appellation Honover, is compared to those celestial birds which constantly keep watch over the welfare of Nature. Its attributes are ineffable light, perfect activity, unerring prescience. Its existence preceded the formation of all things; it proceeds from the first actual principle ; it is the gift of God. Ordained to create and govern the universe, Ahura-Mazda received the Word which in his mouth became an instrument of infinite power and fruitfulness. "I pronounce the Honover continually and in all its might." Ahura-Mazda says to Zoroaster in the Zend-Avesta, "and abundance is multiplied." It is evident that the author of the Zend-Avesta meant the Honover to be understood as a being distinct from Zerwan, or the Eternal, as well as from Ahura-Mazda.

According to the system of cosmogony in the Zend- Avesta, the duration of the present universe is fixed at twelve thousand years, which is subdivided into four terms, and to each of these is appropriated a special series of events. During the first period Ahura-Mazda, alarmed by the appearance of Ahriman "at an immeasurable distance beneath him, covered with filth and putridity," employed himself in creating the universe and the celestial inhabitants. Of these beings the first were Ferohers, or the spiritual prototypes, the unembodied angels of every reasonable being destined to appear upon earth. The Ferohers of the law, of Iran, and of Zoroaster were the most precious in his eyes ; for the law, the expression of the Divine Word, and Iran, which was to be its theatre, was held as ranking high in the scale of intelligence, as well as Zoroaster, its future promulgator.

Ahriman, alarmed at these new instances of Ahura-Mazda's power, flew with malign intent towards the light ; but a single enunciation of the Honover sent him howling back to darkness, 'where he immediately called into being a number of *divs** and evil spirits, designed to oppose the works of Ahura-Mazda. A proposal of peace and an exhortation to resume the paths of virtue were met by him with scorn and defiance, and his rival in self-defence produced six *amshaspands,* or superior guardian angels, pure, beneficent, eternal. "Protect my flocks and herds, O man of God'!" said the holy Brahmin to whose charge was entrusted the animal creation, to Zoroaster. "These I received from the Almighty. Let not the young be slain, nor those that are still useful." "Servant of the Most High," exclaimed the dazzling Ardibihisht, the genius of fire and light, "speak to the royal Gushtasp** for me; say that to thee I have confided all fires. Ordain the Mubids, the Dasturs, and Herboods, † to preserve them, and neither to extinguish them in the water nor in the earth ; bid them erect in every city a temple of fire, and celebrate in honour of that element the feasts ordained by law. The brilliancy of fire is from God, and what is more beautiful than that element? It requires only wood and odours. Let the young and the old give these, and their prayers shall be heard. I transfer it to thee as I received it from God. Those who do not fulfil my words shall go to the infernal regions."

Shahriwar, the spirit of the metal and the mine, spoke next : " O thou pure man! when thou art on the earth tell all men my words; bid those who carry the lance, the sword, the dagger, and the mace, clean them each year, that the sight of them may put to flight those that cherish bad designs. Tell them never to place confidence in wicked men, nor in their enemies." Espendermad, the female guardian of the earth, exclaimed : "Thou who shalt be as a blessing unto mankind, preserve the earth from blood, uncleanness, and from carcasses***; carry such where the soil is not cultivated and where neither man nor water passeth. Fruits in abundance shall reward labour, and the best King is he who rendereth the earth most fertile. Say this unto men from me."

The angel Kourdad, who diffuses the blessings of running streams, next said : " I confide to thee, O Zoroaster, the water that flows and that which is stagnant ; the water of rivers, that which comes from afar and from the mountains ; the water from rain and from springs. Instruct men that it is water which giveth strength to all living things. It makes all verdant. Let it not be polluted with anything dead or

* The Persian word *div* is etymologically connected with the English "devil."

** An early King of Persia.

† Different orders of priests.

*** Because of this injunction, the Parsees (descendants of the ancient Persians), as is well known, expose their dead to be devoured by vultures on the tops of towers.

impure, that your food boiled in pure water may be healthy. Execute thus the words of God."

Last spoke Amerdad, who watches over the growth of plants and trees: " O Zoroaster, bid men not destroy nor pull, except in season, the plants and fruits of the earth, for these were meant as a blessing and a support to men and animals."

Such were the six first angels of Ahura-Mazda ; but no sooner had they appeared than six *divs* arose from the darkness at the voice of Ahriman to counteract their influence. In such contests, three thousand more years elapsed, towards the close of which Ahura-Mazda called into existence the heavens and their celestial systems. Sirosh, the guardian of the earth, and Bahram, armed with a mighty club and arrows, were formed to repel the attacks of Ahriman. Mithra, the mediator between Ahura-Mazda and his creatures, and Rash-in-Rast, the genius of justice, with multitudes of spirits, were called forth to assist in repelling the powers of darkness, and angels were appointed to protect every being. The stars and planets, the months of the year, the days, and even the hours of the day, had each its attendant spirit.

In consequence of the services of these intermediate intelligences, a period of peace and tranquillity ensued. The year was one uninterrupted day ; nor did change of weather or of season disturb the world. But it was a delusive calm, and the cause that awakened the malignant activity of Ahriman was the creation of man. The Feroher or Prototype of Being, delighted with the harmony which reigned on the earth, was bidden by Ahura-Mazda to descend thither and assist in eradicating evil, and was promised that the souls of human beings should finally return to their divine mansions. The Feroher obeyed, and was embodied under the form of the sacred bull, Aboudad the Excellent, the Pure, the Principle of all Good. Ahriman, in the depths of hell, trembled at this intelligence. Stimulated by his *divs*, and particularly by the evil genius Djê, he mustered his spirits, and ascending in the form of a monstrous serpent, covered the earth with noxious animals. In the shape of a huge fly, he polluted everything and insinuated the poison of evil into all nature. By means of a burning drought, he parched the face of the whole earth, and caused his *divs* to strike the sacred bull with a fatal wound. But the benevolent designs of Ahura-Mazda were not so to be defeated. From the right limb of the dying beast issued Kayomurz, the first man ; and from the rest of its members sprang a multitude of vegetable productions, destined to render the earth fruitful. Its seed, carried to the moon and purified by Ahura-Mazda, produced a bull and a cow, from which all animals took their origin.

Kayomurz was of lofty aspect, pure, and of dazzling substance. His body was composed of the four elements—fire, air, water; and earth. Ahura-Mazda added an immortal spirit to this perishable flame, and the human being was complete.

The soul of man, instead of a simple essence, consists, according to the teaching of Zoroaster, of five separate parts, each having particular functions:

1. The Feroher, or principle of sensation.
2. The Bue, or principle of intelligence.
3. The Ruh, or Ravan, the principle of practical judgment and volition.
4. The Akho, or principle of conscience.
5. The Jan, or principle of animal life.

When the first four of these, which cannot subsist in the body without the last, abandon their earthly abode, the Jan mingles with the winds and the Akho returns to heaven with the celestial Ruh, because, its office being to urge man continually to do good and shun evil, it can have no part in the guilt of the soul. The Bue, the Ravan, and the Feroher, united together, are the only principles which are accountable for the deeds of the man, and are accordingly examined at the day of judgment. If good predominates, they go to heaven ; if evil, they are despatched to hell. The body is regarded as a mere instrument in the power of the Ravan, and therefore not responsible for its acts. After death the Akho has a separate existence, as the Feroher had previous to birth.

Such is the soul of man, according to the Zend-Avesta, and such was Kayomurz, created (as the word implies) to be immortal, and sprinkled by Ahura-Mazda with the water of Khei, which rendered him beautiful as a youth of fifteen years. But neither his comeliness nor the power of Ahura-Mazda could avert the malice of Ahriman, who at the end of thirty years, and after a severe conflict of ninety days and nights, succeeded in destroying him. But the principle of regeneration, being preserved and confided to the tutelar genius of fire, was purified by the light of the sun, and after forty years produced a tree, or plant, representing two human bodies. These were Maschia and Maschiana, the parents of the human race. Their names, according to Du Perron, are derived from a word signifying death ; and though they proceeded from the seed of Kayomurz, they were yet deemed children of the earth, which nourished the tree, and of the heavens, which watered it. But, though created pure and capable of perfect and permanent felicity, Maschia and Maschiana were tempted to rebel, and to worship Ahriman instead of their creator, Ahura-Mazda. They thus became *darvund* (accursed), and their souls were doomed to remain in hell until the resurrection. The earth was overrun by *Kharfesters* (or evil spirits clothed with bodies), who inhabited its caverns and recesses. A flood was sent which destroyed them ; but from their foul remains arose noisome animals, reptiles, poisons, and putridity. Maschia and Maschiana plunged still more deeply into sin. Listening to the continued temptations of Ahriman, they drank the milk of a goat (which appears to have been an incarnation of himself) ; they ate forbidden fruit, thereby forfeiting their few remaining privileges ; and poured libations of milk to the powers of darkness in the North. They were separated, but at the end of fifty years again met and had two children, who multiplied and peopled the whole earth.

The power of evil increased with the growth of the universe; nor was any good influence sufficient to arrest its course. The intimate union of the principles of good and evil in all things rendered it impossible to destroy the works of Ahriman, who himself was indestructible. So Ahura-Mazda resolved to rescue from him the creatures whom he had so persecuted, and in order to strengthen them against the future efforts of the Evil One, he gave his law to be promulgated by Zoroaster.

In these struggles must elapse the third period of the duration of the universe, the power of Ahura-Mazda and Ahriman being equally balanced. During the fourth period the latter is to prevail ; misery and desolation will prevail over the earth ; and three prophets will appear, under the last of whom, named Sosioch, a rain of black water will precede the renewal of nature, the resurrection of mankind, and the final judgment.

But annihilation, even for a time, forms no part of the doctrine of Zoroaster. At death the material components of the body rejoin their respective elements—earth to earth, water to water, fire to fire, and life to the air. For three days after death the soul flits round the body in hope of a reunion. On the fourth day the angel Seroch appears and conducts it to the bridge of Chinevad. On this bridge, which connects earth and heaven, sits the angel of justice, Rash in Rast, to weigh the actions of mortals ; and, according to his decision, the dog which guards the bridge permits it to cross and join the souls of its ancestors in heaven or precipitates it into the gulf of hell which yawns below. When its good deeds preponderate over the evil, the soul is met on the bridge by a dazzling figure, which says, " I am thy good angel (*kherdar*). I was pure originally, but thy good deeds have rendered me purer; and passing its hand over the neck of the soul, leads it to Paradise. If, on the other hand, its sins preponderate, it is met by a hideous spectre, which howls out: " I am thy evil *kherdar*. Impure myself, thy sins have rendered me more foul ; through thee shall we be miserable till the resurrection" ; on which it drags the guilty spirit to hell, where Ahriman taunts it with its follies and crimes.

The resurrection, however, is the true triumph of Ahura-Mazda arid his worshippers, and one of the most essential articles of their belief. In that day Kayomurz will first arise, and then Maschia and Maschiana. The judgment of mankind will occupy a space of fifty-seven years. The genii of the elements, which have received in deposit the various substances of the body, must render up their trust; the soul will recognize its earthly companion and re-enter it; the juice of the herb Hom and the milk of the bull Heziosk will restore life to man, who then becomes immortal. Then takes place the final separation of the evil and the good. Sinners who have not in the intermediate state expiated their faults are again sent to hell, but not for eternal punishment. The tortures of three awful days and nights, equal to an agony of three thousand years, suffice for the purification of the most wicked. The voice of the damned ascending to heaven will find mercy from Ahura-Mazda, who will withdraw them from the place of torment. The world shall melt with fervent heat, and the liquid and glowing metals shall purify the universe and fit all beings for everlasting felicity. To the just this ordeal proves as a pleasant bath of lukewarm water; the wicked, on the other hand, shall suffer excruciating agonies, but it will be the last of their miseries. Hell itself and all its demons shall be cleansed; Ahriman, no longer irreclaimable, will be converted to goodness, and become a ministering spirit of the Most High.

Such, according to the Zend-Avesta, is a sketch of the system of cosmogony and theology promulgated by Zoroaster, in all probability compiled and reformed in some degree from the ancient religion of the Magi. The intricate ritual, the multiplication of ceremonies, the narratives of the creation and the deluge, are probably of Jewish origin. The greater part of the mythology, particularly the fable of the sacred bull and the affinity of the Zend with Sanskrit, point to India, while the high, rank assigned to the celestial bodies and planetary system seems derived from Chaldæism.

SPICEMENS OF ZOROASTRIAN LITERATURE.

I. *A Prayer from the Khurda Avesta.*

" In the name of the God Almighty, the bestower of gifts and favours, I praise the name of the Lord Ahura-Mazda, whose name is Izad, God the Excellent, the

7Invisible, the Great, Omnipotent, Omniscient, the Creator of all things, the Protector, the Guardian, the Scurce of all virtue, ever vigilant, the Holy, the Distributor of impartial justice. With all my might I express my thanks and gratitude to the noble Lord of the creation, who has created the universe by His own free-will and wisdom, who has created the six Amshaspands (archangels) that sit beside Him, and numerous other angels ; who created the glorious paradise, the rotatory heavens, the resplendent sun, the glorious moon, the innumerable stars, the seeds of everything, the wind, the air, water, fire, the earth, the trees, the animals, the metals ; who has created men. I adore and praise the Lord of virtue, who has given superiority to men above the rest of the creation, and given them the inestimable gift of speech for the purpose of managing all earthly concerns, for arguing with the enemies of religion, and for abstaining from Satan ; and created man to rule over the earth. I worship the all-wise omniscient God, the universal Protector, who has sent into this world through the virtuous, pure and sanctified Prophet Zartusht* the Mazdayasnan faith for the peace and harmony of the people ; who has created wisdom and pure intellect, knowledge and reason, by which men are enabled to conduct themselves with regard to what is passing, what has passed, and what will come to pass ; who has given the Zend-Avesta as the best of all other knowledges, which enable men to pass the bridge Chinavad in safety and preserve them from hell, which guide us to that glorious place of gladness and felicity which is destined for the righteous. May I, O Lord, obey thy command and profess thy faith, and meditate, speak, and do everything according to thy desire. May I remain firm and steadfast in the path of rectitude. I do hereby abstain from all sin and persevere in virtuous conduct and practise abstinence: May I walk in the path of heaven. May I not be subject to the insufferable rigors of hell. May I pass the bridge of Chinavad in safety, and reach the everlasting paradise, which is adorned, full of perfume, and easy of access. I praise the ever-glorious and ever-vigilant Almighty, who rewards those who practise righteousness. I praise thee, O Lord, who art the Dispenser of justice on the day of judgment, the Redeemer and Liberator of the wicked from hell, who art the Regenerator of the human race. I offer all my praise and adoration to Ahura-Mazda the Omniscient, Omnipotent, the Independent and Absolute, the Creator of the seven Amshaspands and of Bahram the powerful, who is the successful destroyer of enemies. Do thou, O Lord, lend me thine assistance."

(*Translated by* MANAKJI PESTANJI)

2. *From the Arda Viraf* (*circa* A.D. 250).

"It is recorded that when the power of Ardeshir Babagan* was firmly established, he assembled round him forty thousand virtuous Mubids and Dasturs, out of which number he selected four thousand ; of those thus selected he set apart four hundred, who knew by heart the greater part of the Avesta ; of these four hundred he again chose out forty learned doctors ; and from these he selected seven unblemished sages, whom he thus addressed: 'Let whichever of you is able, divest himself of body, and bring us intelligence concerning heaven and hell.' These righteous men made answer:

---

*Zoroaster.

*Founder of the Sassanian dynasty.

'For such a purpose there is required a man who, from the age of seven upwards, has not committed sin.'

"After which these sages selected from amongst themselves one named Arda Viraf, whom they knew to be so qualified, and, accompanied by the King, they all repaired to Azar Khurdad, which was a fire-temple. Having there prepared a golden throne for Arda Viraf, they performed Yazash—*i.e.*, recited prayers according to the prescribed mode. Arda Viraf, having drunk a cup of hallowed wine which he received from the Dastur, lay down on his couch, and did not rise before the expiration of a week ; his spirit, through the efficacy of the divine word, having been separated from the body, those six Dasturs all the while standing round his pillow. On the eighth day Arda, arising from sleep, ordered a scribe to be brought who should commit to writing all his words, and he thus spoke : 'When I fell asleep, Sirushi; the angel of paradise, came near. Having made my salaam, I explained my motives of coming to the other world. He took my hand, and said : "Ascend three steps." I obeyed, and arrived at the Chinavad Pul, or the straight bridge of judgment. The accompanying angel pointed me out the road, when I beheld a bridge finer than a hair and sharper than a razor, and strong, and its length was seven-and-thirty *rasans*, or cords. I beheld a spirit just parted from the body in a state of tranquillity ; on its arrival at the bridge of judgment a fragrant gale came from the east, out of which issued a beautiful nymph-like form, the like of which I never before beheld. The spirit asked her : " Who art thou of such surpassing beauty ?" She replied: "I am the personification of thy good deeds."

"I then saw Mihr Ized (Mithra), at whose side were standing Rash-in-Rast and Sarush Ized, holding a balance in his hand and angels assembled around them. To these I made my salaam, which they returned. Then Sarush laid hold of my arm ; we proceeded to the top of the bridge, one side of which appeared in full splendour of light and the other in total darkness. I heard an uncommon sound, which, on looking forwards, I perceived to come from a dog that was chained with a collar and chain of gold near the light side of the bridge. I asked the angels : "Why is the dog here ?" To which Sarush Ized replied: " He makes this noise to frighten Ahriman, and keeps watch here to prevent his approach. His name is Zering Goash, and the devils shake at his voice ; and any soul that has, during its residence in the lower world, hurt or ill-used or destroyed any of these animals is prevented by Zering Goash from proceeding any further across the bridge. And, Arda Veraf, when you return again to the world, enjoin the taking care of these animals as one of the first duties."

When I proceeded a little onwards, I beheld a lofty portico, where, by order of Sarush, I addressed my prayers towards the place of God, and my sight became darkened through the effulgence of light. Sarush again brought me back to the bridge of judgment, where I beheld a number of persons standing with folded hands. I asked: " Who are these persons ?" Sarush answered: "These are the weak in faith, who remain in this state until the day of judgment. If they possessed an additional particle of virtue equal in weight to one of the hairs of the eyelash, they would be relieved from this calamity." I then beheld another assembly like unto shining stars. Sarush said: " This is the Satra Payah, or the sphere of the fixed stars. In these are the people who with all their wealth observed not the Giti Kharid,* the purchase of the other world." He next brought me to the Mah Payah (or lunar sphere), where I beheld spirits resplendent as the moon.'

"Arda Viraf goes on to describe his progress through the various celestial spheres in a manner somewhat resembling Dante's 'Paradiso.' He then proceeds thus in his account of the infernal regions : 'After this, Sarush and Ardibihisht, taking me out of Paradise, bore me off to behold the punishments inflicted on those in hell. First of all, I beheld a black and gloomy river of fætid water, with weeping multitudes falling in and drowning. Sarush said: "This water is collected from the tears shed by relatives on the death of a person ; and those who are drowning are those whose relatives after their death break out into mourning, weeping, and tears." I next proceeded towards the bridge of judgment, where I beheld a spirit rent from the body and mourning for its separation ; there arose a foul-smelling wind, out of which issued a gloomy figure with red eyeballs, hooked nose, hideous lips, long talons, spear-like fangs, snaky locks, vomiting out smoke. The alarmed spirit having asked, " Who are thou ?" it answered: " I am the personification of thy evil deeds." Saying this, he threw his hands round the spirit's neck and came to the bridge of judgment, which is sharper than a razor. On this, the spirit having gone a little way with great difficulty, at last fell into the infernal regions.

"I then followed him, accompanied by Sarush and Ardibihisht. Our road lay through snow, ice, storms, intense cold, mephitic exhalations and obscurity, along a region full of pits. Into these I looked, and there beheld countless myriads of spirits suffering tortures. They all wailed bitterly, and the darkness was so thick that one was unable to perceive the other. Three days of such punishment is equal to nine thousand years. In all the pits were serpents, scorpions, and other stinging and noxious creatures."

(*Translated by* **SHEA.**)

3. *The Miracle which attended the Birth of Zartusht (Zoroaster). (From the Zartusht-nama.)*

"When the time of his birth drew near, his relations were filled with lamentation. His mother called for the wise women and also for those who were dear to her, in order that they might minister to her and might support her in her travail. The women who were her neighbours and men enchanters surrounded the door of her house. When the moon breathed light on the world, the holy Zartusht was born. As he left the womb, he laughed. The house was enlightened by that laughter ; his father was astonished at him, at his laughter and beauty and loveliness. He said in his heart : 'This is the glory of God.' Save this child, every infant born into the world has wept. They named the child Zartusht. Great and small heard thereof; the word of the seer was fulfilled as he had foretold the birth of the child. The women were envious of his laughter and of the brightness of his destiny ; they remained covetous of him, since the like of him had not been seen. They said: 'We know not how this will be, or what will be the event.' Child like this saw they never; in beauty the world could show no equal to him. The city was filled with the news of the beauty and laughter of the infant; all who were unclean and evil were stung to the heart with that laughter. In those days were many magicians, who filled every place with their art; among them was spread anxiety; their souls were consumed as a torch. They said; 'This is a calamity to us; we must remove this child from the world."

(*Translated by* E.B. EASTWICK.)

* The gift of two rupees, which a man is obliged to give once in his life to a *mubid*, or priest, in order that he may perform a purificatory ceremony in favour of the donor.

2

ISLAM AS MODIFIED BY PERSIAN THOUGHT—PERSIAN HERETICAL SECTS: SHIAHS, ISMAILIANS, MU'TAZILITES ("THE BROTHERS OF PURITY")

OF all the conquests made by Islam at its first promulgation, the most important was that of Persia. It was the Persian theologians, and not the Arabs, who gave clearness and firmness to Islamic doctrines, and it was Persia which gave birth to a variety of extraordinary sects. As M. Dozy remarks in his work on Islam, Muhammad had certainly not foreseen the great influence which his doctrine would have on the Persians. He did not know that he had borrowed many Zoroastrian ideas; he believed that their source was Jewish, and was unaware that the Koran was, so to speak, a second edition of the Zend-Avesta. When the Persian Zoroastrian first studied the Koran he found many of his beliefs already there in a thin disguise—Ahura-Mazda and Ahriman under the names of Allah and Iblis, the creation in six periods of time, the angels and the demons, the innocence of the first pair, the forbidden fruit, the resurrection of the body, heaven, the bridge between heaven and hell, over which the souls of the righteous pass, while the wicked fall from it. It was precisely this lack of originality which favoured the spread of Islam in Persia.

Another cause which favoured the growth of Islam at the time was the bigotry of the Zoroastrian priests under the Sassanide dynasty and the severity with which they had persecuted every form of faith but their own. The battle of Qadysia (A.D 635), which gave Persia to the Arabs, was the signal of deliverance for all those who had been so persecuted. Both Jews and Christians breathed more freely under a religion which declared them " people of the book" (Ahl-i-Kitab), and only required them to pay tribute instead of massacring or deporting them, as the Sassanides had done. Similarly with the number of trades which had been harassed by the Zoroastrian prohibitions regarding defilement of fire, water, or earth—those who carried

---

On this chapter *cf*. R. Dozy : "Essai sur l'Histoire dl' Islamisme"; and W. C. Taylor: " History of Muhammaedanism."

them on became ready adherents of Islam, which had delivered them from the vexatious regulations of the Avesta.

Professor T. W. Arnold, in his work on the "Preaching of Islam," mentions a third which also favoured the spread of Islam in Persia. This was the marriage of Husayn, the son Muhammad's first cousin, with Shahbanu, the daughters of Yazdagird, the last monarch of the Sassanide dynasty. The majority of Persian Moslems are, as is well known, Shiahs—that is to say, they do not acknowledge the first three Caliphs—Abubakr, Omar, and Othman—as legitimate successors of the Prophet, but only the fourth Caliph—Ali—whose claims they exalt to an extravagant degree, according him almost divine honours. The above-mentioned marriage, of course, greatly favoured this tendency, as the descendants of Ali were of Persian blood.

The root-idea of Shiism (as distinct from Sunnism, or orthodox Islam) is that of the need of mediators between God and man. Such mediators the Persians found in Ali and his descendants, the twelve Imams, or leaders. In this scheme All is the successor of Ahura-Mazda, and the Imams replace the Amshaspands, or angels, of the Avesta. Many of the Shiahs believe that Ali is not dead, but that he will return again to reign on earth when men, by their docility and submission, will cause him to forget his earthly sufferings. Others, nearly identifying him with the Deity, claim that he often shows himself to his enemies, " brandishing the lightning in their faces, and terrifying their souls with the crashes of his thunder." It is quite a common proverb in Persia: "Though I do not believe Ali to be God, I believe that he is not far from being so." A great number of the Shiahs declare Ali to be superior to Muhammad. Some say that Ali was chosen by God to propagate Islam, but that the angel Gabriel by mistake delivered the letter to Muhammad. Shah Hossein, one of the last monarchs of the Suffavean dynasty in Persia, described himself on his seal as, "the vilest of the dogs of All." The signet of several other monarchs of this dynasty bore a Persian quatrain to the following effect:

"He who in Ali places not his trust,
Were it myself, myself I should detest.
He who at Ali's gate is not as dust,
On him, though Gabriel's self, may earth be pressed."

Besides Shiism, many other heresies sprang up in Persia soon after the introduction of Islam, especially in the province of Khorassan. There appeared the Ravendis, who taught the doctrine of the transmigration of the soul and successive incarnations of the Deity, and the Zandiks, who were popularly supposed to be atheists. Abu Muslim, the Governor of Khorassan, under the Caliph Al Mansur, was a Ravendi ; his secretary, Hakem Ibn Hashem, adopted the same creed, and resolved to turn it to profit. Hashem was very deformed. He knew that his appearance would prevent his being believed if he proclaimed himself a prophet, And he therefore covered himself with a silver veil, declaring that no mortal could gaze upon the effulgence of his face and live. Hence he is usually called "Al Mokanna," the Veiled Prophet.

In the reign of the Caliph A1 Mahdi, Mokanna began to propagate his teaching, and by some juggling performances persuaded the unlearned that he had the power of working miracles. In particular, he caused the appearance of the moon to rise out of a well for many nights in succession, whence he is called by the Persians "Sazinda Mah," the Moon-maker. His progress was so rapid that in a few months he was at the head of a numerous army, and had garrisoned several strong fortresses. A large force, however, being sent against him, he was compelled to seek refuge in one of his mountain castles, where he was closely besieged. Hopeless of escape, he poisoned the entire garrison and his family, after which he plunged into a vessel containing some corrosive fluid, which consumed every particle of him but the hair, hoping that from the disappearance of the body it would be supposed that he had been taken up into heaven. One of his harem, who hid herself when she saw these preparations, revealed the circumstance ; but many of his former followers continued to believe in the divinity of Mokanna, and clothed themselves in white, to show their hostility to the Abbaside Caliphs, whose distinctive colour was black.

The founder of the Ismailians was Ahdallah, a native of Ahwaz, in the province of Khuzistan. He saw the peril of openly proclaiming himself a religious leader, and therefore resolved to form "lodges," similar to those of the modern Free-masons, in which the members should pass through seven gradations, each having its own peculiar system of doctrines. Missionaries, or Dais, propagated the secret code which Abdallah taught, and initiated gradually those they wished to influence into the various stages of their secret doctrine. In the first stage the neophyte was shown the doubts and difficulties connected with the Koran ; he was inspired with an anxious desire to have its mysteries explained, and some glimpses of the Ismailian doctrine were then afforded him, in order that he might be induced to take an oath of blind faith and unlimited obedience to his Daï, or instructor. In the second stage the nature of the Imamate as a divine institution was explained. The peculiar doctrines of the Ismailians commenced at the third degree, when the neophytes were taught that the number of Imams were seven, and that Ismail, the son of Jaafar Sadiq, the sixth Imam of the Shiahs, was the last and greatest of the Imams. In the fourth stage it was declared that since the creation there had been seven legislators divinely inspired, each of whom had modified the doctrine of his predecessors. These seven prophets were said to be "endowed with power of speech," because they authoritatively declared the divine will; they were each followed by "a mute prophet" that is, one whose duty was simply to enforce the doctrines of the preceding one. The seven legislators were Adam, Noah, Abraham, Moses, Christ, Muhammad, and Ismail ; their seven disciples, or mute prophets," were Seth, Shem, Ishmael (the son of Abraham), Aaron, Simon Peter, Ali, and Muhammad, the son of Ismail.

In the fifth stage it was declared that each of the "mute prophets" had appointed twelve Dais, and that the number twelve was next in sanctity to the number seven. Having passed through these inferior degrees, they were in the last stages initiated into the secret doctrines. Those who attained the sixth degree were told that religious legislation should be subordinate to philosophical; in the seventh stage they were introduced to the mystical speculations characteristic of Oriental metaphysics; in the eighth they were taught the indifference of human actions ; and in the ninth the initiated received their final lesson "to believe nothing and dare everything"—a curious anticipation of Nitzsche.

One branch of the Ismailians acquired the sinister and celebrated title of the Assassins. The founder of this branch was Hasan-ibn-Sabah, whose father, Ali, was a distinguished Shiite. Two of Hasan's schoolfellows were Nizam-ul-Mulk and the famous Omar Khayyam. The three youths entered into a compact that if one of them attained to eminence he would help his old associates. Nizam-ul-Mulk at an early age became the Vizier of the Seljuk monarch, Alp Arslan. Nizam bestowed a pension on Omar Khayyam, who only desired to spend his life in literary seclusion, and obtained for Hasan an introduction to Malek Shah, the successor of Alp Arslan. Hasan, however, soon left the Court, and began to propagate the Ismailian doctrines secretly through the Persian provinces between the Caspian and the Euphrates. At length he made himself master of an impregnable mountain castle, called from its position Alamoot, "the eagle's nest."

Here he formed a confraternity which became famous as the sect of the Assassins. He himself took the simple title of Sheikh, and the name of the "Sheikh-al-Jabal," or Old Man of the Mountain, soon became formidable throughout Asia. He declared himself the Vicar of the invisible Imam, and as such, partially an incarnation of a divine principle. His followers believed that eternal happiness or misery rested on his nod ; for them there existed no crime but disobedience to his orders, and this crime they knew would be promptly punished in this life, and they believed would produce endless torments in the next. The chief importance of the Assassins and Ismailians, from a literary point of view, is that they roused into polemical activity one of the greatest philosophers and theologians of Persia—Al Ghazzali. Of him Professor D. Macdonald says in his "Muslim Theology" : "In 483 A.H. Hasan ibn as-Sabah had seized Alamut. The sect of the Assassins was applying its principles, but the poison of their teaching was also spreading among the people. The principle of authority in religion—that only by an infallible teacher could truth be reached, and that such an infallible teacher existed, if he could be found—was in the air. For himself, Al Ghazzali found the Talimites (or Ismailians) and their teaching eminently unsatisfactory. They had a lesson which they went over parrot-fashion, but beyond it they were in dense ignorance. The trained theologian and scholar had no patience with their slackness and shallowness of thought. The conflict was hot, and Al Ghazzali wrote several books against them."

Another school of broader outlook and deeper influence than the Ismailians were the Mu'tazilites. They maintained the doctrine of man's free-will against the orthodox theologians of Islam, who held that man was a mere puppet in the hands of Allah. They also refused to believe that the Koran was uncreated—a favourite dogma of the other side-declaring that this involved believing in two gods. They went even further, and said that it was wrong to assign any attributes to God, as this impaired the doctrine of His absolute unity. The movement was Persian in its origin and favoured by the Caliphs Al Mansur and Al Mamun, whose mother was a Persian. Unfortunately, the latter Caliph persecuted all those who refused to declare that the Koran was created, and thus provoked a reaction in favour of the narrower orthodox school. While the Mu'tazilites had the upper hand, a great stimulus was given to free-thought in Islam ; commentaries on Aristotle and other Greek works were translated into Arabic, and formed the foundation on which the great Moslem philosophers Avicenna and Averroes built up their systems. The Mu'tazilites also produced a great commentator on the Koran, Az-Zamakhshari, a Persian by birth, whose commentary, the Kashshaf, is widely used at the present day.

The Mu'tazilites received their death-blow as a dominant sect from one of their own number, A1 Ash'ari, who made a public renunciation of his belief in man's free-will, and of the opinion that the Koran was created. This occurred in the great mosque of Basra on a Friday. He was sitting in the chair from which he taught, when he cried out in a loud voice: "They who know me know who I am ; as for those who do not know me, I shall tell them. I am Ali lbn Ismail Al Ash`ari, and I used to hold that the Koran was created, that the eyes of men shall not see God in the next world,* and that we ourselves are the authors of our evil deeds. Now I have returned to the truth ; I renounce these opinions, and I engage myself to refute the Mu'tazilites and to expose their infamy and turpitude." The conversion of Al Ash`ari gave an effectual check to free-thought in Islam—at any rate, for a time. Having been trained in the Mu'tazilite methods, he fought and routed them with their own weapons. A theologian of the time said of him : "The Mu'tazilites went with their heads up till such time as God produced A1`Ash'ari to the world."

Although the Mu'tazilites had suffered a severe blow by the defection of Al Ash'ari, the partisans of free-thought did not altogether become extinct. Greek philosophy had struck its roots too deeply into the Moslem mind to be altogether eradicated.

In the tenth century A.D. an offshoot of the Mu'tazilites sprang up at Basra, called " The Brothers of Purity" (Ikhwan-us-Safa). They published some fifty-one pamphlets, endeavouring to harmonize the tenets of the Koran with Neo-Platonism, and to include all the knowledge of the time in a kind of Encyclopædia. They began with mathematics, which they regarded as an indispensable mental discipline, and also because they had adopted Pythagorean ideas regarding numbers as the basis of everything; then they proceeded to treat of logic, in which they followed Aristotle, as also in natural science, concluding with the Neo-Platonist philosophy. Their works afford the most striking manifestations of the philosophic mind among the Moslems. Most of the compilers appear to have been of Persian birth. They wished to link together all the natural and moral sciences by some one great idea, but their success was only partial. Flügel says of them: "They were opposed to no form of science, avoided no book, cherished no partisan prejudice towards any doctrinal system, but embraced in one scheme all without exception, visible and invisible, uniting the whole body of sciences." They were, of course, much in advance of their time, and their Encyclopædia was burnt at Baghdad in the twelfth century, by order of the Caliph Mostanjid.

The fifty-first and last of the pamphlets forming this Encyclopædia contains an interesting apologue called "Man and the Beasts." The purport of this apologue is as follows: Disputes having arisen between mankind and the brute creation, the latter complaining of man's tyranny, the former of the insubordination of the brutes, both sides appeal to the King of the genii. The animals assert that they are by nature free; a man lays claim to a natural authority over all animals. The King, finding the question to be difficult, determined to take the advice of able counsellors, and to hear

*This was one of the points in dispute between the Mu'tazilites and th orthodax party.

the arguments on both sides. The two parties appear in support of their respective claims. After a full discussion, it was decided, by common consent of the genii, that, men being destined for another world, in which they will be rewarded or punished according to their actions on earth, the sovereignty is theirs-a decree in the justice of which the animals themselves concur.

The following extract will give some idea or the work :

1. *From the Speech of the Parrot before the King of the Genii.*

"You men are proud, again, because you are philosophers and logicians ; but know you not that these sciences only mislead you ?' 'How?' inquired the men. 'Because they induce you to turn your face away from religion, and by pointing out contradictions in your sacred books, shake your faith in them. Opinions and religions then begin to differ. Some consider this world as ancient, and others regard chaos as old. Some say there are two evils existing, some three, some four, five, six, or even as far as seven. Some think the world to be infinite, while others believe it finite. Some believe in its revolving; others do not. Some put faith in the prophets and their sayings; others refuse to do so. Some wander in the mists of doubt; others deny the existence of sense and reason. Besides these, there are several other kinds of false faith and religions which mislead mankind. *We* profess one faith, as we believe in one God, whom we continually worship without vaunting our superiority.

"You also glory in your geometricians and mathematicians, but what are these people ? Night and day they are puzzled in search of proofs. Things beyond comprehension they pretend to elucidate. Thus they waste their lives in learning sciences perfectly useless in themselves, ignorant all the while of that grand science which teaches how to be happy here and hereafter. Some are engrossed in calculating the distances of remote heavenly bodies, some in investigating the heights of mountains and clouds, some in measuring the length of forests and the depth of rivers, and some puzzle their heads in trying to comprehend the laws of the solar system or determining the centre of the earth. And all this time they know nothing of the physiology of their own bodies. They know not how the intestines are placed, and what duties they perform; what strength is possessed by the ribs of the breast ; what are the nature of the heart and brains ; how the bones are arranged, and how the joints strengthened. These particulars, which to know is both simple and necessary, they never study ; whereas it is from these we come to know the Creator, even as the prophet says : "He who knows himself knows God."

"You boast, again, of your doctors ; but you seek their assistance only when lust or intemperance breed a malady in you ; then you run to them. Only the sick go to physicians and druggists, even as the wretched and unfortunate congregate on the doors of astrologers, who are sure to make matters worse, for they have no power to change the evil aspect of a planet ; yet still, for all that, many a professor of that science writes down nonsense on a piece of paper to mislead fools. The same is the case with physicians, who generally increase the malady of their patients by advising them to abstain from things which would have insured a speedy cure. If the diseases were left to nature, they would vanish earlier. Hence, then, it is foolish for you to boast to your physicians and astrologers.

"We do not required these. We regulate our diet, and therefore, never falling sick, never need the prescriptions of the former, not their mixtures. Those who are free depend on no one. Your merchants, architects, and farmers, again, in whom you glory, are worse then slaves, worse treated then beggars. Perpetually toiling, they have no time to rest. They are always building houses, in which they never live; always digging the earth and planting trees, the fruits of which they never enjoy. Who, then, is more foolish than these, who lay by riches for their heirs to spend, and pass their own days in starvation? The merchants, too, are always devising means to accumulate dishonest gains. In hope of a famine, they purchase and lay by grain, and when the time comes sell the same at exorbitant rates, without giving aught to the poor. Thus they go on till misfortune comes: the wealth heaped up with years and years of labour is lost, either swallowed by the ocean, stolen by robbers, or forcibly taken away by some tyrant. Then, poor and dishonoured, they go about beggin from door to door, and live a vagrant life ever after. They imagine in themselves that while trading they lived well; they forget that in living well they had sold their valuable souls. They toil for the world, and at last gain neither this world nor the other. You glory in these shows; we curse them.

"You speak about your Caliphs and Kings, again, as heirs of the prophets. We cannot give them unqualified praise.Is it acting like a prophet to slaughter the race of their founder, to remain always intoxicated with wine, to exact services from thousands of God's creatures, to depreciate the rest of mankind in comparison with themselves, and to regard this world as preferable to the next ? When any of these comes to power, his first act is to imprison some dependent who had faithfully served his father and father's father for long, long years. His good services are all forgotten. Then, again, for worldly considerations he destroys his friends and brothers. In boasting of these persons, you spoil your own cause and aid in establishing our claim of superiority." (*Translated by* **T.P. MANUEL.)**

2. *The Summing-up of the Controversy between Man and the Animals.*

"When the hakim of the genii had finished, the King addressed the men again, and said : 'Have you anything further to adduce?' One of them, from Hijaz, said: 'We have abundance of other excellences to prove that we are the masters and the animals our slaves.' The King said: 'Describe them.' He answered: 'God Almighty has promised us many blessings. One of the greatest is our resurrection from the grave, for the purpose of entering by the bridge Sirat into paradise, where the divine tuba-tree grows, and where the foundatain Salsabil flows with wine, milk, honey, and water; where the mansions are high and the enchanting houris reside. Besides these, there are many other blessing related in the Koran of which the animals never can partake. This sufficiently proves that we are the masters and they our slaves.'

"The nightingale replied: 'These blessings of which you boast as the gift of God, are they not more than counterbalanced by misery and torment? Thus the dread of the day of judgement is being consigned to hell; the dread of hell is being condemned to drink gall and eat of the zakoum-tree, to be close to the King of the infernal regions and to have devils for your neighbours. All this is for you, and many other torments duly enumerated in the Koran. How much better off, therefore, are we than you! We have neither promises of reward nor of punishment, and we are content with what

God has given us. Thus we are at least equal in our proofs, and you have, therefore, no claim whatever to superiority.'

"The man of Hijaz replied: 'How can you be our equals? We can only sink to your degree of degradation if we neglect everything we ought to do. If we continue firmly in faith and obedience to God, we shall live among the prophets and saints in heaven. If we conduct ourselves with propriety and in a virtuous manner, if we employ ourselves in prayer, if we are greatful and resigned, trusting in God and fearing to do evil, our reward will be sure. If, however, we are sinful and walk not in the path of righteousness, even then Muhammad, the last of the prophets (the peace of God be upon him!), will, no doubt, intercede for us with the Almighty to pardon all our offences. After that we shall live in paradise in the company of houris. The angels will say to us : Peace be upon you! be happy and enter into paradise for ever." Not one animal of the winged or finny tribe, not one of the brute creation, will enjoy this privilege ; but after death they will all sink into annihilation, and leave not a trace behind.'

"On hearing these last words, all the *wakils* (pleaders) of the animals and *hakims* of the genii said: 'Now indeed you have hit upon a powerful argument and your proofs are strong. It is praiseworthy to be proud of such distinctions.' 'Then,' resumed the man of Hijaz, 'let me ask the just and equitable King of the genii what is the decision of the court upon this important affair.'

"The King, without further deliberation, commanded that all the animals should continue, as before, under the control and dominion of mankind, and be faithful and obedient. The animals were satisfied with this judgment, and quietly went away from the court of the genii."

3

EPIC POETRY—FIRDAUSI

PERSIA possesses a widely-extended cycle of heroic legends which her first great poet, Firdausi, condensed in his " Shah-Namah," or " Book of Kings." These legends have a double origin : some go back to a very remote age, when the Aryas, who had been up to that time nomadic, settled in Tranoxiana ; others are a distortion or exaggeration of real historical facts. The Persians divide their Kings into four dynasties: (1) The Peshdadian, in which the mythical personages of the Avesta appear as real sovereigns—Jamshid, Feridun, Zohak, etc. ; (2) the Kayanian, corresponding to the historical Achemenides; (3) the Ashganujan, or the Arsacides ; and (4) the Sasamyan, or Sassanides, the last immediately preceding the Muhammadan conquest.

The province of Seistan was especially rich in legends which had collected round the hero Rustam and his father, Zal. Under the later Sassanides existed royal registers in which were contained the accounts more or less fabulous of ancient Kings from Gayomarth to Chosroes the First. These and other legends formed the basis of the "Shah- Namah." They had already been drawn upon by a poet named Daqiqi, who lived under the Sassanides, but he died young, assassinated by a slave, and left his work unfinished for the great Firdausi to take up and carry to completion.

Firdausi, whose real name was Abu'l Kasim, was born near Tus, in Khorassan, about A. D. 935, His father, Fakhr-ed-din Ahmed, was employed as gardener in cultivating an estate in the suburbs of Tus. This estate, which consisted of a canal and four gardens, bore the name of " Firdausi,"* whence the poet derived his name. When he grew up, having experienced some oppression on the part of the Governor of Tus, he went to Ghazni, to prefer his complaint before the Sultan Mahmud. He remained for some time at the Court of Mahmud without being able to bring his affair to a termination ; and as he had no resource for his daily expenses, he employed himself in making verses for any persons who wanted them, and thereby gained what was necessary for his subsistence.

He desired ardently to form an acquaintance with one of the Court poets, Ansari, but the elevated station of the latter prevented Firdausi obtaining access to him.

On this chapter *cf.* Silvestre de Sacy : "Histoire des Poétes Persans" ; also C. Huart : "La Perse."

* Firdaus (whence our "paradise") = garden.

Upon one occasion, however, he succeeded in dexterously obtaining an entrance into the house of Ansari at the very time when the poets Asjedi and Farrukhi, both disciples of Ansari, were present with him. The latter, perceiving Firdausi, was struck by surprise at the appearance of a man in a peasant's dress, and, addressing him, said: "Friend, we are three poets, who have returned from the noise and bustle of the city to enjoy the evening here in private, and we only admit poets to share our conviviality."

Firdausi, nothing abashed, said : " Your slave is also a poet."

" Well," replied Ansari, "our conditions for admission to our repast are that we three shall compose a line each of a particular measure and rhyme. If you finish the quatrain, you shall be welcome to participate in our evening's cheer, but if you fail either in rhyme or measure, we must insist upon your immediate departure."

Firdausi accepted the conditions, and the courtiers already anticipated with joy the impossibility of his fulfilling them, for they had chosen a rhyme in which only three words in the language ended-*i.e.*, "Rushan," "Gulshan," and "Jushan." They thus extemporized:

Ansari. "The moon is not more bright than thy cheek."

Asjedi. " No rose in the garden can vie with thy lovely face."

Farrukhi. " The arrows of thine eyelash pierce the strongest cuirass."

To their great surprise, Firdausi, without hesitation, recollecting the proper name of a warrior in the " Book of Kings," added the following line ending with " Pushan":

"Like the spear of Giv in his fight with Pushan."

All three poets were delighted with this happy impromptu, and Ansari, addressing Firdausi, said : "Your reply is admirable; have you read the history of the ancient Kings?"

" Yes," replied Firdausi ; " I carry the history of the ancient monarchy of Persia along with me."

Ansari thereupon proposed to him as a trial some more difficult verses, and discovering his talents, apologized for the manner in which he had treated him before he knew his merit, and admitted him into their society.

Some time previous Sultan Mahmud had urged Ansari to put into verse the history of the ancient Kings of Persia. The poet, however, always excused himself on the plea that his engagements were too numerous; he probably felt that he did not possess sufficient strength or skill to undertake so great a work. Having hitherto found no person competent to perform the office, he determined one day to propose it to Firdausi, who readily consented to attempt the task. Ansari hastened to inform the Sultan. "Desire him to make some complimentary verses upon me," said the latter. Ansari carried the message to Firdausi, who improvised the following lines:

" Beneath his reign so universal is justice that the lamb and the wolf drink at the same stream.

From Kashmir to the China Sea every nation acknowledges his glory.

As soon as the infant's lips are moistened with its mother's milk.

The first word it articulates is the name of 'Mahmud.'

In the banquet Mahmud is a heaven of liberality; in battle a lion or a dragon.

When he walks in the garden of roses, lilies spring up beneath his feet.

His splendour causes objects to smile like a grove in spring; it makes the air soft and the earth prolific.

The dew of his generosity falling on the ground, renders it like the flowery bowers of Iran."

This panegyric gave much pleasure to Mahmud, who no longer hesitated to entrust Firdausi with the execution of the work which he had offered to undertake. He ordered a house to be built for the poet close to his own palace, so that he might never be interrupted in his composition of the "Shah-Namah." The best painters of the age were employed to adorn the rooms of the house with portraits of Kings and heroes, lions and tigers, elephants and horses, battles and sieges, likenesses of the Kings of Iran (Persia) and Turan (Turkestan), so as to serve as inspirations to the poet's mind whenever he raised his eyes from the great task imposed upon him.

Firdausi passed four years at Ghazni, occupied with the composition of the " Shah-Namah," the Sultan having promised him a dirhem of gold for every distich. He then obtained permission to revisit Tus, his native place ; and after passing four years there without intermission of his toil, he returned to Ghazni, and presented to the Sultan four parts of his poem which were completed. Mahmud was highly pleased with them, and Firdausi continued his labour with the same ardour as before, the Sultan bestowing on him from time to time fresh tokens of his regard.

Unfortunately, Firdausi took no pains to ingratiate himself with the Sultan's Vizier, Meimandi, who, being a Sunni, while Firdausi was a Shiah, conceived a grudge against him and accused him of heresy before the Sultan, who was a bigoted Sunni. The latter immediately began to change his bearing towards Firdausi, and at length, sending for him, reproached him bitterly, observing: " I know you are a heretic, and I will order you to be trampled to death by my elephants as such." The poet fell at Mahmud's feet, protesting that he was no heretic, but an orthodox Sunni, and that some calumniator had wronged him in the Sultan's opinion.

Mahmud replied: "The city of Tus has always given birth to the worst heretics. I am willing to pardon you, providing you consent to renounce your errors."

Henceforward Firdausi lived in perpetual apprehension of the effects of the Sultan's prejudice, and Mahmud never recovered his good opinion of him. The poet, however, having completed the " Shah-Namah," presented it to the Sultan. It contained nearly sixty thousand couplets, and he therefore expected to receive a corresponding number of gold dirhems, as the Sultan had promised. But, owing to the prejudice which the latter had conceived against him, he ordered that the poet should receive sixty thousand dirhems of silver instead.

Firdausi was coming out of the bath when the bags of silver arrived from the treasury. In a fit of indignation the poet gave twenty thousand dirhems to the messenger who brought them, twenty thousand to the proprietor of the bath, and twenty thousand to a seller of sherbet who happened to be present. He then concealed

himself, and having contrived to obtain from the library of the Sultan the copy of the "Shah-Namah " which he had presented to him, he inserted in it a stinging satire, part of which runs as follows:

" I have employed many years in the composition of this poem,

And I expected from the Sultan's magnificence that he would have placed a crown upon my head.

If this King had been the son of a King,* he would have placed a crown upon my head;

But as there is no nobility in his blood, he is incapable of generosity.

The son of a slave, though adorned with a diadem, eventually reveals the baseness of his origin.

Plant even in the garden of paradise a tree whose nature is bitter ;

Water it with streams from the fountain of eternity and bedew its roots with honey ;

Its natural qualities will always appear, and bitter, after all this care, will still be its fruit.

Place beneath the heavenly peacock the egg of a raven formed in infernal darkness;

When it is hatched, feed the young one with fig-seeds from the fig-tree of Eden ;

Cause it to drink of the water of Salsabil, and let the angel Gabriel breathe upon it.

All this will not avail: a raven's egg will produce nothing but a raven.

Put a young viper upon a bed of roses, and nourish it with drops from the fountain of life;

It will, notwithstanding, never become tame, and will infect you with its venom.

Transport an owl from the forest to the charming retreats in your garden ; let it perch during the night upon rose-trees and sport among hyacinths ;

When the day expands its radiant wings, the owl will stretch out its own pinions to return to its native forest.

Consider these words of our prophet, ' Everything returns to its source.'

Pass the shop of a perfumer, and your dress will imbibe the scent of ambergris.

Approach the forge of a blacksmith, and the smoke of the fire will soil your clothes.

Be not surprised, then, at the evil deeds of a wicked man : can night change her hue?

Look not for liberality from a base mind : can the face of an Ethiop become white?

Far better it is to cast dust into your own eyes than to praise an avaricious Prince.

O King ! if thou hadst been noble and generous and hadst walked in the path of virtue,

Thou hadst not thus overturned my hopes, but regarded me with a different aspect."

(*Asiatic Journal*).

The accounts given in the Persian biographies of Firdausi after his departure from Ghazni are vague and unsatisfactory. The remainder of his life was spent in wandering from one kingdom to another, pursued by the emissaries of Mahmud, whose power was too much dreaded by the various monarchs of the East to allow

*** Mahmud was the son of Sabuktagin, who had been a slave.**

them to harbour for any length of time the proscribed poet. He first took refuge with the Governor of Mazanderan, and afterwards fled to Baghdad, where he was hospitably received by the Caliph, Qadir Billah. During his residence in this city he is said to have written the poem "Yusuf and Zuleikha," which consists of nine thousand couplets, in the same measure and style as the " Shah-Namah." But even in the capital of the Abbasside Caliphs he was not secure from the power of Mahmud. The feeble Qadir Billah dared not disobey the commands of the Sultan, and the unfortunate poet was obliged to seek in countries still more remote a safer retreat. It is uncertain at what Court he next took refuge, but he eventually returned to his native town, Tus.

In the meanwhile it happened that Mahmud, during one of his expeditions into India, having occasion to write a letter to the King of Delhi, turned towards his Vizier, Meimandi, and asked him : " If this Indian does not comply with my orders and reply conformably to my wishes, what course will it be best for me to take?" Meimandi, in answer, quoted the following verse from the "Shah-Namah" :

" If the reply is not agreeable to my wishes, beware, Afrasiab, of wielding thy club and of entering the lists."

Mahmud immediately called to mind with regret the injustice of which he had been guilty towards Firdausi, and inquired what had become of him. Meimandi replied that he was old and infirm, and that he lived in poverty and obscurity at Tus, his native place. Struck with remorse, the Sultan ordered the long-withheld reward of sixty thousand gold dirhems to be despatched to the poet. But as the bearers of the money entered one gate of the city of Tus, the body of Firdausi was being carried out at another. The present was carried to his daughter, but she declined accepting it, observing : " I know not what to do with the wealth of Kings." Firdausi died A.D. 1020. His tomb is at Tus, and is much frequented by Muhammadan pilgrims.

Besides the "Shah-Namah" and "Yusuf and Zuleikha," Firdausi left some lyrical poems, but the first constitutes his chief title to fame, and has earned for him the sobriquet of "the Persian Homer." It comprises a mythical history of Persia, from the earliest times to the Arab conquest. First of all, the poet sketches the development of civilization under the early Kings-Gayomarth, who reigned thirty years and fought with the *div* Ahriman ; Hushang, who invented fire; Tahmuras, surnamed "div-band," the "Binder of Devils "; Jamshid, whose reign of seven hundred years witnessed the invention of arms, the division of the nation into four classes, and the introduction of the solar year ; Zohak, the half-fabulous tyrant, from each of whose shoulders grew a serpent, which was fed on human brains. Further on in the history comes the pathetic episode of Sohrab and Rustam, which forms the subject of Matthew Arnold's well-known poem. Sohrab was the illegitimate son of Rustam ; he had left his mother and fought in the ranks of the Turanians, the hereditary enemies of the Persians. Rustam, the Persian champion, who only knew Sohrab by reputation, disguised himself, and engaged him in single combat. At their first encounter they parted by mutual consent, though Sohrab had the advantage; at the second the young warrior was victorious, but spared his father ; at the third Rustam killed Sohrab. The latter, before he died, told Rustam he was his son, and showed him the seal which his mother had fastened on his arm. Rustam was distracted with grief, and would have put an end to his own life, but was dissuaded by his dying son.

The late Professor Cowell well says of Firdausi and the " Shah-Namah ": "Augustus said that he found Rome of brick, and left it marble; and Firdausi found his country almost without a literature, and has left her a poem that all her succeeding poets could only imitate and never surpass, and which, indeed, can rival them all even in their peculiar styles, and perhaps stands as alone in Asia as Homer's epics in Europe. His contemporaries loaded their verses with ornament, and tried to gain by affectation what simplicity and truth to Nature alone can give. Firdausi, uncorrupted by their example, wrote in the purest Persian dialect, avoiding as far as possible all Arabic expressions, the abuse of which was then beginning to corrupt the language, and in a style that for a Persian is marvellous in its simplicity. His versification is exquisitely melodious, and never interrupted by harsh forms of construction ; and the poem runs, on from beginning to end, like a river, in an unbroken current of harmony. Verse after verse ripples on the ear and washes up its tribute of rhyme ; and we stand, as it were, on the shore, and gaze with wonder into the world that lies buried beneath—a world of feeling and thought and action, that has passed away from earth's memory for ever, whilst its palaces and heroes are dimly seen mirrored below, as in the enchanted lake of Arabian story."

EXTRACTS FROM THE " SHAH-NAMAH."

1. *The Last Encounter of Sohrab and Rustam.*

" Again dismounting, each the other viewed
With sullen glance and swift the fight renewed ;
Clenched front to front, again they tug and bend,
Twist their broad limbs as every nerve would rend ;
With rage convulsive Rustam grasps him round,
Bends his strong back, and hurls him to the ground ;
Like lightning quick he gives the deadly thrust,
And spurns the stripling weltering in the dust.
'Thus, as my blood thy shining steel imbrues,
Thine, too, shall flow, for Destiny pursues ;
And when she marks the victim of her power,
A thousand daggers speed the dying hour.'
Groaning in pain, he then in murmurs sighed:
'O had I seen what Fate has now denied,
My glorious father! Life will soon be o'er,
And his great deeds enchant my soul no more !
But hope not to elude his piercing sight,
In vain for thee the deepest glooms of night.
Couldst thou through ocean's depths for refuge fly,
Or midst the star-beams track the upper sky,

His kindled rage would persecute thee there ;
For Rustam's soul will burn with anguish and despair.'
An icy horror chills the champion's heart.
His brain whirls round with agonizing smart ;
O'er his wan cheek no pearly sorrows flow ;
Senseless, he sinks beneath the weight of woe.
Relieved at length, with frenzied look he cries :
'Prove thou art mine! confirm my doubting eyes!
For I am Rustam !' Dire amazement shook
The dying youth, and mournful thus he spoke:
' How oft my heart has throbbed with strong desire,
And fondly claimed thee for my valiant sire !
Now on my arm the dreadful proof behold,
Thy sacred bracelet of refulgent gold !
When parting tears my mother's eyes o'erflowed,
This mystic gift her bursting heart bestowed :
" Take this," she said ; " thy father's token wear,
And promised glory will reward thy care."
The hour is come, but fraught with bitterest woe;
We meet in blood to wail the fatal blow.'
The loosened mail disclosed the bracelet bright—
Unhappy gift!-to Rustam's startled sight ;
Prostrate on earth, he rends his sacred hair
With all the rage and frenzy of despair."

(*Translated by* JAMES ATKINSON)

2. *The Mourning of Sohrab's Mother*

(She rises in the midst of her weeping, and orders her son's war-horse to be brought before her.)

"She seized its hoof in her bosom,
And the horse stood astonished before her.
And she rose and kissed its neck and head,
And anon she laid her cheek on its hoof.
Then she brought her son's royal robe,
And she pressed it to her bosom like a child.
She brought his cuirass and coat of mail, and his bow,
And his javelin and sword and battle-axe,

And she laid the battle-axe on her head,
And thought the while of his arm and of his stature.
She brought his saddle and bridle,
And she laid them in sorrow upon her head ;
And she brought his lasso, seventy feet long,
And she spread it in all its length before her."

(*Translated by* PROFESSOR COWELL.)

3. *Sohrab's Combat with the Gord-Afrid, or Hero-born Damsel.*

"Now the daughter of Gozhdaham was informed that her tribe had lost its Governor ; she was sore afflicted, and wept aloud from pain. She was a woman trained after the fashion of a cavalier and warrior, and had ever distinguished herself in battle ; in somuch that none had been known to excel her, and she had earned, in consequence, the name of the Gord-Afrid, or Hero-born Damsel. She set about equipping herself as a knight for combat. She braided her hair and secured it under a casque and put over this a Roman helmet. With girded-up loins she mounted her charger, and sallied forth from the citadel with the bound of a lion. Poising in her hand a javelin, she dashed across the plain rapid as the flight of a falcon ; like the dust of a whirlwind she drew up in front of the Turkish line, and, with a voice of thunder, called aloud, saying: 'Where are your champions, and which is your chief, and who of all your mighty men of war is the devoted friend of a single combat ? Let me view the man that can pledge his skill in battle and engage me after the manner of a formidable crocodile. Of all those who grace your army ranks, is none so bold as to accept my challenge ?'

"When that lion-overthrower Sohrab observed her, he smiled and bit his lip, and thus addressed her, saying : 'Is the elk returned within the toils and power of the swordsman?' Then with the speed of a squall of wind he drew on his cuirass and put a Chinese helmet upon his head ; he fiercely presented himself before the Gord-Afrid, who seemed to him another noose-ensnaring Amazon".

"She strung her bow and bent it ready, and no bird could safely pass within the reach of her arrow ; she poured a deluge of arrows upon Sohrab and upon the cavaliers on his right and left. On beholding her, Sohrab looked abashed and astonished, but advanced briskly to the fight, and, raising his shield and facing the thick of it, he waded through a field of blood. Gord-Afrid observed her opponent that he was burning like a flaming fire. Throwing her still-strung bow across her shoulders and rising upright in her stirrups, she aimed her javelin at Sohrab, furiously directing its point and the rein of her horse toward him at the same time. On finding himself the object of this fierce assault, Sohrab drew up like a tiger, and giving head to his charger, darted upon her like a flash of lightning. Now the lion was enraged, he made a furious charge, and the point of his spear soon grazed her body ; for the life-seeking weapon, entering at her wrist, found its way out by the crest of her helmet.
Then, aiming a blow at her loins, he made the armour fall piecemeal about her feet ; and, like a ball struck into the air by a club, he was preparing to toss her on his spear from the saddle ; but as she staggered in her seat, the Gord-Afrid unsheathed

a sharp scimitar from her side, and drawing it across his spear, cut it in two ; then, righting herself in her saddle, she recovered her seat. Yet she was not his match in single combat ; hope and fortune might smile for a time upon her, but soon forsook her. The chief gave rein to his horse with such a frown on his countenance as to darken the bright face of day, and, charging with a shout, came in violent contact and threw the helmet from her head, upon which the braided locks escaped from the confinement of her casque, and her face seemed a sun surrounded with rays of glory.

" Sohrab was now aware that she was a Princess, and the curling tips of her hair were the gems of her crown. He was astonished, and asked: 'Are there among the Irani troops in this field many such damsels as this ? and do the cavaliers of war on the day of battle raise the dust up to the clouds under such attractive forms ? If the maidens of Irani are capable of such exploits, what are we to expect from its men of war?' He drew the coil of his noose from his holsters, and adroitly threw and caught her in it by the middle. He said to her: ' Why, O moon-faced charmer, do you court war? Ask me not to release you: such an elk seldom falls into my net."

(*Asiatic Journal.*)

4. *The Adventures of Rustam on his way to Release Kai-Kaus, King of Persia, from the Tower in which he had been imprisoned by the Div-i-Sufid, or White Demon.*

" Fatigued with his first day's journey, Rustam lay down to sleep, having turned his horse, Raksh, loose to graze in a neighbouring meadow, where he was attacked by a furious lion ; but this wonderful horse, after a short contest, struck his antagonist to the ground with a blow from his fore-hoof, and completed the victory by seizing the throat of the royal animal with his teeth. When Rustam awoke he was surprised and enraged. He desired Raksh never again to attempt unaided such an encounter. 'Hadst thou been slain,' he said, 'how should I have accomplished my enterprise ?'

"At the second stage Rustam nearly died of thirst, but his prayers to the Almighty were heard : a fawn appeared, as if to be his guide, and, following it, he was conducted to a clear fountain, where, after regaling himself on the flesh of a wild ass which he had killed with his bow, he lay down to sleep. In the middle of the night a monstrous serpent, seventy yards in length, came out of its hiding-place and attacked the hero, who was awaked by the neighing of Raksh ; but the serpent had crept back to its hiding-place, and Rustam, seeing no danger, abused his faithful horse for disturbing his repose. Another attempt of the serpent was defeated in the same way ; but as the monster had again concealed himself, Rustam lost all patience with Raksh, whom he threatened to put to death if he again awoke him by any such unseasonable noises. The faithful steed, fearing his master's rage, but strong in his attachment, instead of neighing when the serpent again made its appearance, sprung upon it and commenced a furious contest.

"Rustam, hearing the noise, started up and joined in the combat. The serpent darted at him, but he avoided it, and whilst his noble horse seized their enemy by the back, the hero cut off its head with his sword. When the serpent was slain Rustam contemplated its enormous size with amazement, and returned thanks to the Almighty for his miraculous escape.

"Next day, as Rustam sat by a fountain, he saw a beautiful damsel regaling herself with wine. He approached her, accepted her invitation to partake of the beverage, and clasped her in his arms as if she had been an angel. It happened in the course of their conversation that the Persian hero mentioned the name of God. At the sound of that sacred word the fair features and shape of the female changed, and she became black, ugly, and deformed. The astonished Rustam seized her, and after binding her hands, bade her declare who she was. 'I am a sorceress,' was the reply, 'and have been employed by the evil spirit Ahriman for thy destruction ; but spare my life, and I am powerful to do thee service.' ' I make no compact with the Devil or his angels,' said the hero, and cut her in twain. He again poured forth his soul in thanks giving to God for his deliverance.

"On his fourth stage Rustam lost his way. While wandering about, he came to a clear rivulet, on the banks of which he lay down to take some repose, having first turned Raksh loose into a field of grain. A gardener who had charge of it came and awoke the hero, telling him in an insolent tone that he would soon suffer for his temerity, as the field in which his horse was feeding belonged to a *pahlavan,* or warrior, called Oulad. Rustam, always prone to wrath, but particularly so when disturbed in his slumbers, jumped up, tore off the gardener's ears, and gave him a blow with his fist that broke his nose and teeth. 'Take these marks of my temper to your master,' he said, and tell him to come here and he shall have a similar welcome.'

"Oulad, when informed of what had passed, was excited to fury, and prepared to assail the Persian hero, who, expecting him; had put on his armour and mounted Raksh. His appearance so dismayed Oulad that he dared not venture on the combat till he had summoned his adherents. They all fell upon Rustam at once; but the baseborn caitiffs were scattered like chaff before the wind. Many were slain, others fled, among whom was their chief. Him Rustam came up with at the fifth stage, and having thrown his noose over him, took him prisoner. Oulad, in order to save his life, not only gave him full information of the place where Kai-Kaus was confined and of the strength of the Div-i-Sufid (white demon), but offered to help the hero in the accomplishment of his perilous enterprise.

" On the sixth day they saw in the distance the city of Mazandaran, near which the Div-i-Sufid resided. Two chieftains, with numerous attendants, met them, and one had the audacity to ride up to Rustam and seize him by the belt. The hero's fury at this insolence was unbounded; he disdained, however, to use his arms against such an enemy, but, seizing the miscreant's head, wrenched it from the body, and hurled it at his companions, who fled in terror and dismay at this proof of the hero's prowess.

" Rustam proceeded after this action with his guide to the castle where the King was confined. The Divs who guarded it were asleep, and Kai-Kaus was found in a solitary cell, chained to the ground. He recognized Rustam, and bursting into tears, pressed his deliverer to his bosom. Rustam immediately began to knock off his chains. The noise occasioned by this woke the Divs, whose leader advanced to seize Rustam ; but the appearance and threats of the latter so overawed him that he consented to purchase his own safety by the release of the Persian King. After this achievement Rustam proceeded to the last and greatest of his labours—the attack on the Div-i-Sufid. Oulad told him that the Divs watched and feasted during the night, but slept during the heat of the day. As soon, therefore, as the sun rose, he rushed into the camp. The heavy blows of his mace soon awoke the surprised and slumbering guards of the Div-i-Sufid ; they collected in myriads, hoping to arrest his progress, but all in vain. The rout became general, and none escaped but those who fled from the field of battle.

"When this army was dispersed, Rustam went in search of the Div-i-Sufid, who, ignorant of the fate of his followers, slumbered in the recesses of a cavern, the entrance to which looked so dark and gloomy that the Persian hero hesitated whether he should advance ; but the noise of his approach had roused his enemy, who came forth clothed in complete armour. His appearance was terrible, but Rustam, commending his soul to God, struck a desperate blow, which severed the leg of the Div from his body. Irritated to madness by the loss of a limb, the monster seized his enemy in his arms and endeavoured to throw him down. The struggle was for some time doubtful, but Rustam, collecting all his strength, dashed his foe to the ground, and seizing him by one of his horns, unsheathed his dagger and stabbed him to the heart. The Div-i-Sufid instantly expired, and Rustam, on looking round to the entrance of the cavern, from whence the moment before he had seen innumerable Divs issuing to the aid of their lord, perceived they were all dead. Oulad, who had stood at a prudent distance from the scene of combat, now advanced and informed the hero that the lives of all the Divs depended upon that of their chief. When he was slain, the spell which created and preserved this band was broken, and they all expired."

(*Translated by* Sir JOHN MALCOLM.)

4

LYRICAL POETRY

PERSIAN lyrical poetry may be said to commence with Rudaki, born at Bukhara towards the close of the ninth century. He is reported to have been born blind and to have known the Koran by heart at the age of eight. The Samanide prince Nasir, the son of Ahmad, charmed with his genius, attached him to his own personal suite. No poet ever had more favours heaped upon him, not even Ansari, at the Court of Mahmud of Ghazni. He had two hundred pages in his service, four hundred camels to carry his property, and bequeathed his heirs, it was said, " more riches than a poet ever dreamt of."

An anecdote well known in the East illustrates the wonderful power of his poetry over his royal master. The Emir Nasir had left Bukhara for Merv, and was so captivated by the latter city—"the Queen of the World," as it was then called— that the nobles of Bukhara feared the decline of their own city. Accordingly, they begged Rudaki to compose a poem which would arouse in the Emir some regard towards Bukhara. In answer to their request, he composed the following lines :

" The freshness of the waves of Muliyan * is wafted to us ;

The remembrance of the well-loved friend recurs to us ;

The sand of the Amou† and its pebbles glide under the feet like silk;

The waters of the Jehun rise up to the waist of the King.

Rejoice, O Bukhara, and be happy ! the King returns as a guest to thy walls.

The King is the moon, Bukhara is the sky: the moon reascends the sky ;

The King is the cypress, Bukhara is the garden : the cypress returns to the garden."

(*Translated by DARMESTETER.*)

Nasir was so moved by these verses that he at once started for Bukhara, and reached it in a single march. Besides composing many eulogies of the King, Rudaki

---

On this chapter *cf.* James Darmesteter : "Les Origines de la Poèsie Persane."

* A river of Bukhara.

† The Amou Daria, or Oxus.

translated the Indian collection of fables known as "Kalila and Dirnnah" from Arabic into Persian verse, but his translation has been lost. He also composed much amatory poetry, of which the following is a specimen :

"O thou whose face is fair as the moon, whose hair is as fragrant as musk, dost thou know what thy slave was formerly, and how many young maidens used to love him ?

How many hearts, once as hard as stone or an iron anvil, my songs have made soft as silk !

Thou seest Rudaki as he is at present ; thou hast not seen him when he lived with the libertines.

Thou hast not seen him when he went about the world reciting songs, when he was the author of the 'Thousand Stories.'*

Gone are the days when his poems overspread the world; gone are the days when he was the poet of Khorassan.

The times are changed, and I am changed also. Bring me my staff, for the time has come when I must wander with a beggar's staff and scrip."

(*Translated by* DARMESTETER.)

Towards the end of his days Rudaki turned his back upon the world and adopted an ascetic life. "Oh, my soul," he exclaims in one of his poems, "why take so much trouble in nourishing this body ? Should an angel condescend to the care of dogs ? I have a share in the truth taught by the prophets. Why should I seek to draw at the dried-up stream of Greek philosophy?" Rudaki survived his patron, Nasir, and died in poverty and neglect about A.D. 954.

Among the group of poets of which Rudaki was the centre was Shahid of Bactriana. He and Rudaki were mutual admirers, and it is said that Rudaki even preferred the verses of Shahid to his own. The few fragments which remain of the latter seem to justify this preference. Shahid is the pessimist of his century, and has a sombre and grandiose imagination. He was disillusioned as regards the world, and had proved, as he says, by experience - that genius and good fortune are like the narcissus and the rose, which never bloom together. During his lifetime his native country, Khorassan, was laid waste by the ravages of war, and he thus moralizes over the ruins of Tus, one of the chief cities of that province:

"Last night I spent in the desert of Tus. I saw an owl perched where formerly perched the bird of morning (the cock). I said to it: `What news dost thou bring from the desert?' It answered : 'The news is only this : Disaster, disaster !" Elsewhere he says: " Fate has two workmen—the tailor and the weaver. One only sews the apparel of Kings; the other only weaves the black garments of beggars." He journeyed, he says, through the world from one end to another without meeting a single wise man who was content, and condenses his philosophy into the following sombre image :

" If grief were to send up smoke like fire, the world would be buried in perpetual gloom."

* The book of " Kalilah and Dimnah" above mentioned.

Another contemporary poet, Kisai, who died at the age of fifty, takes a similarly gloomy retrospect of life:

" Fifty years ago I entered life to see what good I could do in it by deed or word.

I have passed all my life in this base world, bearing burdens like a camel, the slave of my children, hampered by family ties.

When all is said and done, what have these fifty years left to me ? A book of account with a hundred thousand sins recorded in it.

Alas ! how shall I finally discharge this account, which begins with falsehood and ends with nothingness ?

Alas ! where is the glory of my youth ? where are the things which made life dear ? where is beauty ? where is grace ?

My head is white as milk, my heart is black as pitch. My cheeks are like the water-lily, my body like the slender bough.

Day and night the fear of death makes me tremble like a disobedient child who trembles before the whip.

All is passed, and I have passed; that which was to be has been.

I have been, and my song is no more than a child's tale.

O Kisai! the fiftieth year has laid its five fingers upon thee; it beats down thy wings with blows of the fist and of the claw."

A poet of robuster fibre than either of the two last mentioned was Cabus Shams-al-Maali, Prince of Tabaristan and Jurjan. His writings were held in such estimation that the most casual productions of his pen were preserved as models of composition, and we are told that a famous Vizier of Persia could never open even an official despatch from Shams-al-Maali without exclaiming : "This is written with the feather of a celestial brid."

His energy in reforming abuses roused against him a number of his nobles, who conspired together to deprive him of the sovereignty. Finding a favourable opportunity, they secured his person and placed him in confinement. They then sent messengers to his son Minuchihri, informing him of what they had done, and offering him the throne, on condition that he would unite with them in the deposition of his father. The young Prince pretended to accede to their proposals, and was accordingly proclaimed sovereign of Tabaristan. But no sooner was Minuchihri in possession of the throne than he flew to his father's prison, and, prostrating himself before him, declared that he had only accepted the crown in order to preserve it for his father. Shams-al-Maali, however, though pleased with his son's offer, refused it, saying that he had now done with the world, and intended to dedicate his remaining years to the service of God.

But the conspirators who had dethroned him, dreading his abilities, had resolved upon his death. Having surrounded the castle where Shams-al-Maali was living in seclusion, they unroofed his chamber, deprived him of clothes and every necessary, and left him to die of cold and exposure. The following is one of his shorter poems:

"Why should I blush that Fortune's frown
Dooms me life's humble paths to tread,
To live unheeded and unknown,
To sink forgotten to the dead?"
"Tis not the good, the wise, the brave,
That surest shine or highest rise;
The feather sports upon the wave,
The pearl in ocean's cavern lies".
" Each lesser star that studs the sphere
Sparkles with undiminished light ;
Dark and eclipsed alone appear
The lord of day, the queen of night."

(*Translated by* J. D. CARLYLE.)

There were many poets and men of letters at the Court of Shams-al-Maali before his deposition, the greatest of whom was the celebrated Avicenna, who was not only a philosopher and a physician, but also a poet of no mean calibre. He had formerly been at the Court of Mamun, Emir of Khwarazim Khiva. The great Sultan Mahmud of Ghazni, who, though a bigoted Sunni, liked to patronize literary men, hearing of his reputation, had sent for him. Avicenna, who was anything but orthodox, not caring to come into close proximity with Mahmud, fled to the Court of Shams-al-Maali at Jurjan. Irritated at his flight, the Sultan sent messengers carrying portraits of Avicenna in many directions in order to arrest him; but though Shams-al-Maali had received one of these portraits, he did not surrender Avicenna This, of course, is not the place to speak of the latter as a philosopher. The following are some of the fragments of his poetry which have come down to us :

ON WINE

"Wine is the enemy of the drunkard and the friend of the sober.

A little dose of it is as an antidote ; a strong dose is poison.

A generous wine stimulates the mind, for of a truth its colour surpasses the colour of the rose ;

It is of sharp flavour, like a father's advice, but useful also ; permitted to the intelligent, forbidden to fools.

Is it the fault of wine if a fool drinks it and goes stumbling in the darkness ?

Religion allows it to the wise, if reason forbids it to asses."

(*Translated by Darmesteter.*)

Avicenna's irritation at the frequent and well-founded suspicions of his orthodoxy finds vent in the following:

"In the company of a few fools, so foolish that they imagine they are the pick of the intellectual, one had better play the ass ;

Such are the asinine qualities of these donkeys that whosoever is not one they call a misbeliever."

His poem "On the Soul" is of a higher mood, and tinged with mysticism:

"It descended to thee from a lofty place, a sad-coloured dove, chaste and shy ;

Invisible to the keenest eye, yet it was unveiled.

It came to thee reluctantly, yet perchance it will be loathe to leave thee.

Formerly it was pure, untrammelled by any tie. Now that it is united to thee, it has grown accustomed to the neighbourhood of deserts and ruins.

Why has it fallen from so lofty a height into a pit of such depth ?

If for some reason it is God who has cast it down, this reason is hidden from the subtlest intellect ;

And although it became learned in the secrets of both worlds, the void which it carried within itself has not been filled up.

It is like a flash of lightning over a valley, rapidly extinguished and as if it had not been."

(*Translated by* CARRA DE VAUX.)

Contemporary with Avicenna was Nasir-i-Khusrau, who was descended from the seventh Imam of the Shiahs. He travelled in North India, and was for some years in the service of the Sultan Mahmud of Ghazni, and of his son, the Sultan Masud. About the year 1044 he renounced the courtier's life for the ascetic's, and started on the pilgrimage to Mecca. He passed through Syria, and arrived in Egypt during the reign of the Fatimite Caliph, Mustansir, who received him kindly. On his return from the pilgrimage he occupied himself with literary work in Khorassan, but was attacked by the leading mullahs on account of his supposed heterodoxy. He then went into retirement in Badakhshan, where he died. In the following lines he defends himself against his traducers:

"Thou knowest, O God, what I suffered in Khorassan from great and small.

What was my fault that they so persecuted me, friends and strangers, young and old?

Seeing that I acknowledge the mission of the Prophet, and I never said aught against it.

I believe in the judgment Day, and know the Koran by heart."

One of his apologues strikingly anticipates Byron's well-known lines on Kirke White:

"One day an eagle, flapping his mighty wings, flew from a lofty crag into the air.

Boasting of the strength of his pinions, he said thus :

'To-day the whole earth lies beneath me; who can equal me in flight—what bird, phonix, hawk, or any other ? Although I fly in the lofty firmament high up out of bow-shot, I can see the smallest thing far below ;

If on the surface of the ground a gnat should stir, I can see the movement of its wing.'

Thus he boasted, and sudde .ly by the cruelty of fate an archer in ambush aimed an arrow at him.

Suddenly it transfixed his wing, and flung him down from the height to the depth below.

Prone he fell in the dust, struggling like a fish ;

He turned his eyes to right and left, wondering whence mere iron and wood had obtained this swiftness and power to fly.

When he looked near, he saw it was one of his own plumes which had winged the shaft ;

He said, 'Of whom should I complain, since what has happened to me has come from myself?'

O Nasir, put away boasting out of thy head ;

Remember the fate of the boasting eagle."*

Nasir-i-Khusrau was not only a poet, but a very keen observer. He published an account of his travels under the title" Safar-Nama." The manuscript of this was discovered in 1872, and contains a careful account of the buildings and waterworks of Jerusalem, which he had visited. It was said that if this work had been found a little earlier it might have saved the Palestine Exploration Committee much excavation and considerable outlay.

Not long after the death of Nasir-i-Khusrau was born Abu Ismael, of Ispahan. He was surnamed Tughrai on account of his skill in the kind of writing called " Tughra." He attached himself to the service of the Seljuk Sultans, Malek Shah and his grandson Masoud, by the last of whom he was raised to the dignity of Vizier. Masoud, however, was attacked and defeated by Sultan Mahmud, of Ghazni, in A.D. 1120. The Vizier was seized and thrown into prison, and not long afterwards put to death. A short time before he had written some lines on the birth of a son, which show what his age was at this period:

"This child, born to me in my old age, has charmed my eyes and at the same time inspired me with grave reflections, for fifty-seven years leave traces on the face of the hardest stone."

The most celebrated of his poems is the "Lamiyat-i-ajam," so called because every line terminates with the consonant Lam (1). Of this poem the late Professor Carlyle says : "It has obtained more general approbation than any poem extant in the East ; it is celebrated by the historians, commented upon by the critics, and quoted by the people." It is also one of the very first Oriental poems introduced to English readers, having been edited by Dr. Pococke, of Oxford, in 1661. The poem is pessimistic and distrustful in tone. A portion of it runs as follows:

"No kind supporting hand I meet
But fortitude shall stay my feet ;
No borrowed splendours round me shine
But virtue's lustre all is mine ;

* Hitherto untranslated

A fame unsullied still I boast,
Obscured, concealed, but never lost—
The same bright orb that led the day
Pours from the west his mellowed ray.

* * * *

But wealth, I own, engross'd each thought ;
There was a moment when I sought
The glittering stores ambition claims
To feed the wants his fancy frames.
But now 'tis past ; the changing day
Has snatched my high-built hopes away,
And bade this wish my labours close:
Give me not riches, but repose.

* * * *

Contempt and want the wretch await
Who slumbers in an abject state ;
Midst rushing crowds by toil and pain
The meed of honour we must gain ;
At honour's call the camel hastes
Through trackless wilds and dreary wastes,
Till in the glorious race she find
The fleetest coursers left behind.
If bloated indolence were fame,
And pompous ease our noblest aim,
The orb that regulates the day
Would ne'er from Aries' mansion stray.
I've bent at Fortune's shrine too long ;
Too oft she heard my suppliant tongue,
Too oft has mocked my idle prayers,
While fools and knaves engross'd her cares;
Awake for them, asleep to me,
Heedless of worth, she scorned each plea.
Ah, had her eyes, more just, surveyed
The different claims which each displayed,
Those eyes, from partial fondness free,
Had slept to them and waked for me.

However keen, however bright,
The sabre glitter to the sight,
Its splendour's lost, its polish vain,
Till some bold hand the steel sustain.
Why have my days been stretched by fate
To see the vile and vicious great,
While I who led the race so long
Am last and meanest of the throng ?
Ah, why has Death so long delayed
To wrap me in his friendly shade ?
Left me to wander thus alone,
When all my heart held dear is gone ?"

(*Translated by* J. D. CARLYLE).

We come now to the great name of Omar Khayyam, born at Nishapur about the middle of the eleventh century. Thanks to Fitzgerald's famous translation, or rather paraphrase, he is far better known in the West as a poet than as an astronomer, though in the East the reverse is the case. As regards Fitzgerald's version, Professor Cowell, who was the first to show him a manuscripts of Omar Khayyam's " Rubaiyat," which he had discovered in the Bodleian Library, says : "Fitzgerald's translation is so infinitely finer than the original, that the value of the latter is such mainly as attaches to Chaucer's or Shakespeare's prototypes."

The poet took the title of "Khayyam " from the occupation of his father, who was a tent-maker. As a youth he studied at the college of Nishapur, under the Imam-al-Muwaffik. His two chief friends were Nizam-ul-Mulk, afterwards Vizier to the Sultan Malek Shah, and Hassan-as-Sabbah, founder of the sect of the Assassins. As we have mentioned in a previous chapter, the three friends had agreed that whichever of them was the first to attain a position of eminence should help the other two. Nizam-ul-Mulk, on becoming Vizier, allotted Omar Khayyam a pension of twelve hundred gold pieces per annum.

The following account of Omar Khayyam's death, related by more than one Persian biographer, seems to show that he was not such a confirmed agnostic as he appears in Fitzgerald's version : " It is related that Omar was one day picking his teeth with a toothpick of gold, and was studying the chapter on Metaphysics from Avicenna's 'Book of Healing.' When he reached the section on The One and the Many, he placed the tooth-pick between the two leaves, arose, performed his prayers, and made his last injunctions. He neither ate nor drank anything that day, and when he performed the last evening prayer he bowed himself to the ground, and said as he bowed: 'O God, verily I have known Thee to the extent of my power; forgive me therefore. Verily my knowledge of Thee is my recommendation to Thee.' And, so saying, he died, and may God have pity on him!"*

In one quatrain omitted by Fitzgerald, but included by Whinfield in his version, he avers his belief in the resurrection. It should be remembered, however, that many of the quatrains which pass under his name are of doubtful authenticity.

* "Nuzhat-ul-Arwah." Transtated by E. Denison Ross.

"On the dread day of final scrutiny,
As is thy wisdom, so thy meed shall be;
Strive to get virtues here, for thou wilt rise
Bearing the imprint of thy quality."

As Fitzgerald's version is so well known and so easily procurable, we may insert here as a specimen of Khayyam's work a literal translation of some of the quatrains by Professor Cowell, the poet's first English translator :

"The spring-cloud came and wept bitterly above the grass ;
I cannot live without the purple-coloured wine.
This grass is our festal place to-day,
But the grass that grows from our dust, whose festal place will it be ?
" Ask not for empire, for life is a moment ;
Every atom of dust was once a Kai-Kobad or Jamshid ;
The story of the world and this whole life of ours
Is a dream and a vision, an illusion and a breath.
"When the nightingale raises his lament in the garden,
We must seize, like the tulip, the wine in our hand ;
Ere men one to the other, in their foolish talk,
Say, 'Such an one has seized his cup and gone !'.
"That castle in whose hall King Bahram-seized the cup,
There the fox hath brought forth her young and the lion made his lair.
Bahram, who his life long seized the deer,*
See how the tomb † has seized him to-day !
"By the running stream and the grass, cup-bearer the lamp,
Give the wine, break thy vows, and touch the lute"
Be glad, for the running stream lifts its voice ;
' I am gone,' it cries, 'and shall never return.'
Alas ! that the book of youth is folded,
And the fresh purple spring become December!
That bird of joy whose name was youth,
Alas! I know not how he came or is gone.
" Be glad, for the moon of the festival will be here ;
All the means of mirth will soon be here.
Pale is yon moon, its back bowed and lean ;
You would say it would soon sink in its sorrow.
" Lip to lip I passionately kissed the bowl,

* *Gor*
† *Ibid*

To learn from it the secret of length of days ;
Lip to lip in answer it whispered reply:
'Drink wine, for, once gone, thou shalt never return.'
" I went last night into a potter's shop ;
A thousand pots did I see there, noisy and silent,
When suddenly one of the pots raised a cry :
'Where is the pot-maker, the pot-buyer, the pot-seller ?'
" In the view of reality, not of illusion,
We mortals are chess-men, and fate is the player ;
We each act our game on the board of life,
And then, one by one, are swept into the box.
"Yon rolling heavens at which we gaze bewildered
Are but the image of a magic-lantern :
The sun is the candle, the world the shade,
And we the images which flit therein.
"Last night I dashed my clay cup on the stone,
And at the reckless feat my heart was glad,
When with a voice for the moment outspake the cup:
'I was once as thou, and thou shalt be as I'."

Khwajah Nizami, of Samarcand, one of Omar's pupils, relates the following story about his grave: " I often used to hold conversations with my teacher, Omar Khayyam, in a garden; and one day he said to me: 'My tomb shall be in a spot where the north wind may scatter roses over it.' I wondered at the words he spoke, but I knew that his were no idle words. Years after, when I chanced to revisit Nishapur, I went to his final resting-place ; and, lo! it was just outside a garden, and trees laden with fruit stretched their boughs over the garden wall and dropped their flowers upon his tomb, so that the stone was hidden under them."

Of an entirely opposite character to the poetry of Omar Khayyam is that of Ibn Yamin, who may be described as a Persian Puritan. His father was Yamin-ud-Din, a Minister at the Court of the Khudabendeh Princes in Khorassan in the fourteenth century. Ibn Yamin carried on a literary correspondence with his father, who was also a poet, when one of them was in Asia Minor and the other in Khorassan. The letters contained in this correspondence are, still prized as examples of style, and are much read in Persia and India.

Ibn Yamin's poems took the shape of moral aphorisms, which, it is said, he composed to counteract the sacrilegious quatrains of Omar Khayyam. He seems to have been an unambitious man, and spent his life in retirement looking after his estates. His poems are written in a clear and limpid style, without the constant allusions to wine and roses, mystical or unmystical, which are so frequent in nearly all other Persian poets. He calls things by their plain names, without any fantastic sub-allusions. He lacks lyrical enthusiasm, but makes up for it by sanity and common-sense. He does not "exercise himself in matters too high for him," nor try to solve insoluble riddles, but looks on from his retired corner with quiet and half-compassionate amusement at the world's mad race for honours and wealth. Somewhat like Wordsworth, he seems to have combined aloofness from the world, nobility of character, and austerity of style. The following are some of his pieces :

I. *The World.*

"Jesus (on whom be peace!) called once to God with earnest supplication: O Lord, the world came into being at Thy behest. Show Me the world as it really is.'

"So saying, He walked on, taking His way towards the wilderness, where he saw in a solitary place a veiled woman. 'Who art thou ?' He said to her. The woman replied:'I wait for Thee, O man, who hast desired to see me. I am the world, as Thou art the glory of this age.'

" ' The world!' said Jesus ; 'then unveil thyself, and let Me see thee.' She unveiled herself, and he saw a withered and ghastly hag, with rouged cheeks ; one of her hands exaled sweet perfume and the other was red with blood. Jesus was astonished, and asked her the meaning of the perfume on one hand and of the blood on the other. She answered: 'With one hand I slew one of my suitors to-day, while with the perfumed hand I beckoned to myself another suitor, and yet my virgin veil has never been rent.'

" 'How?' said Jesus, in wrath.'Thou hast had suitor after suitor, and sayest that thy virgin veil has not been rent ?'

"Then she laughed, and said: 'Of all who have wooed and followed me none has shown himself really a man, for he who is indeed a man would never desire me ; therefore, though always wooed, I am ever virgin.' "

(*Translated by* SCHLECHTA-WSSEHRD.)

2. The advantages of Travel

" Travel of a truth brings danger and grief, which those escape who never travel ;

Yet travel brings much blessing also, which those miss who keep at home.

He who always stays in his dark chamber, how can he behold the glory of the moon and stars ?

How shall the divers obtain pearls if they wrestle not with the terrors of the deep ?

He who never constrains his loins to stoop in a mine, how shall he lift ingots of gold and silver ?

The man, however gifted he may be, who cowers at his hearth will never reach the goal,

As the falcon, however strong, which never quits the nest will never catch the prey."

3. Lines written Shortly before his Death.

" Think not that the heart of the son of Yemin is full of grief, but see in what fashion he quits this falling house. In his right hand the Koran, with his eye directed towards his Friend (God) and his face turned towards the Path, he follows the angel of death with a smile."

5

COURT AND PANEGYRIC POETRY

We have already seen how Sultan Mahmud of Ghazni patronized Firdausi and other poets. His example was followed by many other Persian Princes, such as Malik Shah and Sandgar, of Khorassan. In many cases the poets became merely pensioned panegyrists. The vanity of the rulers and the greed of the poets often degraded poetry to the level of mere flattery of despotism. In spite of the Koran's stern prohibition of anything like deification of men, the Court poets often expressed themselves in hyperbolical language which became sheer idolatry. In some cases the sun, moon, and powers of Nature are represented as under the control of the ruler who is the object of their praise.

Chief among the panegyric poets are Unsuri, Anwari, Khakani, and Hilali. Unsuri had the title of " King of Poets " at the Court of Mahmud of Ghazni. He stood at the head of four hundred poets, whose works had to pass through his hands for inspection and revision before they were submitted to the Sultan. An heroic poem on the victories of Mahmud is one of his principal works. The following instance of his readiness and wit is recorded: The Sultan, having one night, while intoxicated, cut off the beautiful tresses of his favourite mistress, was plunged into despair at beholding his rash act when morning came. He became a prey to vexation and remorse, was restless and uneasy, refused all consolation, and became irritable in the extreme by the recollection of his folly. In this state everyone feared to approach him, and the palace was filled with terror and consternation. Unsuri, however, resolved to break the spell, and accosted the monarch in a manner which attracted his attention ; he then, without a moment's hesitation, addressed him in the following lines:

On the Tresses of the Fair One.

"Be this day for ever blest !

None shall sigh, none shed a tear;

Let the grape's rich juice be pressed,

Scatter roses far and near.

These are hours to mirth devoted ;

On this chapter *cf.* Costello: " The Rose-garden of Persia "; and Pizzi : "La Poesia Persiana."

She on whom our monarch doated
Made his cup with bliss run o'er,
Gave his love one charm the more.
" But he grieves. What should he dread ?
See those waving tresses all,
See the curls that deck her head,
One by one like blossoms fall !
Though his hand has pruned the tree,
Why should sorrow cloud his brow,
Since the boughs will fairer be,
More display their treasures now?
"Should the tender cypress sprays
Cast their arms unchecked around,
'Twould become a tangled maze,
Where no grace, no charm, were found ;
But those beauties thinned and shorn,
More its slender shape adorn.
Every ringlet hid a grace—
Now shines out the lovely face ;
Now the clouds are lost to view,
And the sun breaks smiling through."

(*Translated by* **COSTELLO.**)

These lines so delighted the Sultan that he ordered the poet's mouth to be three times filled with jewels, after which, calling for wine, he ordered the poet to be seated beside him, and in his society forgot his grief.

The next important Court poet is Anwari, born at Abiverd, in Khorassan, in the first half of the twelfth century. He studied at Tus, in Khorassan, where he acquired a vast amount of miscellaneous knowledge, to which he refers in the following lines:

" Although I have concentrated my powers on the panegyric and the ode, do not think that I am lacking in the power to express spiritual matters.

On the contrary, I have exercised myself in all the branches of knowledge cultivated by my contemporaries ; I know something of music, of logic, and of astronomy."

In one of his most celebrated odes he expresses regret that he could not have been a second Avicenna. " O God!" he exclaims, "how my soul would have delighted in the joys of philosophy, if my bag were not already stuffed with poetry!"

His works are full of metaphors borrowed from astronomy or mathematics. However, this varied knowledge was not of much practical use to him, and, like many other scholars, he fell into the depths of poverty.One day he was seated at the door of the college at Tus when he saw a horseman pass, attended by a numerous retinue.

" Who is this ?" he asked.

" It is a poet," he was told.

" Wonderful !" he exclaimed. " Learning is so greatly valued, and see how poor I am ; poetry is so little esteemed, and this poet has such a retinue! By the grace of God henceforward I will dedicate myself wholly to poetry, which has been hitherto the least of my merits."

That same night he composed an ode in praise of the Sultan Sandjar. The next day he went to the King's Court and recited it. The Sultan was an accomplished critic ; he recognized the abilities of the poet and asked him :

"Do you wish to be attached to my Court, or have you come for a reward merely ?"

Anwari kissed the ground, and improvised as follows :

"In this world I have no other refuge but the threshold of thy Court. I know not where to betake myself except to this door."

The Sultan assigned him a monthly allowance, and till the death of Sandjar the poet remained in his service, and during this time composed several odes in his honour. In the year 1153 Sandjar marched against the Turkoman tribe of Ghuz, who had withheld their usual tribute of forty thousand sheep. An action ensued, in which he was defeated and taken prisoner. During his long confinement of four years his dominions were ruled by his favourite, Sultana Khatun Turkan. In A. D. 1156 Sandjar managed to escape, but only lived a short time afterwards. During his captivity Anwari composed a pathetic poem, entitled "The Tears of Khorassan," describing the ravages committed on that province by the Ghuz, addressed to Sandjar's nephew, Mahmud-ben-Mohammed, the Governor of Khorassan. Some of the stanzas are as follows :

"Say, dost thou know what wild confusion reigns
Throughout Irania's desolated plains,
And how her sons are drowned in seas of tears?
"Say, dost thou know of all her ancient boast,
And glorious sights that spread her fame the most,
No trace or mournful vestige now appears ?
" The mosque no more admits the pious race ;
Constrained, they yield to beasts the holy place,
A stable now, where dome nor porch is found ;
Nor can the savage foe proclaim his reign,
For Khorassania's criers all are slain,
And all her pulpits levelled with the ground.
" Does some fond mother on a sudden view
Among the victims of this murderous crew
A darling son, her waning age's joy?
Since here the grief is fatal that is known,

Fear checks the rising tear and labouring groan
Nor dares the matron ask how died her boy."

(*Translated by* KIRKPATRICK.)

After the death of Sandjar, Anwari lived at the Court of the last of the Seljuqian dynasty, Tughral III. At Merv it happened that in A.D. 1186 there was a conjunction of all the planets in the sign Libra. Anwari, who plumed himself on his astrological knowledge, predicted that on the night of this conjunction a violent storm would overthrow many buildings and trees in the neighbourhood. Alarmed at this prediction, the people hid themselves for a while in subterranean chambers ; but, as it happened, that night the air was so still that there was not enough breath to move the flame of a torch which had been set up on a minaret. The next day the Sultan sent for Anwari and reprimanded him severely. The poet excused himself by saying that his prophecy would be fulfilled gradually. Here again, however, he was doomed to disappointment, as during the whole year there was so little wind that the people were unable to winnow their corn.

After this Anwari thought it advisable to retire first to Nishapur, and then to Balkh. In the latter town he fell into disgrace for lampooning a rich citizen, and as a punishment was paraded through the town in female dress. From this disgrace he was delivered by the Cadi Hamiduddin, and composed an ode to thank him. The last years of his life were darkened by illness. In one of his poems he complains that gout or some other disease had paralyzed his limbs and prevented him paying his compliments in person to his patron. Like so many other poets of his class, towards the close of life he bade a solemn farewell to poetry, left the Court, and adopted an ascetic life :

"I have renounced panegyric and satire " (he says). " Why ?

Because I had gone astray from the right path.

I have composed, each in their turn, odes, panegyrics, and satires, because my mind was compounded "of passion, cupidity, and hatred.

By night I would torment myself in trying to describe my beloved's sugared lips and her tangled curls ;

By day I would weary myself in solving this problem, Where, with whom, and how shall I get my supper ?

Sometimes I was like the famished dog, whose only comfort is rending one more wretched even than himself.

Now I pray, 'Lord, preserve me henceforth from composing odes, panegyrics, and satires. Too long, alas ! I have done violence to my reason and maltreated my soul.'

Anwari, self-glorification is not worthy of one bearing the name of man. Remain in retirement and seek the path of safety.

The moments of thy life are numbered, and are passing very quickly."

The Sultan endeavoured to induce him to return to Court, but in vain. The poet sent him the following lines, probably the last which he composed :

" I live in a little cell, but enjoy in it peace of mind and good sleep ; all things whereon Kings pride themselves are mine.

He who is at the same time my refuge and my goal has closed for me the path of return.

My tongue cannot answer the King's message ; my dwelling and my manner of life must answer for me."

Anwari died in A.D. 1200, and was buried at Balkh.

Another distinguished Court poet was , Minuchihri, At the commencement of his career he composed poems in praise of the Emir Minuchihr, son of Shams-al-Maali Qabus, whom we have mentioned in the last chapter. When Shams-al-Maali was killed, the Abbaside Caliph, Al-Qadir B'illah, addressed from Baghdad a letter of condolence to the Emir Minuchihr, and conferred on him the honorific title of Falak-al-Maali ("the heaven of loftiness "). The latter succeeded to his father's throne, and ruled in Jurjan and Mazanderan. He was a vassal of Mahmud of Ghazni, to whom he paid a yearly tribute of a thousand dinars. The poet Minuchihri, as was the custom at the time, adopted his patron's name as his own. He afterwards became one of the Court poets of Mahmud of Ghazni and of his successor, Masoud. The following is part of an ode of his in praise of Masoud's Vizier, Ahmed :

"The sun of Viziers, Ahmed, the sun of Abd-us-Samad ; he who is not only the sun of Viziers, but the sun of all creatures, chief of the chiefs of the world, he is at the head of all, as the steel-point tops the lance.

Two little things make him greater than all the creatures of the world-two little things : the heart and the tongue.*

He gives gold, and gets a good name thereby ; he knows that this world is but transitory.

The kingdom is like a body, and the servants of the King are like arteries and veins in this body.

The Vizier is like the physician, who sees when the blood in the veins beats too strongly or too feebly."

In the following complaint of his detractors Minuchihri displays his satirical vein:

"My critic wishes to be considered as clever as I, but he who has consumption will never be stout.

My critic says: ' We are old, whilst thou art young; a young man cannot equal an aged one in wisdom.'

I answer : ' If in vile beings knowledge increased with age, why is Satan in greater disgrace the older he grows ?

My critic says: 'Why are my poems little read, while thine are read by boys and girls ?'

'Because my poems are like clear water, while thine are like ditch-water ; when one can drink clear water, will he drink ditch-water ?'

* An allusion to the Arabic proverb, "A man consist of his two smallest parts—the heart and the tongue."

My critic says : ' Why dost thou pay thy court to the King ?'

I answer : ' Should not the foxes pay court to the lion ?

O envious one, thou wilt never see, so long as thou livest, the face of reason. How can an inhabitant of hell behold the locks and faces of the black-eyed houris ?

Not to make verses is better than to make bad verses ; to be childless is better than to produce an abortion."

Minuchihri was not a highly inspired poet. His merits chiefly consist in a clearance of thought and of diction which is not often found in panegyric poetry, and in an even flow of language. His most sincere panegyrics are not those of Princes, but of wine ; in these he is frankly sensuous, without any admixture of a mystical element such as we have in Hafiz's apostrophes to his cup-bearer.

A more original poet than Minuchihri was Rashidi Watwat, who derived his surname (" Watwat," a swallow) from the smallness of his stature and the sharpness of his tongue. He was a native of Balkh, and one of the most learned of Persian poets. Von Hammer calls him the Boileau of Persia. One day he was holding a public disputation before Atsiz, Prince of Khwarizam ; the latter, hearing him declaim with great vigour, ordered, in jest, the inkstand in front of him to be removed that he might have a good view of him. Upon which Watwat quoted the Arabic proverb we have seen alluded to by Minuchihri : " A man consists of his two smallest parts, the heart and the tongue."

Atsiz showed the poet great favour, and later on, when Atsiz rebelled against Sultan Sandjar, and the latter besieged the fort of Hazarasp, Anwari, who was in Sandjar's retinue, and Watwat wrote very severe satires against each other's side, which they exchanged by means of arrows. When Hazarasp was taken, and Watwat fell into Sandjar's hands, he commanded that the poet should be cut into seven pieces; but Watwat, having begged that, on account of his diminutive size, he should only be cut into two, the Sultan smiled and forgave him.

Watwat spent the last years of his life at the court of II Arslan, son of Atsiz, in whose praise he wrote odes as he had done for his father. He died A.D. 1182.

Contemporary with Watwat was Khaqani, born in Shirwan, a province bordering on the Caucasus. His mother was a Greek by birth, who had been brought into Persia by a slave merchant, and embraced Islam after having been sold to Khaqani's father. The poet seems to have been neglected by his father, but was educated by his uncle, a druggist, who taught him Arabic, medicine, astronomy, and metaphysics.

He made his debut as a poet at the Court of Minuchihri, Prince of Shirwan, who, for one poem in his praise, presented Khaqani with the munificent gift of a thousand golden dinars . Presuming, possibly, on the King's familiarity and kindness, he on one occasion sent the following petition to him:

" Bestow on me a warm vest or a fair slave."

When the King read this, he was enraged at the doubt cast upon his generosity by the word "or," which he thought implied that he would only grant one of his requests, instead of both vest and slave together, and ordered Khaqani to be punished. The poet, with great ingenuity, seized a fly, cut off its wings and feet in the presence of the King's messenger, and sent him back with the dismembered fly and the following message: "I wrote the word 'with' (Persian BA), but this naughty fly alighted on the dot of the BA, whilst the ink was yet wet, and with its feet extended it, so as to make it a YA ('or'), otherwise it would have been, as I originally intended it should be, confident in your Majesty's usual generosity, a request for both vest and slave." His ingenuity was rewarded, and he escaped punishment.

After Minuchihri's death Khaqani obtained leave from his successor, Akhsitan, to visit Mecca on pilgrimage. On the way there and back he received many honours, at Bagdad, at Mecca itself, at Mosul, and at Ispahan. These seem to have somewhat turned his head, and on his return to Akhsitan's court he incurred the displeasure of that prince, and was imprisoned in the fortress of Shabran. During his imprisonment he wrote an ode entitled " Habsyah," or " the prison-ode." The following extract from it shows that he had no small opinion of his rank as a poet:

"I am great ; I am of the number of master-minds ;

I belong to the unseen world, and I am holy by my birth.

How, then, is it possible that my essence should allow itself to be subjugated by matter ?

I am Khaqani, the sovereign of the realm of words, and in the treasury of my eloquence a single jewel is worth the revenue of a hundred satraps.

May I become an infidel if in the seven regions of the earth there is a single man capable of composing two verses equal to mine !"

This ode affords some curious details as to the manner in which prisoners of State were treated at that time in Persia. They were kept in absolute seclusion, and not only were their feet and arms chained, but their legs were fastened in a species of stocks. Spies were placed within hearing to carry to the King any words of lamentation or anger which might escape the lips of the prisoners.

It is not known when or how Khaqani was liberated from prison. In fact, the life of the poet from this time to that of his retirement to Tabriz is veiled in obscurity. We do not know whether it was before or after this time that he lost his little son, Rashid, whom he bewailed in two long elegies. In one of them he says:

"He was a pearl of knowledge and a treasure daily paid, my Rashid ;

An object of worship to his mother and a leader for his father, my Rashid !"

All that is known regarding the last years of Khaqani's sojourn in his country is that he was present at the death of Akhsitan, which he lamented in a long ode. Under the reign of Akhsitan's successor he removed to Tabriz to pass the remainder of his days far from both his friends and detractors. In Tabriz the loss of his wife inspired him with an elegy, remarkable for the depth and sincerity of its grief. Part of it appears to have been written during her illness:

"The world in my eyes has lost its attraction, and I can no longer look on it without grief;

Without the pleasure of seeing thee, who art the essence of my joy, it is impossible to have a joyful heart ;

Without thy caresses, which quickened my life, there is no deliverance for me from the keenness of my sorrow;

Without thy sweet breath, familiar friend of my soul, life for me has lost all its hues and colours ;

Like a dove with a single note, I see, and shall see, nothing but thy name for ever ;

Without thy figure like the cypress, without thy locks curly as the foliage of the box-wood tree, for me there is no more a garden in this world.

Without thee there remains for me, no more in the whole, expanse of heaven, a single sunbeam.

Thoughts of thee darken the mirror of my heart like clouds, and till the moment of our meeting in the next world my heart conceives of no happiness in this one.

Thou biddest me take another wife. Oh, speak not so ! I cannot even conceive such a possibility.

Happiness without thee ! May God pardon me if I even dream about it.

The heart of Khaqani only asks for one thing-that is, never to see a woman again. Before the autumn of my sorrow came I had spring in the garden of my heart."

Khaqani died A.D. 1186, and was buried in the suburbs of Tabriz.

Another court poet who had a chequered career was Hilali, who was originally of a Turkish family from Djagatay, but received his education at Astrabad. In his youth he went to Khorassan, where he established himself at Herat. It is related of him that the first time he presented himself before Mir Alisher, the Vizier and Keeper of the Great Seal of the Sultan Hossein, he addressed him in verse in the following manner:

"The majesty of thy countenance has stricken me to the earth ; I shall never rise again till the last judgment."

Mir Alisher, charmed with the compliment or the poet's ready versification, demanded his surname, to which he replied that it was Hilali (Hilal signifies the new moon). The Vizier, determined not to be outdone in flattery, answered that he ought rather to have been called " Badri," " Badr " being the full moon.

A curious story regarding Hilali is told by Mir Muhammad Taki, an Indian poet, who lived under the Mogul Emperor, Shah Alam, son of Aurangzib. He relates that Hilali one day presented himself before the Governor of Ispahan, who was a patron of poets. The Prince gave orders that he should be received, and welcomed him with great demonstrations of reverence, placing him near him and Conversing with much kindness. Hilali, pleased with his reception, continued to pour forth praises of the Prince. The latter introduced the subject of poetry, in order to try the poet's powers. Hilali did not require much entreaty; he recited his verses, but, unhappily, made many gross errors in metre, which shocked the Prince, who was a fastidious critic. At last, growing more and more annoyed at each new mistake, he ordered a whip to be brought, and applied it unmercifully to the shoulders of the unlucky poet, who fell without signs of life. He was thought dead and carried home.

The event was much talked of in the bazaars of Ispahan. Hilali recovered, and, seeing himself surrounded by pitying friends, exclaimed: "Cease to blame the Prince and to call him the poet's foe; on the contrary, he loves and understands poetry, and rewards those who excel in it. Probably he found defects in mine, and has consequently treated me thus rigorously. It is quite true that the poetry of the present day is execrable, and I have fallen into the bad taste, which is so prevalent, but I am awakened to my defects. I will seek some great master and form myself by his rules, and perhaps I may retrieve my lost fame."

Thus, instead of giving way to despondency or resentment, Hilali immediately set out in search of the greatest contemporary master of his art, the celebrated Jani. With him he passed a considerable time, and did not quit him till he had attained a degree of perfection in poetry which made him worthy to appear again before the Prince whose indignation he had excited. He presented himself therefore once more, greatly to the astonishment of the Court Chamberlain, who, nevertheless, reported to the Prince his request to be admitted. When he entered he was seized with timidity, and dared not advance, but remained with his head cast down in the same attitude, exposed to the rays of the sun.

At length a sign was made for him to approach, and after an interview of some duration the Prince dismissed him, highly satisfied, with a rich present. A friend of his asked the reason of the difference of the two receptions. " In the former," said he, " you received him with honour and dismissed him with ignominy; now you give him a present and send him away happy." " The cause," said the Prince, " is this: poetry had fallen into contempt in consequence of the conceit and ignorance of bad versifiers ; the lesson Hilali received was salutary, or he would have been no better than the rest. The report of his former adventure was spread abroad, and gave a check to the audacity and impertinence of bad authors, who would else have inundated us with their worthless productions, until poetry would have become another word for infamy, and the name of poet a disgrace. Hilali I now find a different man, and worthy of my rewards."

The fate of Hilali was a sad one. Among the Shiahs he was regarded as a zealous Sunni, but Abid-Khan, the Uzbeg Prince, had him put to death as a Shiah, A.D, 1529. Hilali prayed, as a last act of grace, that he might be put to death by the hand of a young man, Seif-ullah ("the sword of God"), who happened to be at the place of execution. His request was granted. The young man, who had probably never before filled the post of an executioner, failed at the first blow, and merely covered Hilali's face with blood. Hilali immediately improvised these lines:

"It is not blood, Hilali, that appears
And gives thy fading cheek a ruddy glow ;
It is thy broken heart whose sanguine tears
For man's injustice and thy fate o'erflow."

The last of the Court poets we shall treat of here is Feizi, born A.D. 1547. Although he lived in India at the court of the Emperor Akbar, his poems were all composed in Persian, and he ranks high among Persian poets. While still a youth, Feizi had been sent by Akbar in disguise among the Brahmins, to investigate the principles of their religion, which they kept secret. So well did Feizi maintain his disguise, that he was received into the house of a learned Brahmin, who taught him

Sanscrit. The Brahmin's daughter fell in love with Feizi, and her father offered her to him in marriage. Feizi, who returned her affection, confessed his secret to the Brahmin, and implored his forgiveness. The Brahmin, struck dumb with astonishment, uttered no word of reproach, but drew a dagger which he always carried in his girdle and prepared to plunge it in his own breast. Feizi seized his hand, and offered to make any atonement in his power for the deceit he had practised. The Brahmin, bursting into tears, told him that if Feizi would grant him two requests he would forgive him and consent to live. Feizi without any hesitation consented, and the Brahmin requested him never to translate the Vedas nor repeat the creed of the Hindus. Feizi seems to have kept his oath, as the Vedas were never translated into Persian during Akbar's reign, though the Emperor incurred the anger of the Muhammadans by the favour he often showed the Brahmins, being doubtless in this influenced by Feizi's reports of them.

Feizi's father was a learned theologian, named Sheikh Mubarak, and his brother the celebrated Abu'l Fazl, Akbar's Vizier, himself the author of the "Ayar Danish," a translation of Sanscrit tales into Persian. In the beginning of his "Diwan," or collection of odes, Feizi thus commemorates his father and brother:

"The name Feiz* came from heaven, and when my father took my horoscope, he saw that I would be a recipient of heaven's favour ;

But when my hopes were shipwrecked in the storms of time, he was my anchor in the tempest.

The gracious hand which he spread out over my head was my guiding star.

He led me to the heights of learning and instructed me in the subtleties of knowledge.

Besides such a father, whom I held dear, I had also a dearly-prized brother,

Abul-fazl. Younger than I by three years, he is a hundred years in front of me in merit.

The gardener prizes not the maple more because it excels the rose-tree in height.

I am an Indian parrot, who, seeing pictures in his dreams, sings songs with the nightingales of Persia.

If thou wouldest find life sweet, be humble ; the sweetest part of the sugar-cane is that which grows next the ground."

In the thirty-third year of the Emperor Akbar, Feizi was honoured with the title Malik-ush-Shuara, or " King of Poets."

Both young and old poets, we are told, from Iran, Khorassan, and other countries, journeyed to Lahore, that they might benefit by his society and conversation. Feizi collected a valuable library of twelve thousand volumes, Arabic and Persian, many of them in the manuscript of the authors.** He composed several works in both those languages, and made an abridged translation into Persian of the celebrated epic poem " Mahabharata" from the Sanscrit. This was undertaken at the command of Akbar, who wished by means of it to do away with some of the enmity between Muhammadans and Hindus. The Emperor also wished to show the Hindus that some of their grossest

* Favour

* Illustrated manuscript in British Museum.

superstitions had no foundation in their most ancient books, and the Muhammadans that they were wrong in thinking that the world had only existed for seven thousand years. The combined efforts of Akbar, Abu'l Fazl, and Feizi, however, were powerless to modify the iron rigidity of orthodox Islam.

It is interesting to notice that Tennyson, in his poem "Akbar's Dream," quotes a phrase, "Thy glory baffles wisdom," from Blochmann's translation of one of Feizi's odes. The ode itself probably expresses Akbar's deism as well as the poet's :

"O Thou who existest from eternity and abidest for ever, sight cannot bear Thy light, praise cannot express Thy perfection.

Thy light melts the understanding and Thy glory baffles wisdom; to think of Thee destroys reason, Thy essence confounds thought.

Thy jealousy, the guard of Thy door, stuns human thought by a blow in the face, and gives human ignorance a slap on the nape of the neck.

Science is like blinding desert sand on the road to Thy perfection ; the town of literature is a mere hamlet compared with the world of Thy knowledge.

Human knowledge and thought combined can only spell the first letter of the alphabet of Thy love.*

Whatever our tongue can say and our pen can write of Thy being is all empty sound and deceiving scribble.

Mere beginners and such as are far advanced in knowledge are both eager for union with Thee ; but the beginners are tattlers; and those that are advanced are triflers.

Each brain is full of the thought of grasping Thee ;

The brow of Plato even burned with the fever heat of the hopeless thought.

O that Thy grace would cleanse my brain ; for, if not, my restlessness will end in madness.

Compared with Thy favour, the nine metals of earth are but as half a handful of dust; compared with the table of Thy mercies, the seven oceans are a bowl of broth,"

(*Translated by* BLOCHMANN.)

Notwithstanding all his excellences as a man and a poet, Feizi did not escape the common snare of Court poets, that of idolatrous adulation of the King, as the following verses show:

"He (Akbar) is a King whom, on account of his wisdom, we call Zufunun** and our guide on the path of religion.

Although kings are the shadow of God on earth, he is the emanation of God's light. How, then, can we call him a shadow?

---

* Thus adapted by Tennyson :

" Thy glory bafflex wisdom; all the tracks
Of science making towards Thy perfectness
Are blinding desert sand; we scarce can spell
The Alif of Thine alphabet of Love." (*Akbar's Dream.*)

** Possessor of the sciences

If you wish to see the path of guidance as I have done, you will never see it without having seen the King.

Thy old-fashioned prostration is of no advantage to thee ; see Akbar, and you see God."

For this extravagant idolatry Akbar himself seems to have been partly responsible. According to the Portuguese missionaries who visited his Court, not only did he adore the sun and make long prayers to it five times a day, he also held himself forth as an object of worship, and though exceedingly tolerant as to other modes of faith, never would admit of any encroachments on his own divinity.

One day, when he was accompanying the Emperor on a long march, Feizi was taken seriously ill, and immediately sent a message to his master, to the effect that "the materials of which he was formed would on the morrow be decomposed," and prayed him to allow his younger brother to come to him instead of accompanying His Majesty to the chase. When Akbar heard these melancholy tidings, he put off his hunting expedition altogether for the purpose of attending at Feizi's bedside. Feizi, even in his dying state, felt this generous act of royal kindness, and composed a verse in gratitude for it.

The poet died A.D. 1595, and was buried at Agra.

6

ROMANTIC POETRY : NIZAMI

NIZAMI is the chief romantic poet of Persia. His much more famous successors, Saadi and Hafiz, have left eloquent tributes to his praise. Saadi says:

"Here is our Nizami, the noble pearl. Heaven created it of purest dew to be the pearl of the world.

It shone long unrecognized by men ; therefore God laid it gently back again in the shell."

Hafiz gives him even higher praise:

"The song of Nizami, to which no other utterance under the ancient sky can be compared."

Nizami was born at Ganja, in Northern Persia, about A.D. 1141. His father died when he was a child, and the poet some years later commemorated him in the following lines:

"Like as my ancestors, so did my father Yusuf, son of Zaki Muwajjad, early depart hence.

Yet what boots it to quarrel with destiny ? Fate spoke, and complaints must be hushed.

Yet whose father died not ? When I saw him depart to his fathers, I tore his image out of my heart.

Whatever has happened to me, bitter or sweet, all I have done is to resign myself."

Little is recorded of Nizami's early years. In his earliest work, the " Makhzan-ul-Asrar," or Treasury of Secrets, he represents his genius, or what a Western poet would call his muse, exhorting him to throw off the trammels of asceticism by which he had been hitherto bound, and to take a part in active life :

" ' Lay not duties on thyself,' a secret voice said to me, 'which thou canst not fulfil;

Pour not water into the pure flame, let not the wind lord it over thy earth ;

Shoot not, when thy own spirit is the mark aimed at ;

Use not the whip when thou thyself art the steed.

On this chapter *cf.* Bacher : "Nizami's Leben und Gedichte."

Henceforth thou must not sit idle ; burst open the doors of thy heart ; avoid the slayers of the senses (ascetics).

Thy heart knows the way ; do thou know thy heart.' "

This work, the "Makhzan-ul-Asrar," in which Nizami was first trying the wings of his genius, consists of various apologues with morals attached, and may possibly have suggested to Saadi the idea of the Gulistan. Two of the apologues are as follows :

1. *The Nightingale and the Hawk.*

"When the rose-bush blossomed in the bower of a garden, a nightingale went up to a hawk and said :

'From all birds how hast thou, being silent, borne away the ball? Produce at length the reason.

Since thou hast drawn breath through thy closed lip, thou hast not spoken a pleasing word to anyone.

Yet thy abode is the wrist of the King; thy food is the breast of the most delicate partridge.

I who, with one twinkling of an eye, by mysterious operation, produce a hundred fine gems from my pocket, why is hunting for worms my nature? Why is my mansion on the top of thorns ?'

The hawk said to him:

' For a moment be all ear; observe my taciturnity, and be silent.

I, who am a little conversant in business, perform a hundred acts and repeat not one.

Go, for thou art beguiled by fortune ; thou performest not one deed, nevertheless thou displayest a thousand.

Since I am all intelligence at the place of hunting, the King gives me the breasts of partridges and his wrist.

Since thou art one entire motion of a tongue eat worms, and sit on thorns ; and so peace be with you."

2. *Christ and the Dead Dog.*

"One evening Jesus lingered in the market-place,
Teaching the people parables of truth and grace,
When in the square remote a crowd was seen to rise,
And stop with loathing gestures and abhorring cries.

"The Master and His meek disciples went to see
What cause for this commotion and disgust could be,
And found a poor dead dog beside the gutter laid ;
Revolting sight at which its face its hate betrayed.

" One held his nose, one shut his eyes, one turned away ;
And all among themselves began aloud to say:
' Detested creature ! he pollutes the earth and air !'
' His eyes are blear !' His ears are foul !' ' His ribs are bare !'

" 'In his torn hide there's not a decent shoe-string left !'
'No doubt the execrable cur was hung for theft !'
Then Jesus spake, and dropped on him this saving wreath:
' Even pearls are dark before the whiteness of his teeth.'

"The pelting crowd grew silent and ashamed, like one
Rebuked by sight of wisdom higher than his own ;
And one exclaimed: `No creature so accursed can be
But some good thing in him a loving eye will see.' "

(ALGER : *Poetry of the Orient.*)

At the time of writing the "Makhzan-ul-Asrar," Nizami had not attached himself to the Court of any potentate, as was the custom of contemporary poets such as Anwari. He reprobates the mercenary spirit in strong terms:

"The poets who sell their lofty art for gold are as heartless as gold itself.

He who barters inspired thoughts for gold exchanges luminous rubies for stones.

These folk [the Court poets] who pride themselves on their learning are low down among the ignorant.

Though to-day a gold crown adorn their brows, to-morrow an iron chain crushes them."

In the prologue to the "Khusrau and Shirin," his first great romance in verse, he speaks of himself as still living a retired life :

"So I live still, turning my back on the world,
Supporting myself on handful of barley bread.
Like a snake which watches over treasure,
I compose at night and shut myself up in the daytime;
Or like a bee which inhabits a narrow cell, but produces much sweetness."

After long deliberation he chose the above, subject, " Khusrau and Shirin," from the pre-Islamic legends of Persia. He tells us that a zealous ascetic friend remonstrated with him for his choice, and said :

" Thou who keepest fasts so strictly,
Break not thy fast on the bones of dead men ;
Throw away the rubbish of the idolaters,
Practise not magic like the heathen Zoroaster.

If thou hast the gift of song, then sing the unity of God.

Why revive the vanished traces of the Magians ?"

To this attack Nizami's reply was to read the opening verses of his poem. The bigot relaxed into admiration, remarking that Nizami, by the magic of his verse, " had surrounded an idol with the Kaaba."*

The legend, indeed, was one admirably fitted to inspire the pen of a great romantic poet. The ancient chronicles related that one of the Sassanian dynasty, Khusrau Parviz, had a mistress whose name was Shirin, and that a certain statuary, or stonecutter, whose name was Ferhad, became enamoured of her. When the King heard this he was much disturbed, and expressed his trouble to one of his courtiers. One of them said: " As this man is a stonecutter, bid him exercise his art." Ferhad was then brought before the King, who promised that if he would, unaided, cut through the impassable mountain of Beysitoun a channel for a river, and hew all the masses of rock into statues, Shirin should be his. Then Ferhad began his work by constructing a recess, or chamber, in the rock, wherein he carved the figure of Shirin, surrounded by attendants and guards, and an equestrian figure of Khusrau. The poet goes on :

"On lofty Beysitoun the lingering sun
Looks down on ceaseless labours long begun ;
The mountain trembles to the echoing sound
Of falling rocks that from her sides rebound.
Each day all respite, all repose denied,
Without a pause the thundering strokes are plied ;
The mist of night around the mountain coils,
But still Ferhad, the lover-artist, toils,
And still, the flashes of his axe between,
He sighs to every wind, 'Alas! Shirin !'
A hundred arms are weak one block to move
Of thousands moulded by the hand of love
Into fantastic shapes and forms of grace,
That crowd each nook of that majestic place.
The piles give way, the rocky peaks divide,
The stream comes gushing on, a foaming tide,
A mighty work for ages to remain
The token of his passion and his pain.
And, sculptured there, amazed, stern Khusrau stands,
And, frowning, sees obeyed his harsh commands ;
While she, the fair beloved, with being rife,

* The sacred shrine at Mecca.

Awakes from glowing marble into life.
Around the pair, lo! chiselled courtiers wait,
And slaves and pages grouped in solemn state.
'Alas, Shirin !' at every stroke he cries,
At every stroke fresh miracles arise.
' For thee my life one ceaseless toil hath been ;
Inspire my soul anew, alas, Shirin !' "

(*Translated by* COSTELLO.)

"When the work was finished," says the poet, "from every quarter came the most expert statuaries and polishers of marble. Beholding the works of Ferhad, they bit the finger of astonishment ; they were amazed at the effects of his chisel upon the marble, and were confounded at the works of that distracted lover."

When Khusrau Parviz heard this, he asked if any person could contrive a stratagem to destroy Ferhad. A certain old woman came before the King and said : "I will engage to trample this statuary under foot, so that his life shall quit his body." Khusrau having promised her many gifts, the old woman proceeded to the mountain of Beysitoun, where she beheld Ferhad still striking with his pickaxe and exclaiming : "Alas, Shirin !" The old woman, coming behind him, said:

" O Ferhad ! what madness is this, or why do you call on the name of Shirin ? For where is she ? Two weeks have now elapsed, and the third week passes away since Shirin died."

When Ferhad heard this he uttered doleful sighs, and flung on the ground the mattock which he held in his hand and precipitated himself from the mountain of Beysitoun ; then he gave up his soul unto God, and as a true lover died for his beloved.

"He heard the fatal news—no word, no groan ;
He spoke not, moved not, stood transfixed to stone.
Then, with a frenzied start, he raised on high
His arms and wildly tossed them towards the sky ;
Far in the wide expanse his axe he flung,
And from the precipice at once he sprung.
The rocks, the sculptured caves, the valleys green,
Sent back his dying cry, ' Alas, Shirin !' "

After composing this poem Nizami was summoned by Kizil Arslan, the Atabeg or Governor of Azerbaijan, to his Court. Kizil Arslan praised the work highly, and presented the poet with two villages, Nijan and Hamd, the revenues of which enabled him to live in comparative independence. His next great work was the "Laila and Majnun," composed at the request of Akhsitan, Prince of the neighbouring province of Shirwan. It was founded on an old Arabian legend, recounting the woes of two lovers belonging to two desert tribes. Nizami did not undertake the work very readily, regarding the subject as not affording sufficient scope for his genius. However, not wishing to displease the Prince, Nizami commenced the work, and completed it in four months. In 1188 he sent it to Akhsitan by the hand of his son, a lad of fourteen, who had a longing for Court life.

The poem commences with the customary praise of God and the Prophet, describing a Muhammad's ascent to heaven. After eulogizing the Prince of Sherwan; and giving some advice to his son, the poet commences the narrative:

"Keis, an Arab youth, afterwards surnamed Majnun, I the mad,' was enamoured of Leila, the daughter of the chief of the Amiri tribe. When Majnun's father demanded Leila for his son, her parents declined to give her, on account of the reported madness of Keis. The latter, hearing from his father of this refusal, became really mad, and betook himself to the desert, where he made the rocks re-echo the name of his beloved. His father went after him, but the frenzied youth paid no attention, saying that he was bound in the chains of love, which none could break. In the meantime an Arab chief named Ibn Selam, passing by the garden where Leila sat, sad and silent, in the midst of her companions, fell in love with her, and asked her in marriage of her parents.

"Majnun, however, had found a friend in an Arab chief named Noufal, who, for his sake, attacked and defeated Leila's tribe. Her father, however, still refused to surrender her to Majnun, who, after reproaching Noufal, betook himself to a still wilder and more remote desert, where a settled melancholy fell upon him.

"And now, remote from peopled town,
Midst tangled forest, parched and brown,
The maniac roams. With double speed
He goads along his snorting steed,
Till in a grove a sportsman's snare
Attracts his view, and struggling there,
Its knotted meshes fast between,
Some newly-prisoned deer are seen ;
And as the hunter forward springs
To seize on one and promptly brings
The fatal knife upon its neck,
His hand receives a sudden check ;
And looking upwards with surprise
(A mounted chief before his eyes!),
He stops, while thus exclaims the youth :
' If e'er thy bosom throbbed with ruth,
Forbear ! for 'tis a crime to spill
A gazelle's blood—it bodeth ill ;
Then set the pleading captive free,
For sweet is life and liberty.

That heart must be as marble hard,
And merciless as wolf or pard,
Which clouds in death that large black eye
Beaming like Leila's lovingly."

(*Translated by* ATKINSON).

" Majnun ransomed this and other animals from their captors and liberated them. One day a passing stranger informed him that Leila's father had married her forcibly to Ibn Selam, and drove him to a still greater excess of grief. Majnun's father then came to visit him, and sought to con sole him, but in vain. On this the old man, bidding a last farewell to his son, returned to his tribe and died. Meanwhile Majnun received a letter from Leila, which was shortly followed by a visit from his beloved herself, who, eluding her guards, came to see her unhappy lover. Their meeting is thus described :

"They met ; but how ? Hearts long to joy unknown
Know not what 'tis to be except alone ;
Feeling intense had checked the power to speak ;
Silent confusion sat upon each cheek ;
Speechless with love unutterable, they
Stood gazing at each other all the day.
Leila, with looks of love, was first who caught
The soft expression of her bursting thought.
' Alas !' she said, as over him she hung,
' What wondrous grief is this that chains the tongue ?
The bulbul, famed for his mellifluous note,
Without the rose can swell his tuneful throat ;
And when in fragrant bowers the rose he sees,
He warbles sweeter still his ecstasies.
Thou art the bulbul of the bright parterre,
And I the rose-why not thy love declare ?
Why, being absent, whilst unseen by thee,
Arose to heaven thy voice and minstrelsy ;
And now at length, when we are met, alone,
Thy love has vanished and thy voice has gone !"

(*Translated by* ATKINSONS.)

" Majnun replied in ecstatic terms, and was much comforted by this visit. Leila returned home, and not long afterwards died. Her death was followed by that of Majnun, whose body was watched by the faithful animals which he had befriended, till taken away by his friends and buried in one grave with that of Leila. The poem concludes with vision of the lovers in paradise:

"The minstrel's legend chronicle,
Which on their woes delights to dwell
Their matchless purity and faith,
And how their dust was mixed in death ;
Tells how the sorrow-stricken Zeyd
Saw in a dream the beauteous bride,
With Majnun seated side by side.
In meditation deep, one night
The other world flashed on his sight.
He saw the ever-verdant bowers,
With golden fruit and blooming flowers ;
The bulbul heard their sweets among
Warbling his rich mellifluous song ;
The ringdove's murmuring and the swell
Of melody from harp and shell :
He saw within a rosy glade,
Beneath a palm's extensive shade,
A throne amazing to behold,
Studded with glittering gems and gold ;
Celestial carpets near it spread,
Close where a lucid streamlet strayed.
Upon that throne, in blissful state,
The long-divided lovers sate.
Resplendent with seraphic light,
They held a cup with diamonds bright ;
Their lips by turns, with nectar wet,
In pure ambrosial kisses met. . . .
The dreamer who this vision saw
Demanded, with becoming awe,
What sacred names the happy pair
In Irem bowers were wont to bear.
A voice replied: ' That sparkling moon
Is Leila still, her friend Majnun ;
Deprived in your frail world of bliss,
They reap their great reward in this.' "

(*Translated by* ATKINSON.)

In another poem, the "Haft Paikar" (The Seven Beauties), Nizami took as his hero Bahram, son of Yezdigird, of the Sassanian dynasty. His father sent him to be educated by Noman, the Arab King of Hira, who summoned the best instructors for him, and had built for him the palace of Khavarnak, one of the greatest wonders of the East. One day, when he was growing towards manhood, Bahram opened a secret cabinet in the palace, and seeing in it the portraits of seven beautiful maidens, fell in love with all seven together. They were Niamat-Naz, daughter of the Emperor of China; Naz-peri, daughter of the King of Khwarezm ; Nesrin-bus, daughter of the King of the Slavs ; Azer-gun, daughter of the King of Morocco ; Humay, daughter of the Emperor of Constantinople ; Durusni, of the race of Kaius, one of the ancient Kings of Iran ; and Khorek, daughter of the King of India.

Bahram, however, could not pursue the matter any further, as the death of his father, Yezdigird, recalled him to Persia. The luxurious nobles of the Persian Court dreaded a monarch who had been educated among Arabs, and raised another Prince, Chosroes, to the throne. But this proceeding only afforded to the true heir, Bahram, an opportunity of showing his courage and magnanimity. He proposed that the crown of Persia should be placed on the ground between two untamed lions, that he and Chosroes should come to the spot, and whichever should have courage to take the crown should retain it as being the one most worthy of the sovereignty. Accordingly, the Persian chiefs found two fierce lions, kept them fasting for three days, and on the fourth caused them to be conveyed out of the city in two iron cages. These lions each had an iron chain round his neck, fastened to an iron stake. The two stakes were fixed into the ground, the crown was placed where both could reach to defend it, the cages were opened and the two lions came forth. Bahram first invited Chosroes to seize the crown, but he declined. He then himself flew at the lions, and, though almost unarmed, slew both, and seized the crown, amid the shouts of his subjects. His first act was to reward Noman, the Arabian who had educated him ; his second to pardon those who had endeavoured to deprive him of the crown.

When he had become King, Bahram returned to his favourite occupation of hunting. In these expeditions he was often accompanied by a female slave named Fitna, concerning whom Nizami relates the following somewhat grotesque incident : "One day Bahram, who was a skilful archer, had by a single shaft fixed the hoof of an antelope to its horn. Turning to Fitna for applause, he was annoyed by her coolly remarking: `Practice makes perfect.' Enraged at this uncourtly observation, the King instantly ordered her to be sent into the mountains to perish. Her life was saved by the mercy of one of the Ministers of the Court, who allowed her to retire to a small village on the side of a hill. She there lodged in an upper room, to which she ascended by twenty steps. Immediately after her arrival she bought a small calf, which she regularly carried once up and down the flight every day. This exercise she continued four years, and the improvement of her strength kept pace with the increasing weight of the animal. Bahram, who had supposed his favourite dead, happened after a fatiguing chase to stop one day at this village. He saw a young woman carrying a large cow up a flight of twenty steps. He was astonished, and sent to inquire how strength so extraordinary had been acquired by a person of so apparently delicate a form. The lady said she would communicate her secret to none but Bahram, and to him only on his condescending to come alone to her house. The monarch instantly went, and on his repeating his admiration, she bade him not lavish his praises where they were not due. 'Practice makes perfect,' said the lady in her natural voice, and at the same time she lifted her veil. The monarch recognized and embraced his favourite. Pleased with the lesson she had given him, and delighted with that love which had led her to pass four years in an endeavour to regain his esteem, he ordered a palace to be built on the spot to serve as a hunting-seat and a commemoration of this event." After a time Bahram be-thought himself of the seven Princesses whose pictures he had seen in the castle of Khavarnak, and sent to demand their hands from their respective fathers. They were willingly granted to him, and he built for them a great palace, with seven divisions, each coloured separately. In this he lodged the Princesses, visiting them in turn, and they in turn related to him seven stories, which compose a great part of the work. The apartments of the Indian Princess were hung with black, those of the Moorish with yellow, those of the Chinese with green, and so on. Each of them corresponded to some particular planet, according to the old Chaldæan astrology.

Bahram's death, as related by Nizami, was a melancholy one. He was drowned in a quagmire during one of his hunting expeditions, and his body was never recovered :

"And Bahram, that great hunter—the wild ass
Stamps o'er his grave, but never breaks his sleep."

Nizami's longest work is the "Sikander-nama," a free poetical handling of the legend of Alexander, as handed down in Oriental tradition. The first part treats of Alexander as a world-conqueror ; in the second he is portrayed as a sage and prophet, on the strength of a mention of him in the Koran. The introduction contains the following touching address by the poet to his son :

"Many, like me, already slumber in the grave,
And yet they are forgotten by the living.
Think of me, O young partridge,
When thou passest by my grave ;
When thou seest grass growing out of my dust,
And the plain headstone all broken down ;
The dust of my couch scattered by the winds,
And unremembered by any of my coevals.
Lay then thy hand upon that heap of clay,
And remember my pure spirit ;
Shed over me one tear, and I shall shed upon thee light from heaven ;
Whatever thou prayest for, I will contrive that it be granted.
Pronounce my praise, and I will pronounce thine ;
Approach me, and I will approach thee from above ;
Consider me living as thyself: I will come to thee in the spirit, if thou comest to me.
Think me not unable to companion thee, for though thou seest me not, I still see thee."

After an introduction, in which Alexander holds intercourse with various philosophers, including Socrates, and receives the gift of prophecy; the poet describes his journeys. He first visits Jerusalem and delivers the inhabitants from a tyrant who oppresses them—a reference possibly to Antiochus Epiphanes. Then he goes by way of North Africa to Andalusia, in Spain, where he embarks on a sea-voyage.

"Many islands he saw uninhabited by men ;
Still he sailed on from isle to isle.
Many living beings he met, both men and others,
Yet all were shy, and none approached him,
But flew before him from mountain to mountain."

Afterwards he arrives at a barren coast the sand of which is yellow and glittering, and in its composition and inflammability like sulphur. After a month's march through this desert, Alexander arrives at the great ocean. Here is the end of the world, the place of the sun's going down, "the limit beyond which thought cannot pass." Nothing surprises the King so much as a warm spring, which he finds bubbling up through the sea. The sage whom he consults regarding it can only tell him that many have inquired about it in vain. Alexander bathes in the sea, and finds the water as heavy as quicksilver. Many of his councillors advise him not to attempt to cross it, as it conceals many dangers, especially a monster who kills men with one look, and a shore full of shining stones which destroy people by causing irresistible laughter. Alexander, however, causes some loads of the stones to be taken away by men with bandaged eyes, and subsequently, on reaching an island, has a castle built with these stones. This building, says Nizami, has caused the death of many travellers, who, finding no entrance, have climbed the walls, but been hurled lifeless to the ground by the magic power of the stones.

Then follows a six months' march through the desert, on accomplishing which Alexander conceives the desire of finding the " yet unbeheld " sources of the Nile. After a long march over hills and valleys, he comes to a very steep mountain, in colour "like to green glass," from which the Nile descends. He sends some explorers up the mountain, but none of them return. At last he sends a man and his son, commanding the man when he has reached the summit to write what he has seen, and cast the note down to his son waiting below. The latter returns without his father, but bearing with him the following description:

"The grief of the toilsome path caused such anguish in my soul that I believed I was treading the way to hell.

The way was as narrow as a hair, and he who trod it was within a hair's-breadth of death.

To go down again also seemed impossible. When I reached the top of the precipitous rock, the narrow way led me into a strait place.

What I saw on one side tore my heart and senses with sights of terror ;

But on the other side were gardens ranged by gardens, abounding in springs of water and fresh verdure and roses, where echoed the clear song of melodious birds.

An Eden on this side and hell on that! Who would turn back from such an Eden to hell ?

Think, O King, of all the deserts and wastes we have passed through! Who could have the heart to turn back from Paradise to such a wilderness ?

I remain here and greet thee, O King, May joy be allotted to you all, as it is to me!"

Alexander conceals the enticing description from his army, and hastens onwards. After he has traversed another desert with fatiguing marches, he reaches the famous enchanted gardens of Irem, planted with golden trees. Nizami describes at length the beauties of this garden, with the golden fruits and jewels which adorn it. In it Alexander finds a vault with an inscription containing the lament of Shedad, the former owner of the garden, over the transitoriness of earthly greatness, which moves the King to tears. He quits the place hastily, without taking any of the treasures with him.

The next march leads through a desert, in which they find a number of wild beasts in the form of men, who live in caves, are ignorant of the use of fire, and whose only means of subsistence is catching fish. The sun by day serves them for fire and the night-dews for drink. Alexander makes inquiries from them regarding the other inhabitants of the desert, and learns that they are still wilder and more unsociable, but—

"Beyond, where the heat of the sun is felt no longer,
Rises a city, nobly built and fair,
Inhabited by men with white faces,
Of clear intelligence and civilized.
Their life endures for five hundred years,
And yet no trace of age is seen in them."

Passing over Alexander's marches to the south and the east, too lengthy for description here, we come to his march to the north, which conducts him to a kind of Utopia, the inhabitants of which thus describe their manner of life, in answer to his questions :

"Since thou askest after our condition, O King, we will tell thee all.
Our race is a pious one, swerving not a hair's-breadth from the right ;
All our intercourse with each other is harmonious, unmarred by discord ;
Under no circumstances do we tell a lie, therefore we have no bad dreams by night;
We put no useless questions, for idle questioning is abhorrred of God ;
And to whatsoever He ordains we submit without murmuring.
We share all our possessions alike, and look upon each other as equals;
Therefore none of us ever exults at the misfortune of another.
We fear no thieves, therefore we have no watchmen in our cities or fields ;
We have no bolts or bars on our houses, and our flocks feed shepherdless.
The wild beasts fly not from us, for no hand is raised to molest them.
When anyone dies, we are not sorrowful, fot of what use would sorrow be ?
We say behind no one's back what we would not say to his face."

Alexander is much impressed by these people, and exclaims :

"If these are the true morals, what are ours ?
If these are genuine men, then what are we ?
Oh! had I but known of this folk before,
Never would I have roamed all over the earth,
But secluded myself in a corner,
And devoted myself to the worship of God."

This conclusion evinces the latent vein of mysticism in Nizami, which is present more or less in nearly all the Persian poets. Shortly after this Alexander returns home, is taken ill, and dies near Babylon. Before his death he says:

"Naked I came out of my mother's womb, therefore return me naked to the earth again ;

Born with nothing, shall I go hence laden ? Better it is to depart as I came.

A bird flew from the mountain where he sat ; what did he add to the mountain, what did he take from it ?

I am the bird, and my kingdom is the mountain; I go hence ; what does it matter to the world ?

My body, indeed, is given to the earth, but my soul flies to the abode of the blessed ;

Therefore cover not your heads with dust, but employ your tongues in asking forgiveness for me."

This tone of austere exultation probably expresses the mind of the poet himself as he drew near his end. He died at Ganjah, where he had spent most of his life, in A.D. 1203.

7

SUFISM

AT the close of the last chapter we referred to the vein of mysticism, or, as the Persians call it, Sufism, which runs through Nizami's poetry. After his time Sufism so generally pervades Persian poetry that for an adequate appreciation of it some knowledge of that system is necessary. We therefore in this chapter give a brief account of it, basing our remarks chiefly on Tholuck's Latin treatise, "Sufismus."

The name "Sufi" is derived, in the opinion of Tholuck, from the Arabic *suf* (wool), in allusion to their garments, which, as with the early Quakers, were a distinguishing mark of these Eastern, quietists. Others have referred it to the Arabic *safa* (pure), and some to the Greek *sophos* (wise), but the first derivation is probably correct.

A variety of opinions have prevailed likewise with regard to the origin of the Sufic doctrines.

Some have been disposed to look for it in the Vedantic philosophy of India ; others in Neo-Platonism ; and Tholuck was at one time inclined to the opinion that it took its rise among the Zoroastrian Magi. All these sources have probably contributed to Sufism, but there is no doubt that the early Muslim mystics derived their mysticism from their keen sense of the terrors of the world to come, as portrayed in the Koran itself. This led to asceticism and separation from, worldly matters, and that in its turn led to mysticism. It is true that Muhammad had said, "There is no monkery in Islam," and enjoined marriage on all his followers, but in less than thirty years after his death hermits had become numerous in the deserts of Arabia and Syria. Two of the first four Caliphs, Abu-bekr and Ali, were founders of monastic communities. These were the forerunners of later similar organizations, and from them up to the twelfth century came the most famous Sufi teachers. Among the most distinguished of these early Muhammadan pietists was a woman named Rabia. It is related of her that, having undertaken the journey to Mecca, when she came in sight of the Kaaba, its sacred shrine, she exclaimed :

"What is the Kaaba to me? For I indeed have approached so near unto God that I may claim the promise, 'He who comes a hand's-breadth towards Me, toward him will I go an ell.' What is the Kaaba, then, to me ?" This anecdote well illustrates the tendency of Sufism, as, indeed, of mysticism in general, to value outward ceremony

Cf. for this chapter : "Bibliotheca Sacra," vol. v. ; and Tholuck "Sufismus."

little in comparison with inward experience. When one of Rabia's friends inquired by what method she had arrived at this knowledge of God, she replied :

" Thou hast known after a method and through certain means, but I immediately (*sine modo*)."

Of another of the early mystics, Hasan Basri, the following saying is reported : "It will happen that the blessed, through the unveiling of the Divine Majesty, will be lost in ecstasy for seven hundred thousand years ; through their awe of Him they will perish, and having beheld His loveliness they will be absorbed into His unity."

In such sayings as these we have the seeds and elements of the entire Sufic system. But it was not till the second century of the Hegira* that this mysticism began to show its most extraordinary developments. This age holds a marked place in the history of Muhammadanism. Scarcely had the Grecian philosophy been introduced to the followers of the Prophet than a great conflict of opinions arose. The old traditional ways of teaching and of believing were in some places modified, in others abolished. Men sought in the solitude of ascetic life a refuge from the zeal of party. This age witnessed the rise and progress of the Mu'tazilites (*vide* Chapter II.), the establishment of numerous Dervish Orders, and finally the rise of Sufism. When all things were in dire confusion, and doubt of the truth of their religion was filling the minds of men with uneasiness, mysticism, as is usual at such periods, secured an immense number of adherents, and spread its branches far and wide. From the most diverse classes appeared those who, moved by conscientious impulse, gave up their accustomed habits, and devoted themselves to stirring up religious zeal in their fellow-countrymen. In some cases persons of high rank, such as one of the sons of the Caliph Haroun-al-Raschid, and even brigands from the mountains, assumed the coarse garment of the Dervish Sufis.

A saying of one of these converted brigands has been preserved by Jami in the " Biharistan": " Fudhail Ayaz being asked 'who was base,' replied: 'He who worships God out of fear or from hope of reward.' Again, when they inquired, But, then, in what way dost thou worship God?' `In love,' said he, `and friendship; for by the bond of love am I held in subjection to Him.' "

That the foundations of Sufism were laid at this time is evident from the fact that from the two-hundredth year of the Hegira onwards, we find frequent mention made of it by authors whose writings still remain. There is extant in the "Tazkirat ul Auliya" of Attar a saying of the learned Imam Shafi, the chief theologian of his age, in which the Sufis are mentioned with commendation. Shafi was accustomed to say: " The science of the whole world cannot compare with mine ; but not mine even can compare with that of the Sufis." And Hanbal, another of the four great Imams, bestows no less praise upon them, affirming that, "the Sufi's quiet trust in God excels the most anxious zeal of other men."

The founder of Sufism as a distinct system was Abu Said ibn Abu'l Khair, born in Khorassan about A.D. 970. He was unpopular in his life time and regarded as an infidel. It is related that the women used to mount on the roofs of the houses and cast dung upon him as he passed by. Tennyson has recorded one of his sayings, " Love is the net of truth," in his poem " Akbar's Dream." Regarding the philosopher Avicenna,

* The flight of Muhammad from Mecca to Medina, A.D. 622.

his contemporary, he is reported to have said : "All that he knows I *see.*" When asked, " What is Sufism ?" he replied: "What thou hast in thy head, resign ; what thou bearest in thy hand, throw away; and whatsoever cometh upon thee, turn not back." He founded a monastry for Dervishes, and commanded his followers to take food twice a day.

Sufism, however; did not long restrain itself within the limits of simple piety and devout mysticism. In the third century of the Hegira a leading Sufi named Bayazid Bistami began to teach open Pantheism. When asked, "What is the throne of God ?" "I am the throne of God," was his reply. "What is the Tablet?" (on which the eternal decrees are written), "I am the Tablet." " I," he said, "am Abraham, Moses, Jesus ; I am Gabriel, Michael, Israfil ; because, whatever has attained unto the true essence is absorbed into God, and therefore is God."

Contemporary with Bayazid, but more moderate in his opinions, was Junaid. He was asked, "When can a servant of God be said to be truly His servant ?" and replied : " When he is satisfied that from God all things have their source, that they remain in Him, and will at last return to Him." The end and aim of Sufism was thus described by him: "To free the mind from the too frequent assaults of passion, to extirpate human nature, to repress sensual instinct, to assume spiritual qualities, to attain the heights of true knowledge, and to do whatsoever is good-behold the end of Sufism."

Another Sufi, Abu'l Hussein Nuri, said: " Sufism is neither a rule nor a doctrine, but something inborn. For, were it a rule, the good of it might be procured by diligent observance ; if a doctrine, by study. But it is a something innate ; according to the words of the Koran, 'We are created with a divine nature.' Evidently no one is able by diligent observance or study to possess himself of a divine nature." He was also accustomed to say: " If God veil Himself from thee, no guide and no direction can lead thee to Him." The most extravagant of all the Sufis seems to have been Mansur Hallaj, who was put to death at Bagdad, A.D. 922, for repeatedly exclaiming : "I am the Truth." The disciples of Mansur were accustomed to write to their master in language like the following: "Oh, of all essences the essence, summit of all delights, we testify that thou assumest diverse forms, but now thou has taken the form of Mansur. Grant us thine aid ; we seek assistance from thee !"

The inquiry naturally arises whether these pantheistic notions were of foreign origin, and were engrafted upon the simple mysticism of Abu Said, or whether they are developments from a basis of Muhammadan doctrine. Tholuck inclines decidedly to the latter opinion, and considers that all the peculiar dogmas of the Sufis-their views respecting the annihilation of the distinction between good and evil and the rejection of all ceremonial laws—depend, as it were, on that one doctrine of the " mystic union " between God and man. This is referred to in the Koran (chap. vii.), where God is represented as saying to all creatures in the stage of pre-existence: " Am I not your Lord?" and they answer, "Yes." Since then every Sufi hears in his soul the mystic vibrations of that question: " Am I not your Lord ?"

This dogma of the mystic union does not seem to have been held in specific form during the first two centuries of the Hegira; but whether known by name to Rabia and the mystics of her age or not, it was really familiar to them, and well understood. Many of the sayings ascribed to Muhammad himself have a strong mystic colouring—

e.g., the saying, " I have moments when neither prophet nor angel can comprehend me." The Persian mystics seem never to have practised the extravagant austerities so common among the ascetic devotees and fakirs of India, such as keeping a limb immovable till it withers, etc. Sir John Malcolm, in his" History of Persia," says: " The Persian Sufis, though they may have borrowed much of their belief and many of their usages from India, have not adopted, as a means of attaining beatitude, those dreadful austerities which are common among the visionary devotees of India." Although they practised monastic life, they seem not to have subjected themselves very strictly to monastic rules.Those who were able to attain the loftiest heights of contemplation considered that if the mind were only free for divine meditation all outward action was of small consequence. Thus Jalaluddin Rumi, in his " Masnavi," of which we shall treat in the next chapter, has the following anecdote: " When on a certain occasion a Dervish was accused to his superior of garrulity, sluggishness, and gluttony, and was reminded by him of the trite proverb, 'The middle course is the best,' he is said to have repliedas follows: 'Although to hold a middle course is wise and good, yet even this is to be done with reason. I am lord of meditation, not subject to it.' Therefore," adds Jalaluddin, 'he to whom a cake becomes divine light, eats whatsoever pleases him. It is permitted. If charges, then, of dissolute life are brought against the Sufis, it is impossible altogether to deny their correctness."

But although these Persian mystics rejected the absurd austerities of some of their Indian brethren, we still find certain rules for such as wished to enjoy the divine approach. The first injunction laid down for their observance returns to the of Plotinus-a pure simplicity of soul-as may be seen from the following extract from the "Gulshan-i-Raz " (Rose-garden of Mystery) of Shabistari :

"It becomes thee to lay aside every impurity and defilement that may by chance adhere to thee-the depraved doubts that rise in secret spontaneously and the instincts of our brute nature. Freed from these hindrances, thou mayest attain that which is the highest attainment of all—the expulsion of all thoughts whatever; then, believe me, thou wilt be honoured with the divine approach, and all distinction between the knower and the known will cease." This is the Sufi ideal—to polish the mind from the rust of concupiscence and selfishness till it becomes a perfectly clear and unspotted mirror, reflecting the rays of the Godhead.

The same fact is illustrated in the following sentences from Jalaluddin Rumi : " Ho! thou who goest bowed down beneath the burden of thy knowledge, how is it that thou art contented with the name merely? Hast thou ever gathered roses from the letters R-O-S-E ? Seek for the moon in the heavens, and not its reflection in the water. What more shall I say? That thou mayest the better know my pure essence, it is necessary that thou become a pure mirror, all individual qualities being rejected. For the Prophet hath said: 'He belongeth to the number of my people who becometh my essence and my delight. And thus will he become when his soul shall behold me by the same light by which I see him—*i.e.*, not through mere traditions and opinions, but in the drinking of the water of life.' "

Again, in the "Masnavi" of the same author we find the following:

"Once, early in the morning, the Prophet inquired of Zaid : 'How hast thou arisen, my child ?'

"To which he replied: ` Faithful.'

"Then the Prophet said: 'But hast thou any sign that the garden of faith hath bloomed in thee ?'

"And Zaid answered: 'Day and night have passed over me as a sword glances by a shield; for in a single act of thought I have comprehended the perpetuity of time-both that which has preceded the creation of the world and that which comes after it. In such a state it is all the same whether thou numberest a hundred years or one single hour.' "

Like some of the European quietists, these Oriental mystics permitted themselves at times to adopt terms and figures from the marriage relation. In the "Masnavi," Muhammad is said to have been admitted to kiss the right hand of the bride. Yet the phrase seems to have been rather an unusual one, for in the same book Jalaluddin begs that it may not be imputed to him as a fault that he applies the word " bride " to the Deity.

One of the topics on which the Sufis were divided was whether God could be seen by man or not. It is related that a certain person came to Jaafer Sadiq and said to him: " Show me the Lord!"

Jaafer replied : " Art thou ignorant what the divine oracle said to Moses: ` Never shalt thou behold Me' ?"

He replied:

"That indeed I know well; but now the religion of Muhammad is our religion, and people are found who cry aloud: ` My heart seeth the Lord,' or ` I worship not a Lord whom I do not see,' or other like things."

When Jaafer heard this, he commanded the importunate man to be thrown into the Tigris. This was done, and so long as he kept afloat on the surface of the stream he implored Jaafer with loud outcries to save him; but when he began to sink, and seemed just ready to drown, he began to pour forth prayers to God. Where upon Jaafer bade them draw him forth from the river; and as soon as his strength and senses returned, said to him: "Tell me now, my friend, hast thou seen God now?"

Then the man answered: " While I was calling upon thee, O Jaafer, I was in a cloud; but from the moment I commenced praying to God I beheld what I desired through a window opened in my breast."

It seems, on the whole, probable that the Sufis did not in general believe in any manifestation of the Deity visible to sense.

In reflecting upon the examples above quoted from Sufi writers, one is struck with the variety and even the contrasts of opinion which are found among them. While some use such language only as is natural to every devout meditative spirit, others rise to heights of extravagance and impiety that are absolutely insane. Some appear to be seeking after mere tranquillity and purity of soul ; others are bent on attaining a certain unknown and ineffable absorption in the Deity—a sort of religious dream, in which all rational and voluntary action shall be annihilated. It is the teaching of this latter class, rather than that of the Koran, which is responsible for

* Koran.

much of the apathy and fatalism commonly ascribed to Mohammadans. The Koran, however much stress it lays on the omnipotence and foresight of God, constantly addresses man as responsible for his actions ; this is also the case with the saner kind of Sufis, such as Jalaluddin. Bayazid, on the other hand, appears to have reached a pitch of conceit which amounted to insanity. He declared himself to be identical with the Deity and with all the angels and patriarchs. His philosophy of the matter was somewhat as follows:

"There is only one original, eternal, absolute essence, the true essence of all things. This essence is *one*—absolute unity. Men who are individual and personal existences are somehow separated from this great unity of being; but they may return to it, be reabsorbed, and again become one with this infinite, undivided, invisible Power. All the angels and patriarchs have long since reached this state, and I, Bayazid, have reached it last; and so I am one with God, who is the absolute Unity. Hence I am one with whatsoever else is one with Him, for His Unity is perfect. I am one with Gabriel, and Abraham, and Moses, and with the creative 'Word. ' "

Furthermore, since in the view of Bistami the Deity Himself is nothing more than this primal absolute Power, in which, as in a vast sea of latent force, all other powers, now embodied in specific forms, were originally held in solution, and into which all these individual natures will ultimately merge, it follows that the real *essence of* the human spirit is Deity. In man, then, Bayazid argued, this divine Power recognizes itself, and sees itself to be divine ; and so, "while men suppose that they are worshipping God, it is in reality the Deity who is paying adoration to Himself. In like manner Mansur Hellaj, regarding himself thus as a specific form of Deity, believed that he was God temporarily clothed in a finite appearance.

The account of the Sufis given by Sir John Malcolm in his " History of Persia "agrees with the above description. "It was the theory of the Sufi," he says, "that God is diffused over all His creation. He exists everywhere and in everything. They compare the emanations of His essence or spirit to the rays of the sun, which they conceive are continually darted forth and reabsorbed.* It is for this reabsorption into the divine essence, to which their immortal part belongs, that they continually sigh. They believe that the soul of man and the principle of life which exists throughout all nature are not *from* God, but *of* God, and hence those doctrines which establish an equality of nature between the created and the Creator. Some, believing that the principle which emanates from God can do nothing without His will, and can refrain from nothing that He wills, altogether deny the existence of evil. They are complete optimists : everything is good with them-religion and infidelity, the lawful and unlawful. 'The Nazarenes,' say they, 'are not infidels because they deem Jesus a God, but because they deem Him alone a God.'

" Unceasingly," says Jami, "a divine influence flows from the world unknown into souls." Jalaluddin writes : " Into the breast of Omar floweth the voice of God, which is the root of all speech and of every language. All other tongues whatsoever—that which the Turk, the Persian, the Arab undersands—are but echoes of this. But

* Jalaluddin says :

"I am the sunlight falling from above,
Yet never severed from the sun I love."

why speak of Turk and Arab? Nay, even the wood and stone are but repercussions of this voice ; for in what moment soever it shall please God to cry aloud, ` Alastu' (`Am I not thy Lord ?'), matter replies, 'Bala' ('Even so')."

Another figure much used by Sufis to express the relation of the human to the divine is that of attraction. Thus we read that God in the first place draws towards Himself by attractive influences, so that His servant may turn his mind in the direction whence the attraction comes, and may be illumined with love. Then follows the "journey," which is divided into two parts, the journey *unto* God and *into* God, but ends at last in the "ascent up to heaven."

This doctrine, or something very like it, is found in Moslem theologians of approved orthodoxy and sobriety, such as Ghazzali. In his chapter on prayer, in his " Ihya-ul-ulum " (Revival of the Religious Sciences) we find the following:

" Prayers are of three degrees, of which the first are those that are simply spoken with the lips. Prayers are of the second kind when with difficulty, and only by a most resolute effort, the soul is able to fix its thoughts on divine things without being disturbed by evil imaginations ; they are of the third kind when one finds it difficult to turn away the mind from dwelling on divine things. But it is the very marrow of prayer when He who is invoked takes possession of the soul of the suppliant, and the soul of him who prays is absorbed into God, to whom he prays, and, his prayer ceasing, all consciousness of self has departed, and to such a degree that all thought whatsoever of the praying is felt as a veil between the soul and God. This state is called by the Sufis 'absorption,' for the reason that the man is so absorbed that he takes no thought of his body, or of anything that happens externally, or even of the movements of his own soul, but is first engaged in going *toward* his Lord, and finally is wholly *in* his Lord. If even the thought occurs that he is absorbed into the Absolute, it is a blemish, for that absorption only is worthy of the name which is unconscious of itself. And these words of mine, though they will be called, as I well know, but foolish babbling by raw theologians, are yet by no means without significance. For consider : The condition of which I speak resembles that of a person who loves any other object, such as wealth, honour, or pleasure. We see such persons so carried away with their love, and others with their anger, that they do not hear one who speaks to them, nor see those passing before their eyes. Nay, so absorbed are they in their passion that they do not perceive their absorption. Just so far as you turn your mind on your absorption you necessarily turn it away from that which is the object of it."

Elsewhere Ghazzali says: "The commencement of this is the going to God ; then follows the finding Him, when the absorption takes place. This at first is momentary, as the lightning swiftly glancing upon the eye, but afterwards, confirmed by use, it introduces the soul into a higher world, where, the most pure essential essence meeting it, fills the soul with the images of the spiritual world, while the majesty of Deity discovers itself."

The Sufis have technical terms for the transitory ecstasies experienced by the novice as contrasted with the permanent exaltation of the ripe mystic. The former is called "Hal" (condition), the latter " Maqam " (station). Human life is regarded as a pilgrimage, the object of which is to obtain the knowledge of God, to whom the soul returns as an exile after its long banishment and imprisonment in the flesh, as a bird in a cage. This view of life as a journey, and of the soul as an emanation from God, is founded on a verse in the Koran: " Verily we are from God, and to Him we return." Sir John Malcolm, in the work quoted above, gives the stages of the Sufi journey thus: " The first stage is humanity ('Nasut'), in which the discsiple must live according to the law ('Shariat'), and observe all the rites, customs, and precepts of his religion. The second is the nature of angels ('Malakut'), for which there is the pathway of purity ('Tariqat'). The third is the possession of power ('Jabrut'), to which corresponds knowledge ('Marifat'), and the fourth is absorption into the Deity ('Fana f'illah')."

Such is a brief outline of the Sufi philosophy, which forms the mental background of all the greatest Persian poets-Jalaluddin Rumi, Hafiz, Jami, and Saadi, though in the last it is not so strongly marked as in the other three. These poets have a technical vocabulary corresponding to their Sufi tenets—*e.g.*, wine means devotion, sleep is meditation on the divine perfection ; perfume, hope of the divine favour ; zephyrs are outbursts of divine grace ; the tavern is a secluded oratory where they become intoxicated with the wine of love ; beauty denotes the perfection of the Deity.

The first important Sufi poet after Abu Said was Hakim Senai, born at Ghazni, in Afghanistan, in the early part of the twelfth century. He was the forerunner of two poets greater than himself, Fariduddin Attar and Jalaluddin Rumi. The latter said : " Attar was the soul itself and Senai its two eyes ; but 1 come after both Senai and Attar." The whole of Senai's poetical works amount to more than thirty thousand distiches, of which the most important is the " Hadika," or Garden, a mystical work on the unity of God, self-mortification, and the attainment of the knowledge of spiritual truth. This work was at first viewed with suspicion as heterodox by the mullahs of Ghazni, but was afterwards pronounced orthodox by a special decree from the theologians of Baghdad. Senai had originally been one of the Court poets of Sultan Ibrahim of Ghazni. When the latter determined on attacking the idolaters of India, Senai composed a poem in his praise, and was hurrying to the Court to present it before that monarch's departure. There was at that time in Ghazni a madman known as Lai Khur, who often in his wanderings made sage remarks. It so happened that Senai, in passing a garden, heard the notes of a song, and stopped to listen. After some time the singer, who was Lai Khur, addressing the cupbearer, said: "Cupbearer, fill a bumper, that I may drink to the blindness of our Sultan, Ibrahim." The cupbearer remonstrated, and said that it was wrong to wish that so just a Sultan should become blind. The madman answered that he deserved blindness for his folly in leaving so ,fine a city as Ghazni, which required his presence and care, to go on a fool's errand in such a severe winter. Lai Khur then ordered the cupbearer to fill another cup, that he might drink to the blindness of Hakim Senai. The cupbearer still more strongly remonstrated against this toast, urging the universally esteemed character of the poet, whom everyone loved and respected. The madman contended that Senai deserved the malediction even more than the King, for, with all his science and learning, he yet appeared ignorant of the purposes for which the Almighty had created him; and when he came, as he would do in a short time, before his Maker, and was asked what he brought with him, he could only produce panegyrics on Kings and Princes, mortals like himself.

These words made so deep an impression on the sensitive mind of the poet that he secluded himself from the world from that time, and gave up all the luxuries and vanities of Courts. Not long after this the Sultan Bahram Shah offered him his daughter in marriage, which honour, however, he gratefully declined, and immediately set out on a pilgrimage to Mecca and Medina. In the following lines of the " Hadikah " he alludes to his refusal of the royal bride:

" I am not a person desirous of gold, or of a wife, or of exalted station ; by my God, I neither seek them nor wish them. If through thy grace and favour thou wouldst even offer me thy crown, I swear by thy head I should not accept it."

Senai died A.D. 1180, and was buried at Ghazni, where his tomb is visited by pilgrims and is called the "Mecca of Ghazni."*

1. *From the " Hadikah " of Senai.*

"A lover on his death-bed lay, and o'er his face the while, Though anguish recked his wasted frame, there spread a fitful smile;

A flush his sunken cheek o'erspread, and to his wasted eye
Came light, that less spoke earthly bliss than heaven-breathed ecstasy.
And one, that weeping o'er him bent and watched the ebbing breath,
Marvelled what thought gave masterv o'er that dread hour of death.
' Ah, when the fair,* adored through life, lifts up at length,' he cried,
'The veil that sought from mortal eye immortal charms to hide',
'Tis thus true lovers, fevered long with that sweet mystic fire',
Exulting meet the lov'd one's gaze, and in the glance expire.' "

(*Translated by* FALCONER.)

2. "At one period of his sovereignty the Caliph Mamun became a persecutor, and shed the innocent blood of his people. To the race of Barmak he acted with such injustice that no one remembers the like. After he had put to death the innocent Yahya, fortune looked upon him sternly and harshly. The injured Yahya had a mother, aged and frail, when thus deprived of the beloved of her heart. She became the companion of sorrow in this world ; consolation, which should be all sweetness, to her became poison. They told this circumstance to Mamun, and laid before him the pitiful case of the afflicted matron. They said : 'She invokes evil upon thee, and prays for the downfall of thy sovereignty. Go, comfort her heart, and cease from thy hatred ; beg pardon of the aggrieved mother for thine injustice.' At night Mamun went to her house, unattended by any of his people, with the view of speaking in mitigation of his crime. Pearls and jewels he proffered to her in abundance. That he considered his best way of proceeding. He said to her :

" 'O mother, all that has come to pass had been predestined. Since destiny hath taken its course, of what avail is your sorrow? Henceforth be resigned and forget your evil wishes towards me. Although Yahya is no more, having undergone his doom, yet from this moment I will be your son ; I will occupy his place. Let your heart be

* Ouseley, "Biographical Notices of Persian Poets."

* God.

comforted ; abandon all hatred, malice, and evil wishing.' The aged mother spoke, and said:

" 'Tell me, O cruel Prince, how can I help lamenting such a son? How can a King like thee be his substitute? How can thy jewels and offerings be an equivalent ? With all the grandeur that hath come to thee, canst thou ever occupy his place in my heart? When thou mentionest his name, is it possible for his mother to refrain from shedding tears ? As for thee, with thy thousands of retinue and all thy regal pomp, my heart will none of thee. Canst thou fill the place of him who is gone?'

"These few words, precious as royal pearls, remain as a memorial of that noble and injured woman. Mamun felt humbled and abashed before her, and from that day forward he never allowed the blood of any one of his people to be shed."

(*Translated by* **D. FORBES.**)

To, these we may append the noble eulogy on Senai by Jalaluddin Rumi, who looked upon him as one of his two masters in Sufism, Fariduddin Attar being the other. It has been translated by Professor. R. A. Nicholson, of Cambridge, in his version of the " Divan-i-Shams-i-Tabriz":

"Quoth someone, 'Master Senai is dead.'
The death of such a master is no little thing.
He was not chaff which flew on the wind ;
He was not water which froze in winter ;
He was not a comb which was broken with a hair ;
He was not a seed which the earth crushed.
He was a treasure of gold in this dust-pit,
For he valued the two worlds at a barley-corn.
The earthly frame he flung to the earth,
Soul and intellect he bore to heaven.
The pure elixir, mingled with the wine-dregs,
Came to the jar's surface, and the lees settled apart.
The second soul, which the vulgar know not,
I protest by God that he surrendered to the Beloved."

8

MYSTICAL POETRY

FARIDUDDIN ATTAR AND JALALUDDIN RUMI

FARIDUDDIN ATTAR was born at Nishapur A.D. 1119. The name Attar signifies "perfumer " and refers to his occupation, which was that of a druggist. One day when he was sitting in his shop a Dervish passed, and, contemplating Attar and his goods, heaved a profound sigh. Attar, feeling annoyed, bade the Dervish go about his business. " You are right," the Dervish replied ; "the journey to the next world is easy for me, for I have nothing but my Dervish frock to take with me. It is not so with you, who possess so much valuable property. Had you not better think of preparing for the journey ?" These words made a profound impression on Attar's mind. He gave up his trade in order to devote himself exclusively to the service of God. For several years he practised ascetic exercises, and then made the pilgrimage to Mecca.

In his old age he retired to Nishapur, where his successor as a mystic poet, Jalaluddin Rumi, met him. Attar gave the latter one of his works, the "Asrar Nama," or Book of Secrets, and is said to have prophesied his future greatness. Attar wrote several other works, the most important of which are the " Tadhkirat-ul-Auliya," a collection of lives of the Sufi saints, and the " Mantiq-ut-Tair," or Parliament of Birds. The latter is an allegory, in which several birds, representing souls, such as the parrot, the partridge, the falcon, the nightingale, the peacock, the pheasant, the dove, etc., assemble themselves, under the guidance of the hoopoe, to seek the Simurgh, the mysterious king of birds, who resides in Mount Kaf, at the extreme limits of the world. After the usual praises of God and Muhammad, the poem opens by speeches from each of the birds and the hoopoe's replies. Thus the nightingale says :

"The secrets of love are known to me ; all the night I chant songs concerning it. It is in imitation of me that the flute laments. I stir with emotion the beds of roses, as well as the hearts of lovers. Whoever listens to me loses his reason and is carried out of himself. If I am for long bereft of the sight of my well-loved Rose, I am desolate and cease from singing. Whenshe spreads her sweet perfume abroad in the springtime, I joyfully open my heart to her and cease from bitter lamentation. My secrets are not known to all the world ; to the Rose alone are they revealed. The love

For this chapter, *cf.* Garcin de Tassy, "La Poesie philosophique et religieuse chez les Persans."

of the Rose is enough for me ; how can I reach the Simurgh ? All her hundred petals bloom for me; how, then, should I not be happy ?"

To this the hoopoe replies: " O thou who laggest behind, content with external forms, cease to boast of an attachment which misguides thee. The love of the Rose has planted in thy heart many thorns. The Rose is beautiful, truly, but her beauty disappears in a few days. Those who aim at perfection should not take delight in the love of such a transitory thing. If the gracefulness of the Rose arouses thy love, it is only to draw daily and nightly lamentations from thee. She laughs at thee every new spring, but she does not smile for thee."

Then appears the parrot, with a morsel of sugar in its beak, apparelled in green, and with a gold collar round its neck. "People," it says, "with hearts of steel have enclosed me in a cage of iron. Held in this prison, I ardently long for the spring of the water of life, guarded by Khizr.* Like him, I am clothed in green, for I am the Khizr of birds. I wish to quench my thirst at the source of this mysterious water. I have no ambition to soar as far as the Simurgh. The well of Khizr suffices me." The hoopoe rebukes it, saying that it has no idea of real happiness, to acquire which one should be willing to renounce even life itself. Something beyond personal immortality must be desired ; one must not be content with the husk, but find the almond within.

The peacock next presents itself, adorned with plumage of a thousand colours and gay as a newly-married bride in her attire. "To adorn me," it says, " the Painter of the invisible world handed his brush to the Genii. Although I am the Gabriel of birds, destiny has appointed me a lot far below that angel ; for, having formed a friendship with the serpent in the terrestrial paradise, I was ignominiously chased out of it.† Obliged to quit the lofty rank which I occupied, I was forced to live in solitude, humiliated by the ugliness of my feet. But I hope some day to quit this obscure sojourn for the mansion of eternity, and repose in paradise, though I cannot hope to reach the King (the Simurgh) of whom thou speakest." The hoopoe replies: " O thou who wilfully wander-est from the true path, know that the palace of the King is worth more than the paradise of which thou speakest. It is the eternal habitation of the aspiring soul, the abode of the heart, the seat of truth. Real Being is a vast ocean, of which Eden is a mere drop. When thou canst have the ocean, why be satisfied with a drop of nightdew ? He who can share the secrets of the sun, will he be content with a grain of dust ? He who is the whole, can he concern himself with a part ? Does the soul need the members of the body? Wouldst thou be perfect, consider the whole, seek the whole, choose the whole."

Thus, with somewhat tedious peculiarity, each bird states its various fears and objections regarding the pilgrimage, and to each the hoopoe replies. At last they start on the perilous journey, which leads them through eight mysterious valleys-the Valley of Search, the Valley of Love, the Valley of Knowledge, the Valley of Independence of External Things, the Valley of Unity, the Valley of Astonishment, the Valley of Poverty, and the Valley of Annihilation. These various valleys correspond in some degree, though not exactly, to the stages of the Sufi pilgrimage mentioned in the last

* A mysterious figure in Muhammadan tradition who roams about the earth clothed in a green mantle. Some suppose him to be the prophet Elijah.

† Muhammadan tradition makes the peacock admit the snake into paradise.

chapter. Of the enormous number of birds who start, all perish in one or another of these stages except thirty. Some are drowned in the ocean; some die of thirst on the tops of high mountains; some have their plumes burnt and their hearts dried by the scorching heat of the sun; some are devoured by wild beasts, falling paralyzed with terror into their jaws ; some die of exhaustion in the desert; some fight and kill each other for a few grains of corn. The thirty who arrive, having lost their wings and feathers in the terrible journey, find that they have arrived, after all, at *themselves,* for the Persian word *Simurgh* signifies " thirty birds." The Simurgh thus addresses the unfortunate pilgrims :

" All you have been and seen and done and thought,
Not *you*, but I, have seen and been and wrought ;
I was the Sin that from Myself rebelled,
I the Remorse that toward Myself compelled ;
I was the *Tajidar** who led the track,
I was the little Briar that pulled you back ;
Sin and Contrition—Retribution owed
And cancelled—Pilgrim, pilgrimage, and road,
Was but Myself toward Myself, and your
Arrival but Myself at my own door."

(*Translated by* E. FITZGERALD.)

Such is the close of this curious allegory. Attar somewhat relieves the monotony of it by interspersing anecdotes, of which the following are examples:

The King and the Slave.

"A kindly King once handed a favourite slave of his a fruit to eat. The latter took it with gratitude and began to eat it with delight, saying he had never tasted anything more delicious. This aroused in the King a desire to taste it also, and he requested the slave to hand him the part that was left. Accordingly, the slave handed it to the King; but when the latter tasted it, he found it so exceedingly bitter that his eyes watered, and he could not speak for some minutes. At last he said, with a frown, to the slave:

"'How did you find this bitter fruit sweet?'

The slave, who had entered the path of spirituality, replied:

" 'Your Majesty, I have received from your hands so many gifts that I could not refuse one bitter fruit. Since Your Majesty has heaped upon me benefits, how can I repine at a single bitterness ?' "

Shah Mahmud and the Idol.

"When Sultan Mahmud invaded India, he found at Somnat an enormous idol. The Brahmins offered him, if he would spare it, ten times its weight in gold; but

* Lit., "the crown-wearer"—*i.e.*, the hoopoe—so called becuase of the tuft of feathers on its head.

Mahmud refused to sell it, and ordered a great fire to be kindled in order to burn it. One of the Sultan's officers ventured to suggest that it would be better to accept the Brahmin's offer. 'No,' said Mahmud ; 'I fear lest at the dread day of account the Creator should say to me before the assembled universe: "Mahmud is a seller of idols.'

"When the idol was actually burnt, a great store of precious stones was found therein, which Mahmud thus obtained for nothing.

" Do thou also," says Attar to the reader, " break the idols which thou worshippest, in order not to perish miserably, like this idol. Burn up thy soul as Mahmud burnt that idol, and thou wilt discover precious stones in it."

The Muhammadan Warrior and the Christian.

"A Muhammadan warrior, engaged in battle with a Christian,* asked for an interval in which to say his prayers. The Christian assented, and the Muhammadan performed his devotions; then they resumed the combat vigorously. Presently the infidel asked for an interval in which to perform *his* devotions. He retired to one side, chose a suitable spot, then bowed his head in the dust before his idol. When the Moslem saw his opponent in that attitude he said to himself, 'Victory is now actually within my grasp,' and was preparing treacherously to strike him with his sword, when all of a sudden a voice from above addressed him:

" 'O disloyal and dishonourable man, is this the way thou exercisest faith and keepest thy word? This infidel drew not the sword on thee when thou wast at prayer, and thou wouldst strike him ! Hast thou not read the words of the Koran, "Fulfil your promises faithfully" ? Be not worsted by an infidel in generosity; return not evil for good. Deal with him as he has dealt with thee; if thou art a true believer, keep faith with him.'

"At these words the warrior paused and burst into tears. When the infidel saw the Moslem standing astonished, in tears, and with his sword in his hand, he asked him the reason, and the Moslem told him. When the infidel heard it he also burst into tears, and exclaimed:

"Since God, on behalf of His miserable enemy, thus blames His friend for not keeping a promise, why should I continue to act disloyally towards Him? Teach me the principles of Islam, that I may embrace the true faith, that I may burn up polytheism, and adopt the path of the Law. Oh! how I lament the blindness which has hitherto prevented me from thinking of such a master!' "

Attar lived to the great age of one hundred and ten. The account of his death, as recorded in Ouseley's "Biographical Notices of Persian Poets," seems to show that he had really attained to that indifference to life and the world which he so strenuously enjoins. When Jengiz Khan invaded Persia, one of the Moghul soldiers seized Attar, and was about to put him to death, when another Moghul, pitying the aged man, and interested by his unaffected piety and resignation, offered to purchase his life for a thousand dirhems. The offer would have been gladly, accepted but that Attar, anxious that the bird (his soul) should be emancipated from the cage of its mortal coil, advised his captor to refuse the price offered, as he might depend on meeting with a better

* Attar lived at the time of the Crusades.

customer. After waiting some time another Moghul came up, and, remarking on the great age of the captive, offered for him a bag of horse-fodder. Attar, smiling, said: "This is my full value; sell me." Then the Moghul, annoyed at having refused the first good offer, in a passion immediately murdered him. His death took place A.D. 1229.

JALALUDDIN RUMI.

To Jalaluddin Rumi might be applied Dante's phrase regarding Homer: "He flies above other poets like an eagle." He was a mystic first and a poet afterwards—that is, he valued his poetic gift as a means of spreading his ideas, and did not, like Hafiz, use Sufi phrases as a mere poetic ornament. Thoroughly imbued as he was with the doctrines of ideal Pantheism—*i.e.*, that the soul must aspire to and finally be absorbed in God—he was Puritanical in the sternness with which he inculcated the necessity of mortifying the flesh in order to reach this final goal. He differs from many Pantheistic teachers in emphasizing the reality of sin and the free-will and responsibility of man. In common with the other Persian mystics, he regards outward rites as insignificant in comparison with the spiritual truths which they embody. Even of the Koran itself, which orthodox Muhammadanism declares to be uncreated, he says:

" I extracted the marrow of the Koran,
And flung the bone to the dogs."

He is perfectly aware that religious belief is based upon an accumulation of probabilities, but in the Sufistic stage of *wajd,* or ecstasy, he can rise into the sunlight of clear assurance. The cast-iron dogmas of Muhammadanism are molten into universal religious truths, in the alembic of his poetry.

To him the true Ka'ba is not the square shrine which the Muhammadan pilgrims perambulate at Mecca, but the human heart. "You may circle round the Ka'ba a thousand times," he exclaims. "God cares not for it if you hurt one heart." So, with regard to the incessant ablutions enjoined by Islam, he says: "Yes, your hand can wash your body, but what hand can wash your heart?" He is almost Hebraic in his sense of the sinfulness of man as contrasted with the holiness of God: "Do not sin, for even our good acts are sinful in the sight of our Beloved. Man was placed on earth to prove him bankrupt towards God " (" Masnavi," Book II). In this he rises far above the average morality of Muhammadans, who dispute whether sins of thought are sins at all. So, again, in contrast to the common Muhammadan idea of God as an Almighty Despot, damning or saving whom He will, Jalaluddin says:

" Union exists beyond all thought and speech,
Between great Allah and the soul of each."

His view of woman is probably unique among Muhammadan writers:

" Woman is a ray of God, not a mere creature."

Jalaluddin Rumi, of the royal line of Khwarezm, was born at Balkh, in Central Asia, A. D. 1207. His father, Bahauddin, was a leading theologian, but, having fallen under the displeasure of the reigning Prince of Balkh, left that city and went on the pilgrimage to Mecca, finally settling at Iconium, in Asia Minor, or Rum, whence the poet received the sobriquet " Rumi." After the death of his father, in 1231, Jalaluddin succeeded him as spiritual guide to his many disciples, about four hundred in number. He had previously studied Sufism at Aleppo and Damascus, but the man who exercised the profoundest influence on him was a fakir named Shams-ud-din ("The Sun of Religion"), from Tabriz. The story of their first meeting is thus told in the "Menaqib-ul-Arifin" (Acts of the Adepts), translated by the late Sir James Redhouse :

"Shams-ud-din arrived at Iconium in December, 1244. He engaged a lodging at an inn, and pretended to be a great merchant. In his room, however, there was nothing but a broken waterpot, an old mat, and a bolster of unbaked clay. He broke his fast once in every ten or twelve days with a damper soaked in broth of sheep's trotters. One day, as he was seated at the gate of the inn, Jalaluddin came by, riding on a mule, in the midst of a crowd of students and disciples on foot. Shams-ud-din arose, advanced and took hold of the mule's bridle, addressing Jalaluddin in these words:

"'Tell me, was Muhammad the greater servant of God or Bayazid Bistami ?'

" Jalaluddin answered him:

" 'Muhammad was incomparably greaterthe greatest of all prophets and all saints.'

" 'Then, rejoined Shams-ud-din, 'how is it that Muhammad said, " We have not known thee, O God, as Thou rightly shouldst be known," whereas Bayazid said, " Glory be to me! how very great is my glory!'"

" On hearing this question, Jalaluddin fainted away. On recovering his consciousness, he took his new acquaintance home with him. They were closeted together for weeks or months in holy communications."

Shams-ud-din, however, was not popular in conium. From the same authority we learn: " He likened his auditors to oxen and asses." Jalaluddiu's disciples were intensely jealous of him for monopolizing the attention of their master. Finally he perished in some obscure way in a street riot, and not long after Jalaluddin's son, Ala-ud-din, died also. In token of his sorrow Jalaluddin founded the famous order of the " Mevlevi," or whirling Dervishes, whose gyrations are supposed to signify the revolutions of the planets round the sun.

Of Jalaluddin, as of Shelley, it might be said, " He learnt in suffering what he taught in song." His great "Masnavi," a collection of apologues and moral reflections, in twenty-six thousand couplets, opens with the plaintive notes of the reed-flute longing to return to its osier-bed, even as the soul longs to return to God :

"Hear how yon reed, in sadly-pleasing tales,
Departed bliss and present woe bewails !
'With me from native banks untimely torn
Love-warbling youths and soft-eyed virgins mourn;
O ! let the heart, by fatal absence rent,
Feel what I sing and bleed what I lament ;
Who roams in exile from his parent bower
Pants to return, and chides each lingering hour ;

My notes, in circles of the grave and gay,
Have hailed the rising, cheered the closing day;
Each in my fond affections claim'd a part,
But none discerned the secret of my heart.
What though my strains and sorrows flow combined,
Yet ears are slow, and carnal eyes are blind.
Free through each mortal form the spirits roll,
But sight avails not. Can we see the soul?
Not he who reasons best this wisdom knows;
Ears only drink what rapturous tongues disclose.
Nor fruitless deem the reed's heart-piercing pain—
See sweetness dropping from the parted cane.
Alternate hope and fear my days divide :
I courted grief, and anguish was my bride.
Hail, heavenly love ! true source of endless gains !
Thy balm restores me, and thy skill sustains.
Oh, more than Galen learned, than Plato wise,
My guide, my law, my joy supreme, arise !
Love warms this frigid clay with mystic fire,
And dancing mountains leap with young desire.' "

(*Translated by* SIR W. JONES.)

The " 'Masnavi" throughout the Muhammadan world, especially in Turkey, Persia, Afghanistan, and India, is looked upon as almost divinely inspired, and is called "The Koran in the Pehlevi tongue." Professor Cowell says of it (" Oxford Essays," 1855): "The stories themselves are generally easy, and told in a delightful style; but the disquisitions which interrupt them are often ' darker than the darkest oracles,' and unintelligible even to the Persians themselves without a copious commentary. When he is clear, no Persian poet can surpass his depth of thought or beauty of imagery; the flow of fine things runs on unceasingly as from a river-god's urn,"

The following are three of the apologues from the " Masnavi".

1. *The Caliph and Satan.*

" In heavy sleep the Caliph lay,
When someone called, 'Arise and pray!'
The angry Caliph cried, 'Who dare
Rebuke his King for slighted prayer ?'
Then from the corner of the room
A voice cut sharply through the gloom :

' My name is Satan. Rise ! obey
Muhammad's law ! awake and pray.'
'Thy *words* are good,' the Caliph said,
'But their intent I somewhat dread,
For matters cannot well be worse
Than when the thief says, " Guard your purse.!"
I cannot trust your counsel, friend ;
It surely hides some wicked end.'
Said Satan : ' Near the throne of God
In ages past we devils trod ;
Angels of light, to us 'twas given
To guide each wandering foot to heaven ;
Not wholly lost is that first love,
"Nor those pure tastes we knew above.
Roaming across a continent,
The Tartar moves his shifting tent,
But never quite forgets the day
When in his father's arms he lay ;
So we, once bathed in love divine,
Recall the taste of that rich wine.
God's finger rested on my brow—
That magic touch, I feel it now !
I fell, 'tis true—oh, ask not why,
For still to God 1 turn my eye ;
It was a chance by which I fell:
Another takes me back from hell.
'Twas but my envy of mankind,
The envy of a loving mind :
Jealous of men, I could not bear
God's love with this new race to share.
But yet God's tables open stand ;
His guests flock in from every land.
Some kind act towards the race of men
May toss us into heaven again.
A game of chess is all we see,
And God the player, pieces we.

White, black, queen, pawn, 'tis all the same,
For on both sides He plays the game.
Moved to and fro, from good to ill,
We rise and fall as suits His will.'
The Caliph said : ' If this be so,
I know not, but thy guile I know ;
For how can I thy words believe
When even God thou didst deceive ?
A sea of lies art thou-our sin
Only a drop that sea within.'
' Not so,' said Satan ; ' I serve God,
His angel now, and now His rod.
In tempting I both bless and curse,
Make good men better, bad men worse.
Good coin is mixed with bad, my brother ;
I but distinguish one from th' other.'
' Granted,' the Caliph said ; ' but still
You never tempt to good, but ill.
Tell, then, the truth, for well I know
You come as my most deadly foe.'
Loud laughed the fiend. ' You know me well ;
Therefore my purpose I will tell.
If you had missed your prayers, I knew
A swift repentance would ensue ;
And such repentance would have been
A good outweighing far the sin.
I chose this humbleness divine,
Born out of fault, should not be thine,
Preferring prayers elate with pride
To sin with penitence allied.' "

(*Translated by* JAMES FREEMAN CLARKE.)

2. *The Jewish King and the Martyrs.*

"The Jewish King seized a mother with her child,
And brought them both before the fire.
'Oh, woman,' he cried, ` bow down before the image,
Or thou shalt burn in thy silence in yonder fire !'

The woman was a pure and holy believer,
And she refused to do homage to the idol.
He seized her child and flung it in the flame,
And the mother feared and turned her heart from its faith.
She prayed that she might be allowed to worship the idol,
When the voice of her child was heard from the fire :
' Oh, come hither, my mother, for here I am happy,
Though to outward appearance I may be in the midst of a flame ;
Oh, come hither, my mother, and behold the proofs of truth ;
Oh, come hither, and learn the secrets of Abraham,
How he found in the furnace roses and jessamines.*
It was death which I saw when I was born from thee,
It was death when I was delivered from the womb.
When I was born, I escaped from a prison
Into a world of fresh air and fair colours ;
But now I see that the world is but a prison,
Since I have tasted the rest which is in this fire.
Oh, come hither, my mother, for our good fortune hath arrived ;
Oh, come hither, nor throw away prosperity from thy hand.
Thou hast seen the power of the tyrant ; come hither,
That thou mayst know the power and mercy of God.
Oh, come hither, and call others with thee,
For the King hath made a banquet in this fire.
Come ye hither, my friends, like moths round a taper,
Leap into the fire in the eyes of your persecutors ;
Plunge ye all into this deep sea,
That your souls may be washed and purified.'
Then the mother flung herself into the flames,
And the sympathy-seeking child seized her hand in his ;
And the mother also burst into speech ;
She also strung the pearls of the praise of God's mercy ;
She shouted to the people from the midst of the fire,
And the hearts of the crowd were astonished at her speech.
After this the people, forgetful of themselves,
Leaped into the fire, both men and women ;

* **Muhammadan tradition says that Nimrod threw Abraham into a furnace, which forthwith turned into a rose-garden.**

Without other allurements through sole love of the Loved One,

For this love maketh even the bitter to be sweet."

(*Translated by* COWELL.)

3. *The Existence of Evil.*

"A Sufi said to a Qazi (judge) : 'Could not the Almighty have given us pure profit without loss ?

He who made Abraham's furnace a rose-garden, could He not have done this for us and no harm ensue ?

He who produces a rose from a thorn, could He not have turned our winter into spring ?

He who makes the cypress lofty, can He not turn grief into joy ?

He who calls existence out of non-existence, would it hurt Him to make it permanent ?

He who breathes the soul into the body, if He prevented the body dying, what loss would He incur ?

What harm would there be if that Generous One gave His servants their desires without their struggling, and protected weak mortals altogether from the deceits of the flesh and the devices of the devil ? if He did not cause the seeker to waste so much time and made his heart at once like a pure mirror ?'

The Qazi answered : 'If there were no bitterness, and no contrast of beautiful and ugly, of stone and pearl ; if there were no Satan and flesh and lust, and no war and wound and fraud, then by what title would the King call his servants ?

How could He say, "O patient one," or "O meek one," or " O brave one," or " O generous one " ?

How could there be any patient or just or devout men it there were no tempter couched in ambush ?

The heroes Rustam and Hamza and an effeminate eunuch would be all one ; wisdom and knowledge would be vain and confused.

The object of wisdom is to point the right way ; if there were only one way, wisdom would be of no avail.

Do you wish to ruin two worlds for the sake of a mean cottage ?

I know, however, that you are ripe and not raw, and that you put these questions only for the benefit of the commonalty.

The tyranny of fortune and every imaginable pain are easier to bear than alienation from God and neglect of Him ;

For those things pass away and these do not, and he is truly wealthy whose soul is awake."'

(*Translated by* FIELD.)

4. *The Suppliant.*

"All night the lonely suppliant prayed,

All night his earnest crying made,

Till, standing by his side at morn,
The tempter said in bitter scorn :
'Oh, peace! What profit do you gain
From empty words and babblings vain ?
" Come, Lord-oh, come !" you cry alway ;
You pour your heart out night and day,
Yet still no murmur of reply,
No voice that answers, " Here am I." '
"Then sank that stricken heart in dust;
That word had withered all its trust ;
No strength retained it now to pray,
While Faith and Hope had fled away.
And ill that mourner now had fared,
Thus by the Tempter's art ensnared,
But that at length beside his bed
His sorrowing angel stood and said :
' Doth it repent thee of thy love
That never now is heard above
Thy prayer, that now not any more
It knocks at heaven's gate as before ?'
' I am cast out ; I find no place,
No hearing at the throne of grace.
" Come, Lord, O come :" I cry alway ;
I pour my heart out night and day,
Yet never until now have won
The answer, "Here am I, my son." '
"Oh, dull of heart, enclosed doth lie
In each 'Come, Lord,' a ' Here am I';
Thy love, thy longing, are not thine—
Reflections of a love divine ;
Thy very prayer to thee was given
Itself a messenger from heaven.
Whom God rejects, they are not so ;
Strong bands are round them in their woe;
Their hearts are bound with bands of brass,
That sigh or crying cannot pass.

All treasures did the Lord impart
To Pharaoh save a contrite heart.
All other gifts unto his foes
He freely gives, nor grudging knows ;
But Love's sweet smart and costly pain
A treasure for His friends remain."

(*Translated by* R. C. TRENCH.)

The general character and effects of the "Masnavi " have been well summed up by Mr. P. Z. Easton, who resided many years in Persia:

"The richness of ideas in this work make it as it were a very seed-bed, where there is ofttimes more meaning in a single sentence than in learned tomes; comprehensive as well as rich, the truth of Muhammadanism supplemented by the truths of all other religions. Not only does it furnish a centre for the multitudinous sects of Islam, but it presents a platform on which theistic Hindu and Muhammadan meet. Another important characteristic is that we find Jalaluddin addressing all classes of men, unfolding the highest themes to the lowest as well as to the highest intelligence. To make a learned man a philosopher were nothing. The soldier, the muleteer, the lowest ranks of men-them would he teach the lessons of divine wisdom. A still more important practical feature of this system is, that it is not a mere philosophy: it is an institution whose disciples and propagators are the thirty-six Dervish sects scattered over the Muhammadan world."

The influence of the "Masnavi" has been very great, in Turkey especially, where numerous commentaries have been written on it. D'Ohsson, in his " Oriental Antiquities," has preserved a curious anecdote regarding Ertoghrul, the founder of the Ottoman dynasty, and Jalaluddin :

"Moulana Jalaluddin Rumi lived at that time at Iconium, with the reputation of a saint. This Sheikh, surnamed Mullah Hunkiar ('The Royal Mullah'), was the founder of the order of Mevlevi Dervishes, one of the most distinguished of those which exist still in the empire. Ertoghrul frequently visited him. He one day carried with him Osman, his son, while an infant, and recommended him to his prayers. The Sheikh took him by the hand and said : ' I regard and cherish thee as my son ; may the blessings of Heaven descend upon thee! May thy fortune be most illustrious; and may the prosperity of thy arms and family be as durable as the attachments which thy descendants and successors shall entertain for mine.' "

It is from this Osman (afterwards Osman L) that the present Sultan, Muhammad V., is descended in a direct line. He has himself, during his thirty years' imprisonment under the late Sultan Abdul Hamid, been a great student of the " Masnavi," and, like

* One stanza of "In Memoriam" rather aptly sums up the characteristics of Jalaluddin's poetry :

"And all the breeze of fancy blows,
And every dewdrop paints a bow;
The wizard lightnings deeply glow,
And every though breaks out a rose."

his predecessors, was on his accession to the throne girded with the sword of Osman by the head of the Mevlevi Dervishes, whose order was founded by Jalaluddin.

The "Diwan-i-Shams-i-Tabriz," Jalaluddin's other great work, may be described as a kind of mixture of the Song of Solomon and Tennyson"s "In Memoriam," if such a blending is conceivable.

Nearly every ode is inscribed with the name of his dead friend, and couched in erotic language. Here philosophy is in abeyance, and the reader is carried onward on a current of unwavering lyrical impetus. The following ode, translated by Professor Falconer, is in the original in Arabic, which some of the Persian poets seem to have handled as easily as their mother-tongue:

1.

He comes—the bearer of the draught divine !
See mantling in that cup no mortal wine !
Drink ! and each earthly appetite forgot,
Each sense abolished (Spirits need them not),
Hear without ears ; be, without vocal breath,
Divinely eloquent, yet mute as death !
Now, mystic lovers ! wild with strange delight,
To heavenly mansions wing your rapturous flight.
Tread of yon halls august the marble floor,
Behold the Eternal Fair and face to face adore.
Heard yc that shout ? The Archangel Herald cries,
'Tis Resurrection's morn ! Ye saints, arise !
Rise ! Of pleasure everlasting
Drink your fill at Heaven's call !
Long were ye condemned to fasting,
Welcome now the Festival !'

2.

" Seeks thy spirit to be gifted.
With a deathless life ?
Let it seek to be uplifted
O'er earth's storm and strife.
"Spurn its joys, its ties dissever,
Hopes and fears divest;
Thus aspire to live for ever,
Be for ever blest.
"Faith and doubt leave far behind thee,

Cease to love or hate ;
Let not Time's illusions blind thee—
Thou shalt Time out-date.

"Merge thine individual being
In the Eternal's love,
All this sensuous nature fleeing
For pure bliss above.

" Earth receives the seed and guards it,
Trustfully it dies ;
Then what teeming life rewards it
For self-sacrifice !

"With green life and clustering blossom
Clad and golden fruit,
See it from earth's cheerless bosom
Ever sunward shoot.

" Thus, when self-abased, man's spirit
From each earthly tie
Rises, disenthralled, to inherit
Immortality."

(*Translated by* FALCONER)

3.

" Soul of mine, thou dawning light: Be not far, O be not far !
Love of mine, thou vision bright: Be not far, O be not far !
Life is where thou smilest sweetly ; death is in thy parting look ;
Here 'mid death and life's fierce fight : Be not far, O be not far !
I am East when thou art rising; I am West when thou dost set.
Bring heaven's own radiant hues to sight : Be not far, O be not far !
See how well my turban fitteth, yet the Parsee girdle binds me ;
Cord and wallet I bear light : Be not far, O be not far !
True Parsec and true Brahman, a Christian yet a Mussulman,
Thee I trust, Supreme by right : Be not far, O be not far !
In all mosques, pagodas, churches, I do find one shrine alone ;
Thy face is there my sole delight : Be not far, O be not far !"

(*Translated by* W. HASTIE.)*

* By permission of Messrs. Maclehose and Sons.

It is interesting to find that, according to the "Menaqib-ul-Arifin " above quoted, Jalaluddin was appreciated by his great contemporary, Sheikh Sa'di of Shiraz. That work informs us that the Prince of Shiraz wrote to Sa'di begging him to select the best ode with the most sublime thoughts that he knew of as existing in Persian, and to send it him for presentation to the great Khan of the Moghuls, who then ruled over nearly all Asia. It so happened that an ode by Jalaluddin had just become known at Shiraz, commencing thus :

"Divine Love's voice each instant left and right is heard to sound :

"We're bound for heaven. To witness our departure who'll be found?' "

This ode had captivated the minds of all the men of culture in the city, and Sa'di copied it out and sent it to the Prince with the remark: " A monarch of auspicious advent has sprung up in the land of Rum, from whose privacy these are some of the breathings. Never have more beautiful words been uttered, and never will be. Would that I could go to Rum and rub my face in the dust under his feet!"*

Up to a recent period Jalaluddin Rumi was comparatively neglected by English translators, though Sir William Jones and Professor Falconer had translated some fragments of his works. Now, however, considerable portions of the " Masnavi " have been translated by Mr. Whinfield and Professor Wilson, and of the " Diwan-i-Shams-i-Tabriz " by Professor Nicholson and Dr. Hastie.

Jalaluddin died in 1273, and was buried at Konia, where successive heads of the Dervish order which he founded have resided ever since. His son, Sultan Veled, succeeded him as head of the order ; he was also a poet, but belongs rather to Turkish literature than to Persian.

* Redhouse's translation of the "Menaqib-ul-Arifin."

9

DIDACTIC POETRY : SA'DI

SA'DI, the most popular of all the Persian poets, was born at Shiraz in A.D. 1184. His father, named Abdullah, was attached to the service of the Atabeg Sultan, Sad-ben-Zangi, who governed the province of Fars from A.D. 1195 to 1226. It was from him that the poet took the name "Sa'di," his real name being Muslih-ud-din (" Reformer of Religion"). He lost his father and mother at a comparatively early age, and mentions both affectionately in his works. Of the former he says in the " Bostan " : " I remember in the days of my childhood my father (may the Divine mercy rain beneficence upon his tomb!) bought me a writing tablet, a desk, and also a ring of gold. A pedlar came, and in exchange for some dates carried off my gold ring." Regarding his mother he says in the " Gulistan": " Once in the insolence of youth I dared to lift up my voice against my mother. She sat down in a corner, and with broken heart said to me, weeping: `You who are so cruel now towards your mother, have you forgotten the days of your infancy?'" In other passages of his writings he refers in a feeling way to the trials of orphans. At an early age he showed strong religious tendencies, rising during the night for prayer and practising fasting.

After having made some progress in his studies at Shiraz, he removed to Bagdad, then the seat of the Caliphate and resort of the most learned men of Islam. He obtained a scholarship at the Nizamiya College, founded by the Vizier Nizam-ul-mulk, the friend of Omar Khayyam. Sa'di there formed a friendship with a celebrated Sufi philosopher, Shihab-udin Suhrawardy, who was afterwards put to death as a heretic by the Sultan Saladin. It is doubtless to this friendship that the traces of mysticism in his works, especially in his Ghazals, or Odes, are chiefly due.

On the conclusion of his studies, finding Shiraz much disturbed owing to the constant incursions of the Mongols, he betook himself to travel. According to his biographer, Daulat Shah, he accomplished the pilgrimage to Mecca fifteen times, and for the most part on foot. Besides Arabia, he journeyed over a large part of the then known world, and among the countries and cities which he visited he mentions in his poems Damascus, Jerusalem, Baalbec, Bassora, Egypt, Mauritania, Diarbekr, Turkestan, Abyssinia, Asia Minor, and India. It was while wandering in the neighbourhood of Jerusalem that he was taken prisoner by the Crusaders. He thus relates the adventure and its consequences in the second chapter of the " Gulistan".

"Once on a time a weariness of my friends at Damascus came over me. I betook myself to the desert of Jerusalem, and associated with animals up to the time when I became a prisoner in the clutches of the Franks, and they set me to earthwork in the fosse of Tripoli along with a lot of Jews. One of the leading men of Aleppo—an acquaintance existed between us previously—passed by and recognized me.

" He said : 'What state is this ? and how art thou passing thy life ?'

" I replied :

" 'I was flying from men to the mountains and the desert,
That I might have nothing to do with any other than God;
Imagine what my state must be at the time
When I must needs have to do with a gang of inhuman wretches !'

He took compassion on my state, and got me freedom from the captivity of the Franks by the payment of ten gold pieces, and took me with him to Aleppo. He had a daughter; he gave her in marriage to me, with a portion of one hundred gold pieces. Some time elapsed; the girls, who was bad-tempered and quarrelsome, began to give loose to her tongue, and embittered my life.

" A bad woman in a good man's house
Is his hell in this world itself.
Beware of an evil companion, beware !
' And keep us, O our Lord, from the torment of hell.'*

" Once she gave vent to taunting speech, and was saying ;

" 'Art thou not he whom my father bought back again for ten gold pieces ?'

" I replied : 'Yes ; he set me free from the captivity of the Franks by payment of ten gold pieces, and made me a captive to thee for a hundred pieces of gold.

" 'I heard that a good man set free a goat from the jaws and clutches of a wolf ;
At night he drew a knife across its throat ;
The ebbing life of the goat to him thus plained,
" Thou snatchedst me away from the claws of the wolf;
When I looked closely, lo! thou wert ultimately a wolf for me.", "†

Sa'di's unfortunate marriage seems to have occurred about A. D. 1204. In the " Bostan" he gives a vivid account of another adventure which befell him at Somnath, in India, and the way in which he discovered the knavery of the Hindu priests. After describing how he gained their confidence by pretending to be a convert to their religion, he says:

"One night, after having securely fastened the door of the temple, I hurried to and fro like a scorpion. Examining the platform carefully, I noticed a curtain embroidered with gold ; behind it sat one of the priests, holding the end of a cord in

* Koran, chap. iii.

† Platt's translation of the "Gulistan."

his hand. Every time he pulled the cord the idol outside the curtain lifted its hands towards heaven. When he saw me the priest was greatly troubled, and overwhelmed with shame to see that his trick had been discovered. He fled ; I pursued and caught him and cast him head downward in a well, for I knew that if I let him survive he would have plotted against my life in order to preserve his secret. In order to be secure against him I cast stones upon him, for dead men tell no tales, and fled from that place as quickly as possible ; when one has fired a jungle it is well to fly from the lions which lurk within it."*

It is rather doubtful whether Sa'di has not been giving the rein to his fancy in this piece of autobiography. After having thoroughly satisfied his taste for travel, he returned to Shiraz, which was now in a state of peace, owing, as he says in the preface to the "Gulistan," to the wise rule of Abu Bakr bin Sad Zangi.

" No fear is there for Persia's clime from the calamities of fortune
So long as such as thou, God's shadow, art at its head.
At this time no one can point out on the earth's wide surface
An asylum of tranquillity like the threshold of thy gate."

Sa'di took up his abode in a hermitage outside the city, and gave himself up to religious meditation and the completion of his two great works, the " Gulistan" and " Bostan," which were finished about A. D. 1257. These are the finest products of his genius, and contain the fruits of his long travel and experience. The "Gulistan" is probably more read in the East than any work except the Koran. Professor Cowell says of it:

" When we open the book we step at once into life and action, far away from the disputations and logic of the schools, into the street and the bazaar. We are no longer talking of abstractions and shadows ; we are face to face with living agents ; we are jostled in the crowd. Behind Sa`di's book rises in perspective Sa'di's own long life of adventure and travel, and it is this which gives to it its freshness and reality. The old man, as he writes, recalls the past scenes in which he himself has felt and acted ; every desert journey, every night adventure, every caravanserai's guests, have added some figure to the long succession of images which his memory calls up from the past. His childhood and its quiet home, his studious youth, his restless manhood and settled age, are summoned in turn to the sessions of sweet silent thought,' and each brings its store of memorials."

Like other great poets, Sa'di was not without his detractors. In the fifth book of the " Bostan " he says;

"One evening, when I had kindled the torch of poetry at the brilliant flame of inspiration, a man with envy in his heart heard me recite my verses. He could not help applauding them, but a kind of malignity mingled with his praises. Can one prevent the wounded complaining?

" 'Behold, 'he said, 'what fine thoughts and noble ideas! Sa'di is skilled in the language of piety, of mysticism and of moral philosophy, but there are no martial tones in his lyre. He leaves to other poets the honour of celebrating the feats of the javelin, the battle-axe, and the massive mace.'

* "Bostan," chap. viii.

"Ignorant man! he does not see that I have no taste for warlike epics, otherwise it would be easy for me to attain distinction in that domain also. I too could draw the warrior's blade and eclipse the glory of my rivals."

But popular acclamation raised Sa'di high above the murmurs of envy. He was revered not only as a great poet, but as a saint, and accredited with supernatural powers by the more superstitious. It is related that a religious man at Shiraz, who was possibly envious of Sa'di's great reputation for sanctity, frequently affected to doubt its being genuine and to disbelieve his being a favourite of Heaven. One night in a dream this man was transported to Paradise, where the souls of the blessed were singing the praises of the Almighty. On inquiry he found that they were chanting a verse of Sa'di's composition, which, they said, was more acceptable to God than one year's adoration of the whole choir of angels. He awoke and approached the Sheikh's door ; great was his surprise to find him arisen and in the act of chanting in holy ecstasy the identical couplet which he had heard in his dream:

"The foliage of a newly clothed tree, to the eye of a discerning man, in every leaf displays a volume of the wondrous works of our Creator."

The religious man fell at Sa'di's feet, related his dream, and having obtained his blessing, returned home his most enthusiastic admirer.

Barbier de Meynard has well summed up the chief characteristics of Sa'di's poetry:

"Of all the Eastern poets," he says, "Sa'di is perhaps the only one who can sustain in Europe the popularity which the enjoys with Muhammadan readers, because he combines in himself those qualities which modern taste requires. His unfailing good sense, the charm and wit which animate his stories, the tone of indulgent raillery for human shortcomings—all these merits, so rare in his countrymen, give him a right to our admiration. Sa'di had by nature only a moderate leaning towards mysticism, but he was a product of his age, and could not resist the current of ideas which drew in that direction every cultivated and imaginative mind. Those of his pieces which are most strongly impregnated with the spirit of Sufism have something strained and artificial about them, with a lukewarmness which is as far removed from the sincerity of Jalaluddin as it is from the disordered inspiration of Hafiz. In the last we see the greatest lyrist and in Sa'di the most human and large-hearted moralist of Islam."*

Sir John Malcolm has recorded in his " Sketches in Persia " that the works of Sa'di are not merely enjoyed in his own country as poetry, but have had a real effect upon Persian character.

" 'Have you no laws,' said I one day to Aga Meer, 'but the Koran and the traditions upon that volume ?'

" 'We have,' said he gravely ; 'the maxims of Sa'di.'

" Were I to judge from my own observations," adds Malcolm, " I should say that these stories and maxims, which are known to all from the King to the peasant, have fully as great an effect in restraining the arbitrary and unjust exercise of power as the laws of the Prophet."

* Barbier de Meynard, "La Poesie en Perse."

Sa'di died in A.D. 1292, at the age of 108. From that time to this his grave, like that of his fellow-townsman Hafiz, has been a place of pilgrimage.

FROM THE "GULISTAN" OF SA'DI*

Sic Transit !

"One breath of life each moment flies,
A small remainder meets my eyes.
Sleeper, whose fifty years are gone,
Be these five days at least thy own.
Shame on the dull departed dead
Whose task is left unfinished.
In vain for them the drum was beat
Which warns us of man's last retreat.
Sweet sleep upon the parting day
Holds back the traveller from the way.
Each comer a new house erects,
Departs—the house its lord rejects.
The next one forms the same conceit—
This mansion none shall ere complete.
Since good and bad alike must fall,
He's blest who bears away the ball.†
Send to thy tomb an ample store ;
None will it bring—then send before.
Life is like snow in July's sun :
Little remains, and is there one
To boast himself and vaunt thereon ?
With empty hand thou hast sought the mart ;
I fear thou wilt with thy turban part.
Who eat their corn while yet 'tis green
At the true harvest can but glean ;
To Sa'di's counsel let thy soul give heed :
This is the way—be manful and proceed."

2. *The Dervish's Revenge.*

" They relate that an oppressor smote a pious man on the head with a stone. The Dervish had not the power to retaliate ; but he kept the stone carefully beside him until a season when the King was wroth with that officer, and confined him in a pit. The Dervish came and smote him on the head with that stone.

"He said: 'Who art thou ? and why hast thou struck me on the head with the stone?'

"The Dervish replied: `I am such a one, and this stone is the same which, on such a day, thou didst cast at me.'

"The other rejoined: 'Where hast thou been this long while ?'

"The Dervish answered: 'I was awed by thy rank ; now that I behold thee in the dungeon I take advantage of the opportunity ; as the wise have said :

" ' "Seest thou that fortune crowns the unworthy, then Choose thou submission, too, with wiser men.

Hast thou not sharp and rending claws? Then yield—

For so'tis bst—so beast the battlefield.

He that has grappled with a hand of steel

Will in his silver arm the anguish feel ;

Wait thou till fortune shall his arm restrain,

Then at thy will thou mayst thy foeman brain." ' "

3. *The King and the Dervish.*

"A solitary Dervish had fixed himself in the corner of a desert. A King passed by him. The Dervish, inasmuch as cessation from worldly pursuits is the kingdom of content, raised not up his head and heeded him not. The King, through the domineering character of royalty, was offended, and observed: 'This tribe of tatterdemalions is on a level with brutes.'

" The Vizier said to the Dervish : The King of earth's surface passed near thee ; why didst thou not do him homage and perform thy respects ?'

"He replied : 'Tell the King to look for service from one who expects favours from him, and let him know that Kings are for the protection of their subjects, not subjects for the service of the King, as they have said :

" 'Kings are but guardians who the poor should keep,
Though this world's goods wait on their diadem.
Not for the shepherd's welfare are the sheep ;
The shepherd, rather, is for pasturing them.
To-day thou markest one flushed with success,
Another sick with struggles against fate ;
Pause but a little while, the earth shall press
His brain that did such plans erst meditate.
Lost is the difference of King and slave
At the approach of destiny's decree ;
Should one upturn the ashes of the grave,
Could he discern 'twixt wealth and poverty ?'

(*Translated by* EASTWICK.)

"The discourse of the Dervish made a strong impression on the King.

"He said: 'Ask a boon of me.'

"The Dervish replied: 'I request that thou wilt not again disturb me.'

"On this the King rejoined: 'Give me some piece of advice.'

"The Dervish said :

" 'Now that thy hands retain these blessings, know
This wealth, these lands, from hand to hand must go.' "

4. *Sa'di and his Father.*

" I remember that in the time of my childhood I was devout and in the habit of keeping vigils, and eager to practise mortification and austerities. One night I sat up in attendance on my father, and did not close my eyes the whole night, and held the precious Koran in my lap while the people around me slept.

" I said to my father: 'Not one of these lifts up his head to perform a prayer. They are so profoundly asleep that you would say they were dead.'

" He replied : 'Life of thy father! it were better if thou too were asleep, rather than that thou shouldst be backbiting people.

"Naught but themselves can vain pretenders mark,
For conceit's curtain intercepts their view ;
Did God illume that which in them is dark
Naught than themselves would wear a darker hue.' "

5. *Sa'di and the Old Man.*

" I was engaged in a dispute with some learned men in the principal mosque of Damascus. Suddenly a young man entered the door and said:

" 'Is there any among you who knows the Persian language ?'

"They pointed to me. "I said : 'Is all well ?'

"He replied : 'An old man of a hundred and fifty years of age is in the agonies of death, and says something to me in Persian which is not intelligible to me. If thou wouldst be so kind as to trouble thyself so far as to step with me, thou wilt be rewarded. It may be that he wants to make his will.'

"When I reached his pillow, he said this:

"'Methought a few short moments I would spend
As my soul wished. Alas! I gasp for air.
At the rich board where all life's dainties blend
I sat me down, partook a moment there,
When, ah ! they bade me leave the scarcely tasted fare.'

"I repeated the meaning of these words to the Damascenes in Arabic. They marvelled at his having lived so long and yet grieving for worldly life.

"I said to him : 'How dost thou find thyself under present circumstances?'

"He replied : ` What shall I say ?

" 'Hast thou ne'er marked his agony
Out from whose jaw a tooth is wrenched?
Then think what must his feelings be
Whose life, dear life, is being quenched !'

" I said: 'Dismiss from thy mind the idea of death, and let not thine imagination conquer thy nature ; for the philosophers have said, " Though the constitution may be vigorous, we are not to rely upon it as gifted with perpetuity, and though a disease may be terrible, it furnishes no positive proof of a fatal termination." If thou wilt give us leave, we will send for a physician in order that he may use remedies for thy recovery.'

"He replied: 'Alas!

"The master's bent on garnishing
His house, which, sapped, is falling in.
The skilful leech in mute despair
Together smites his hands, as there
He marks, like broken potsherd, lie
The poor old man outstretched to die.
The old man groans in parting pain,
His wife the sandal* rubs in vain ;
But once unpoise our nature frail,
Nor cure nor amulet avail.' "

(*Translated by* EASTWICK.)

FROM THE "BOSTAN."

1. *The Drop of Water.*

" A solitary drop of water falling from a cloud blushed when it saw the huge extent of the sea, saying:

"Where the ocean exists, what place is there left for me to occupy, if that immense body of water be present, my God ? What an inconsiderable atom of matter am I ?'

" While it was after this manner reviewing itself with an eye of humility, an oyster took it into the bosom of its shell and nourished it with its whole soul; the revolution of fortune raised it to an exalted station, for it ripened into a precious pearl, and became the chief jewel of the imperial crown of Persia. It rose into dignified eminence, because its walk was humble, and knocked at the door of annihilation till it was ushered into an illustrious existence."

(*Translated by* GULCHIN.)

* Preparations of sandal-wood are used in the East as restoratives.

2. *The Fire-worshipper.*

" A fire-worshipper had abandoned all intercourse with the world, and girt up his loins in the service of an idol.

After some years destiny involved that votary of a reprobate faith in circumstances of difficulty;

And the helpless wretch, grovelling in the dust of the temple at the feet of his idol, thus piteously implored, in the hope of a blessing :

' I am in distress ; succour me, O idol ! I am in peril of death ; have mercy upon me !'

Repeatedly did he pour forth his soul in supplication, but his prayer was still unanswered.

How could an idol, which cannot even brush away the flies from itself, fulfil the desire of anyone ?

At length he was provoked, and said : ' O idol, that enthrallest in delusion, in vain have I worshipped thee for several years!

Fulfil the present object of my anxiety ; otherwise I will ask it of God.'

He thus spake, and, raising with sincere devotion the hand of supplication, exclaimed : ' O mighty Creator!'

While his face was even yet defiled with dust from the worship of that idol, the true God fulfilled his desire.

An enlightened sage was confounded at this, and the serenity of his soul was darkened with perplexity

That a vile and erring idolater, with his head still intoxicated from the flagon of the pagod,

With his heart still unpurged from infidelity and his hands from perfidy—

That even to such a one God had fulfilled the object of his desire !

While his thoughts were thus deeply absorbed in this mystery, a divine intimation reached the ear of his heart :

'That old man of deficient understanding fervently implored his idol, but his prayer was not accepted ;

Should he be repulsed at My Court also, what difference were there between an idol and the Eternal ?"'

(*Translated by* FALCONER.)

3. *The Humble Youth.*

"An intelligent and virtuously disposed youth arrived by sea at a port of Rum (Asia Minor).

Men discerned in him excellence, humbleness of spirit, and discretion, and assigned him an appointment within a sacred edifice.

One day the chief of the holy brotherhood said to the stripling: 'Clear away the rubbish and dust of the mosque.'

The moment that this traveller in the path of piety heard the order he went forth, and was seen no more there.

The brethren and the senior of the mosque ascribed the fakir's disappearance to his dislike for menial service.

Next day one of the ministering attendants met him in the way, and reproached him, saying :

You have acted unbefittingly, and have followed a pernicious counsel !

Knew you not, O self-conceited boy, that it is through service men attain to dignity ?'

The youth, bursting into tears, exclaimed with heartfelt emotion :

'O friend, nourisher of my soul and enlightener of my understanding,

I beheld within these precincts neither dust nor rubbish ; I was the only impure thing in that holy place ;

Therefore it was that I withdrew from it, for it was meet that the mosque should be clear from all defilement."'

(*Translated by* FALCONER.)

4. *The Spilt Pearls.*

" His courtiers of the Caliph crave,
'Oh, say how this may be,
That of thy slaves, this Ethiop slave
Is best beloved by thee ?
" 'For he is hideous as the night;
But when has ever chose
A nightingale for its delight
A hueless, scentless rose ?'
"The Caliph then— 'No features fair
Nor comely mien are his';
Love is the beauty he doth wear,
And Love his glory is.
" 'Once when a camel of my train
There fell in narrow street,
From broken casket rolled amain
Rich pearls before my feet.
"' I, winking to my slaves that I
Would freely give them these,
At once upon the spoil they fly,
The costly boon to seize.
" ' One only at my side remained—
Besides this Ethiop, none ;
He, moveless as the steed he reined,

Behind me sat alone.
" ' "What will thy gain, good fellow, be,
Thus lingering at my side ?"
"My King, that I shall faithfully
Have gurarded thee! he cried.
" ' True servent's title he may wear,
He only who has not;
For his Lord's gifts, how rich soe'er,
His Lord himself forgot!'
"So thou alone dost walk before
Thy God with perfect aim,
From Him desiring nothing more
Beside Himself to claim.
"For if thou not to Him aspire,
But to His gifts alone,
Not Love, but covetous desire,
Has brought thee to His throne."

(*Translated by* R.C. TRENCH)

5. *The Gem.*

"A venerable and discerning worthy records of the son of Abdul-aziz.

That he possessed a gem upon a finger-ring the worth of which it baffled the calculation of the jeweller to estimate.

You would have said that, at night, the world-enlightening substance was a pearl in brightness like the day.

There chanced to occur a year of famine so severe that the full moon of the face of mortals became the new.

When the Prince no longer beheld comfort and vigour among his subjects, he considered it inhumane to remain unconcerned himself. When one sees poison on the palates of his fellow-creatures, how can the sweetest draught pass his lips ?

He ordered the gem to be converted into money, taking compassion on the needy and the orphan.

In a single week he had expended the sum, bestowing on the poor, the wretched, and the indigent.

The censorious assailed him, and said that another such gem was not again to be procured.

I have heard that he replied, while tears trickled down his cheeks as from a wasting taper :

'Ornaments are unseemly on the Prince while the heart of a subject is pining with want. A ring without its gem I can bear with, but I cannot endure that the hearts of my fellow-men should be filled with dejection."

(*Translated by* FALCONER.)

10

HAFIZ

It isa curious coincidence that the two Persian poets who are best known outside their own country should have belonged to the same city, Hafiz, like Sa'di, being born at Shiraz. His name, Hafiz (" Remembrancer "), implies that he knew the Koran by heart. He also had the title Shams-*ud-din* (" Sun of Religion "). He was well versed in jurisprudence and theology, which he taught publicly in the college founded by Haji Kivam. The poet Jami, who lived in the fifteenth century, says that he neither knew the teacher of Hafiz nor the sect to which he belonged ; but he adds that his writings show that he was an adept in Sufism, and he gives him the titles of *Lisan-al-Ghaib* ("The Tongue of the Unseen ") and of *Tarjuman-al-Asrar* ("The Interpreter of Secrets").

Hafiz lived for the most part a life of ease and retirement in a quarter of Shiraz named Mosella. Muhammadan writers relate that in his old age, incapable of longer enjoyment of the pleasures of this world, he set himself to preparing for another by the practice of austerities and devotions. From that time he consecrated all his talents to celebrate the unity of God and the praises of the Prophet. There is nothing inherently improbable in this, as the same might be said of several other Persian poets.
But this tardy conversion did not gain for him the pardon of the more zealous Moslems. Shocked at the fact that he had publicly indulged in the use of wine and sung its praises, they persisted in regarding him as a Kafir (infidel). Nor did their hatred stop with his life ; they tried to deprive him of the honours of sepulture as a Mussulman. On the other hand, the admirers of *Hafiz*, fearing that the execution of this project might be followed by the works of their favourite poet being placed on the index of forbidden books or altogether destroyed, maintained his orthodoxy, and declared that a certain levity of conduct should not be too severely scrutinized. After a lively discussion it was decided to cast lots for the decision ; several couplets from the Diwan of Hafiz were transcribed on pieces of paper and cast into an urn. A child then putting in his hand at hazard, drew out one on which was written :

" Do not fear to approach the corpse of Hafiz, for though stained with sin, he will enter heaven." Accordingly the poet was interred with suitable honours.

Later on a magnificent tomb was erected over his remains, which Sir Gore Ouseley thus described in his " Biographical Notices of Persian Poets":

"When I saw it in 1811, on my way as Ambassador from King George III, to the Court of Persia, it was in excellent order. The Vakil had directed a slab of the finest alabaster to be placed over the tomb, with two odes from the Diwan beautifully sculptured on it in bas-relief of the finest Nastalik characters. He also built a neat pavilion or hall (in which a superb copy of the poet's works is open for perusal), with apartments adjoining for the Mullahs and Dervishes who attend the tomb ; and he beautified the little garden in which the poet's remains are interred in such a manner as to render it the most delightful retreat in the vicinity of Shiraz."

The following is one of the odes inscribed on the tomb :

"Announce the glad tidings that my soul may rise in thy enjoyment.
I am a bird of paradise, and will fly from the snares of world.
Were I but a servant at the table of thine elect,
I should rank above all the great men of the universe.
O Lord, let the cloud of guidance rain,
That I may arise, encircled with Thy glory.
Sit on my tomb with wine and music,
That I may arise out of it amid dancing lovers,
O image of sweet actions, arise and show on high
That I, as Hafiz, soar above the world and evil spirits !
O my heart ! submit to the Sovereign of the universe, and govern thy passions !
Show a sense of gratitude for divine protection.
Many who put on an outward show are not worth a single barleycorn ;
Let such hypocrites be banished to the mountains.
This day I am living with thy people, O Ali,
And to-morrow I may be summoned before the tribunal of the saints.
He who is not Ali's friend lives in infidelity.
Tell him to depart, and spend his days in solitude.
O Hafiz, prepare the way for the King's servant,
And guard it whilst man is on his passage.
Khwajah Hafiz, the lamp of the wise,
Seek the date in the soil of Mosella,*
If you wish to know it, when you approach my tomb,
Which will be the resort of pilgrims and travellers
From all parts of the world."

(*Translated by* **E. POCOCK.**)

* The letters of the words "earth of Mosella" in Persian, when combined, give the date A.D. 1338.

The habit of consulting the works of Hafiz on occasions of perplexity has continued in Persia since the death of the poet. One of the most celebrated coincidences to which this has given rise is the following:

After having conquered the province of Fars, Shah Thamasp, uncertain whether to return to Khorassan or to undertake the conquest of Azer-baijan, opened the Diwan of Hafiz at random. His eye fell on these lines, addressed by Hafiz to himself: "By the charm of thy verse, Hafiz, thou hast conquered Iraq and Fars. Go forward, and attack Bagdad and Tabriz (the capital of Azer beijan)." Shah Thamasp acted on the advice, and made an expedition which resulted in the conquest of that province.

Many anecdotes of doubtful authenticity are related of Hafiz, but they serve to show what the Persians think of their favourite poet. In his youth Hafiz loved a young girl who was also courted by Shah Shujah, son of the Prince of Shiraz. At the same time he had received a mysterious intimation that he would obtain the highest gifts of poetry if he watched forty nights without intermission in a place called Pir-i-Sabz (" The Green Old Man "). He had already passed thirty-nine sleepless nights, when, while he was walking during the day near the door of his mistress, she invited him in. He had never received a similar encouragement before, but when the shades of the fortieth night came on he tore himself away from her and went to keep his vigil.

That very night Khizr, the green-mantled prophet, came to reward his perseverance ; he presented Hafiz with a cup of nectar, whence the poet imbibed the exquisite sweetness which permeates his verse.

This allegorical story seems to allude to the nights which Hafiz consecrated to study, to the obstacles he had to surmount, and to the efforts he had to make to scale the Oriental Parnassus. He had a rival as a poet in the Prince of Shiraz, to whom he is reported to have said, after the latter had been disparaging his poetry : " It is evidently the mediocrity of my verses which causes them to spread all over the world, while yours, in spite of their incontestable superiority, never cross the frontiers of Shiraz." The Prince sought to revenge himself upon Hafiz by citing him before the Ulema (theologians) on account of an alleged heretical couplet in one of his poems. Hafiz was warned in time, and saved himself by inserting a couplet immediately before the one in question, which made it appear to be the speech of a Christian :

"How sweetly the song stole on my ear this morning from the Christian cup-bearer at the door of the tavern, accompanied by the drum and the flute, when he said :

" 'If this be the true faith which Hafiz professes, alas ! that to-day should be followed by to-morrow.' "

Though not in favour with his own Prince, Hafiz received many compliments and gifts from others. Sultan Ahmed, who at that time reigned at Bagdad, was extremely desirous of seeing Hafiz at his Court ; but, notwithstanding all his solicitations, the poet could never be prevailed upon to quit his own country in order to reside at Bagdad ; he preferred, he said, a morsel of dry bread at the place where he had been accustomed to dwell, and had no desire to visit a foreign country. He sent, however, to Bagdad a copy of complimentary verses to Sultan Ahmed, wherein he told the Sultan "that he might be justly designated the soul of the universe; that he was the most precious gift of divine bounty ; that the splendour of birth, the excellency of all the virtues, centred in him ; and that the power of the Khusrau's of Persia and the glory of Jenghis Khan had united to give birth to Ahmed of Bagdad."

The celebrated story of Hafiz and the Emperor Timur rests on the authority of Daulat Shah, the author of the " Tazkirat-us-Shuara," or History of Poets. When Timur had made himself master of the province of Fars, he sent for Hafiz, and when the poet arrived, Timur said to him :

"I have subjected with this sword the greater part of the earth ; I have depopulated a vast number of cities and provinces in order to increase the glory and wealth of Samarcand and Bokhara, the ordinary places of my residence and the seat of my empire; yet thou, an insignificant individual, hast pretended to give away both Samarcand and Bokhara, as the price of a little black mole setting off the features of a pretty face, for thou hast said in one of thy verses:

"' If that fair maiden of Shiraz would accept my love,
I would give for the dark mole which adorns her cheek Samarcand and Bokhara.' "

Hafiz bowed to the ground before Timur, and said to him:

"Alas! O Prince, it is this prodigality which is the cause of the misery in which you see me." This repartee delighted Timur so much that, instead of finding fault with him, he treated him with kindness.

Another Prince-patron of Hafiz was Sultan Mahmud Shah Bahmani in South India, who invited Hafiz to his Court, sending him a large sum of money for the journey. When Hafiz reached Lahore in the Panjab, he gave all the money he had remaining to one of his friends who had been robbed. Obliged in consequence to return homeward, he met at Ormuz two merchants, who offered to take him to South India for nothing. Hafiz accepted their offer, but the ship on which he embarked was driven back by a gale of wind ; he found that he had enough of the sea, and refused to start again, contenting himself with sending an ode to the Vizier of Mahmud Shah, which contained the following lines :

" The whole world is dearly bought by a single moment spent in sorrow.
Let us sell our Dervish garments for wine ; there is naught better than this.
The pomp of a Sultan's crown, under which is folded ceaseless fear for one's life ;
It may be a heart-stealing cap, but it is dearly bought by loss of the head.
The evils of the sea at first seemed easy to me in the hope of the pearl ;
But I erred, for one single wave is dearly bought by a hundred 'mans' of gold."

Hafiz seems to have been happily married, and he lamented his wife, who died young, in terms which dispose of the common Western idea that pure marital affection is unknown among Muhammadans:

"That beloved friend, by whose charms my house seemed the abode of an angel.
She was an angel herself all over, pure and free from every imperfection."

The poet himself died A. D. 1388.

The chief work of Hafiz is his Diwan, or collection of odes, which was edited after his death by the poet Kasim-al-Anwar. The chief characteristics of his poetry are purity of style, naturalness of expression, harmonious verse, and lyrical spontaneity. A great number of his couplets have passed into proverbs in Persia. As regards his praises of wine and love, it is impossible to say how much is to be taken in a literal and how much in a mystical sense, Sir William Jones says :

"It has been made a question whether the poems of Hafiz must be taken in a literal or a figurative sense ; but the question does not admit of a general and direct answer, for even the most enthusiastic of his commentators allow that some of them are to be taken literally, and his editors ought to have distinguished them, as our Spenser has distinguished his four odes on Love and Beauty, instead of mixing the profane with the divine by a childish arrangement, according to the alphabetical order of the rhymes."

The following versions of a few of the odes were made by the late Professor Cowell:

1.

"The lost Joseph shall return to Canaan ; do not despair.
One day the cell of affliction shall be a rose-garden ; do not despair.
O heart forlorn, thy condition shall mend ; act not the craven.
This bewildered head shall yet reach its goal ; do not despair.
If the spring returns once more on the throne of the garden,
O bird of the sweet song, thou shalt yet spread the rose's pavilion over thy head ; do not despair.
If the revolution of the heavens be for a little space not as we wish,
Their revolving shall not be for ever in one fixed course; do not despair.
Take heed and never despond ; thou knowest not the secrets of futurity.
There are hidden games behind the veil ; do not despair.
Our state of separation from the beloved, the rival pressing his suit—
God knoweth it all, God the bringer of change; do not despair.
If through desire to reach the Kaaba thou once set foot in the desert,
Should the thorns of the acacia wound thee, do not despair.
O Hafiz, in the cell of poverty and the seclusion of the dark night,
While prayer and the Koran are thy constant employ, do not despair."

2.

"Glad news has come that the days of grief will not last ;
Joy did not endure, so neither shall sorrow now.
What though in my loved one's eyes I am but the dust path,
Yet neither shall my rival remain in his place of honour.
Count as a gain, O taper, the coming of the moth,
For this thine interview will not last till morning.

An angel from the unseen world gave me the joyful tidings
That none shall remain for ever a constant prey to sorrow.
The eunuch who holds the veil smites all alike with his sword ;
None remaineth a fixed inhabitant in this harem's sacred enclosure.
What place is there for our thanks or complaints at fortune's pictures of good or ill ?
For on the pages of existence the writing will not last.
They say that this was the song at ancient Jamshid's banquet:
'Bring the cup of wine, for Jamshid will not last !'
O man of riches, bring thou thy poor heart in thy hand,
For treasure of gold and store of money will not last.
They have written in letters of gold on yonder sapphire canopy :
'Save the virtue of the munificent, nothing else will last:'
O Hafiz, despair not of thy mistress's love,
For the pictures of fortune's oppression and the signs of her tyranny will not last."

3.

"The red rose is in bloom and the nightingale is intoxicated;
'Tis the proclamation of gladness, O mystical worshippers of wine,
The foundations of our penitence whose solidity seemed as of stone.
See a cup of glass, how easily it has shattered them !
Bring the wine ; for in the audience-hall of the soul's independence
What is sentinel or Sultan ? what the wise man or the intoxicated ?
Since from this caravanserai with its two gates* departure is inevitable.
What matter whether the arch of life's lodging be high or low ?
Only by toil and pain can the post of joy be won—
Yea, they have annexed the condition of evil to the compact of 'Alast.'†
For existence or non-existence vex not thy soul ; be glad of heart,
For non-existence is the end of every perfection that is !
The pomp of Asaf ‡ and his steed of the wind and his flying circle of birds,
All have passed to the wind, and their lord derived no profit.
Rise not on the wing to quit the path, for the winged arrow
Takes the air for a little space, but it sinks to earth at last.
The tongue of thy pen, O Hafiz, what thanks shall it utter
That men carry the gift of thy words from hand to hand ?"

* Birth and death.

† The Sufis hold (*cf.* Chapter VII.) that at the creation God called the various created spirtis before Him and asked them each, "Art thou not My creature?" To which they all replied, "Bala" (Yes). This primeval compact is frequently alluded to in Persian mystical poetry.

‡ The Vizier of Solomon.

4.

" Hither, hither, O cup-bearer, hand round and give the cup,
For love at first showed easy, but difficulties have come *
At the odour of musk which the breeze will unfold from those tresses,
From the curls of those musky ringlets, what blood hath fallen in our hearts !
Stain thou with wine thy prayer-carpet if the old man of the tavern commands thee,
For the traveller is not ignorant of the ways and customs of the inn.
To me in the inn of my beloved, what peace or Joy when every moment
The bell proclaims the summons, 'Bind on your burdens, O travellers !'
Dark is the night ; there is fear of the wave and a dreadful whirl pool;
How should they know our state, the careless ones on the shore?
Wilfully ye distort my every deed to my reproach ;
How should that secret remain concealed, when they make it their common discourse ?
If thou desire her presence, O Hafiz, forsake her not ;
And when thou attainest thy desire, quit the world, and let it go."

5.

"At the hour of the wanderer's evening prayer, when I begin weeping,
I finish my story with a wanderer's lamentations ;
I weep so forlorn at the memory of my beloved and my country
That the custom of travelling I would fain abolish from the world.
I come from the country of the beloved, not the city of the stranger ;
O God the Protector, restore me safe to my friends.
The air of the dwelling-place of my beloved is the water of life to me ;
O breeze of the North, bring me one breath from the land of Shiraz.
Except the morning breeze, none else knoweth me here ;
Only the morning breeze is the friend of my bosom.
Why should Reason remind me that I am old ?
For love hath made me young again playing with my beloved.
I have heard the harp of the planet Venus, and it said in the early morning :
' I am the disciple of the sweet-voiced Hafiz."'

6.

"I proclaim it aloud, and am glad at the utterance ;
I am the slave of love and free from the two worlds !

* Jalaluddin Rumi has a line which maintains the opposite of this; and a story is related of two of their respective admirers who were discussing the inconsistency, when Jalaluddin's partisan clenched the dispute by the repartee : " The wise Sufi saw at a glance what poor Hafiz only found out by experience."

How shall I explain my absence, a bird of the heavenly rose-bush—
How I fell into this region of the snares of circumstance ?
I was an angel once, and the highest heaven my dwelling-place ;
Adam brought me hither to this ruined tavern.
The shadow of the heavenly tree, the charms of the houris and the bank of the Lake—
All have gone from my memory, at the breath of the breeze from thy street.
No astrologer knoweth the star of my fortune ;
O Heaven ! for what fate was I born of my mother the world ?"

7.

"What curse has fallen on the earth,
That each revolving moon gives birth
To crimes, to violence ? I see
No corner from this pest is free.
" Fraternal hearts no longer beat
In kindred concord pure and sweet ;
Daughters against their mothers wage
A ceaseless strife with fiendish rage,
And the son's breast is all on fire
With evil thoughts against his sire.
" The proud, majestic Arab steed,
His sides with galling panniers bleed ;
The stupid, stubborn ass has got
A golden bridle and what not.
" For brainless fools' and idiots' food
Ambrosia, nectar—nought's too good ;
The sage, the wit, must thankful live
On what his bleeding heart can give.
" The good look on with anxious eyes,
Expecting better days to rise ;
When, lo ! the mystery darkens still,
For worse alone succeeds to ill.
"Yet, though desponding doubts may brood,
Thus Hafiz counsels, 'Go, do good !'
This Heaven-taught lesson far outvies
The fleeting wealth the world supplies."

(*Translated by* FALCONER.)

We may conclude this brief account of Hafiz with some words in which a Western mystic has admirably summed up the characteristics of the Eastern poet:

"We do not wish to strew sugar on bottled spiders," says Emerson, "or try to make mystical divinity out of the Song of Solomon, much less out of the erotic and bacchanalian songs of Hafiz. Hafiz himself is determined to defy all such hypocritical interpretation, and tears off his turban and throws it at the head of the meddling Dervish, and throws his glass after the turban. But the love or the wine of Hafiz is not to be confounded with vulgar debauch. It is the spirit in which the song is written that imports, and not the topics. Hafiz praises wine, roses, maidens, boys, birds, mornings, and music, to give vent to his immense hilarity and sympathy with every form of beauty and joy ; and lays the emphasis on these to mark his scorn of sanctimony and base prudence. But it is the play of wit and the joy of song that he loves ; and if you mistake him for a low rioter, he turns short on you with verses which express the poverty of sensual joys. Sometimes it is a glance from the height of thought, as thus :

" 'Bring wine ; for in the audience-hall of the soul's independence
What is sentinel or Sultan ? what is the wise man or the intoxicated ?'

And sometimes his feast, feasters, and world are only one pebble more in the eternal vortex and revolutin of fate—

" 'I am: what I am
My dust will be again:'

In all poetry Pindar's rule holds *συν ∊ τois φων ∊ i* (it speaks to the intelligent) ; and Hafiz is a poet for poets, whether he writes, as sometimes, with a parrot's or, as at other times, with an eagle's quill."

To this we may subjoin a quatrain from Goethe's "West-œstlicher Diwan":

" Over the Mediterranean Sea
Bright the Orient sun has sprung ;
Only he who Hafiz knows and loves
Knows what Calderon has sung."

11

JAMI

JAMI, the last of the great Persian poets, was born at a village named Jam, in Khorassan, in A. D, 1414. His early years were devoted to the study of science and literature at Samarcand, in which he soon outstripped all his contemporaries. After a while, being eager to be initiated into the mysteries of Sufism, he betook himself to Herat, where he wished to become a pupil of Sheikh Saad-ud-din Kashgari, the head of the Nakhshbandi Dervishes. Some time, however, elapsed after his arrival at Herat before Jami ventured to present himself before the Sheikh. The latter was accustomed to sit with his friends in front of the great mosque of Herat before or after prayers, and had often noticed the youth passing to and fro. At last Jami summoned up courage to enrol himself among Saad-ud-din's pupils. The Sheikh quickly perceived his genius, and said to his friends : "I have caught a falcon in my net." One of Saad-ud-din's opponents, Maulana Shihab-ud-din, observing Jami's devotion to his instructor, remarked : ,"After five hundred years Khorassan has produced a genius among the students, and him, too, Saad-ud-din has seduced."

Jami profited so well by the lessons of his master that he was appointed to succeed him as spiritual director. His genius, eloquence, and the beauty of his poetical compositions, attracted many persons of high rank. The Vizier, Ali Sher, became his intimate friend, and Abu Said, the Sultan of Herat, called him to his Court and showed him much favour. Jami also corresponded with two successive Sultans of Turkey, Muhammad II. and Bajazet II. To the former he dedicated a political treatise entitled " Irshadiyat " (The Direction), and to the latter a collection of lives of Sufis entitled " Nafahat-ul-uns " (Breathings of Intimacy.) His affability of manner won the regard of the common people, a number of whom he used to teach under the portico of the great mosque of Herat. In his youth he had been addicted to sensual pleasure, but in mature life he gave himself to asceticism and meditation. In this latter period the works which he composed related exclusively to moral philosophy or mystical theology. One of these is the " Beharistan," or Garden of Spring, a work much resembling the " Gulistan " of Sadi, though it has not attained a tithe of the popularity of the latter. It consists of stories, with verses and sayings of celebrated Sufis interspersed. The following are a few specimens of this work :

For this chapter, *cf.* Rosenzweig, Preface to the Odes of jami.

1.

It is easier to uproot a mountain with a needle than to eradicate pride from the heart of man. Boast not of having no pride, for pride is more hidden at the bottom of the heart and more imperceptible to the eye than the steps of an ant on a black stone in a dark night."

2.

"Fudhail Ayaz (may the Lord be gracious to him !) said: ' I serve the Lord from pure love to Him, because I cannot bear not to serve Him.' Certain of his tribe asked him: 'Who is the foolish man?' He replied: 'He who serves the most high God from hope or fear.' "

" 'My life ! I cannot keep myself far from Thy door ;

I cannot be content with paradise and the houris ;

I lay my head at Thy door for love, not for the hope of gain,

And from that door I have not the patience to remove.

How should the burning of him whom love for Thee has slain be hid in the darkness of the dust,

Since this flame arises from his lighted heart ?

How can the lover remove his head from the collar of devoted attachment?

Like the ring-dove, that collar sits upon his neck.' "

3.

"Shibli (may the Lord make his tomb holy!) was seized with delirium, and they took him into a hospital. A number of people went there to see him, of whom he asked : 'Who are you?' They said: 'Thy friends.' Then he took up a large stone and ran upon them, and they all fled. But he said : 'Come back, you pretenders, for friends do not fly from friends, nor do they regard the stones of unkind treatment from them.'

" 'He is a true friend who is the more steadfast the more enmity he experiences from his friend;

A thousand stones of ill-treatment thrown upon his head by him

Serve but as foundation-stones to establish the building of his love.'

"They tell of him, too, that once he was sick, and the Caliph sent a Christian physician to cure him.

"The physician asked him as he entered :

" 'What does thy heart desire?'

"He replied: 'That thou shouldst become a Mussalman.'

"He said: 'If I do so, wilt thou recover?'

"He said: 'Yes.'

"So he offered Islam to the Christian, who made the confession of faith ; and Shibli rose from his bed of sickness, and no mark of it remained upon him. They both went together to the Caliph and told him the story.

"He said: 'I thought I had sent the physician to the patient ; but I find that I sent the patient to the physician.' "

4.

"Abu Bekr Wirak said, 'If you should ask Avarice, "Who is thy father?" it would say, "Distrust in the care of the providence of the Omnipotent "; and if you should ask, " What is thy occupation?" it would say, "The acquisition of meanness and vileness "; and if you should ask of its end, it would answer, " Calamity and disappointment and bondage.' "

"One day Alexander was sitting with his courtiers, and one of them said to him :

" 'The Lord (whose name be magnified!) has given to thee a great dominion ; take to thyself many wives, that thou mayest have many children and thy memory remain on the earth.'

"He answered : 'A man is remembered, not by his sons but by his just principles and good dispositions ; it is not good that he who has conquered the men of this world should be conquered by women.'

" 'Since a man is not certain of even so much as this,
Whether his son will be of the number of the wise or of the foolish,
Then is nobleness of disposition son enough for a wise man.
What need of weak women for hope of children ?"'

The subject of Alexander seems to have attracted Jami, for he wrote a work entitled " Khirad Namah Sikandari " (The Book of the Wisdom of Alexander). In it he represents Alexander on his accession to the throne as receiving a book of advice from each of several philosophers. He studies these books, and profits so much from their perusal that he becomes capable of composing one himself. On his death the same philosophers compose elegies on him, and Aristotle writes a letter to his mother, who sends a reply. The work terminates with the constantly recurring theme of the fragility of human fortunes.

Jami's " Salaman and Absal" is an elaborate allegory, which is probably better known to the English reader than any of his other works, owing to Fitzgerald's beautiful paraphrase. The plan of it is as follows:

Prince Salaman, enamoured of Absal, who had been his nurse, flies with her to an unknown island. Satiety and repentance bring him back to the King his father, who makes him promise to renounce his love. But the young man falls into melancholy, to escape from which he returns to his old habits, and again experiences remorse. At last, in order to escape the alternative of living in pleasure, but with a troubled conscience, or of sacrificing pleasure to obtain peace of mind, he casts himself into the fire, together with his mistress. She alone is consumed, but he receives no injury. Her death plunges him into deep sorrow, and in the hope of recovering her he becomes the disciple of a Sufi, who promises him as a reward that he will bring Absal back. By this artifice the Sufi gains the ear of Salaman, and contrives to substitute in his heart love of the divine in place of love of the earthly.

The allegory is not very difficult of interpretation. Salaman represents the soul which gives itself up with the body to illicit pleasures, Repentance brings it back to God, though it leaves Him again more than once ; but it is purified by penitence, and finally recognizes the True Beauty, which is only to be found in the Creator. At the close of the poem Jami himself thus interprets it:

"The Incomparable Creator, when this world
He did create, created first of all
The First Intelligence-First of a chain
Of Ten Intelligences, of which the last
Sole Agent is in this our universe,
Active Intelligence so called ; the One
Distributor of evil and of good,
Of joy and sorrow. Himself apart from matter
In essence and in energy—His treasure
Subject to no such talisman—He yet
Hath fashioned all that is ; material form
And spiritual sprung from Him-by Him
Directed all and in His bounty drowned.
Therefore is he that Firman-issuing Shah
To whom the world was subject. But because
What he distributes to the universe
Himself from a still higher Power receives,
The wise and all who comprehend aright
Will recognize that higher in the Sage
His the Prime Spirit, that, spontaneously
Projected by the "Tenth Intelligence,
Was from no womb of matter, reproduced
A special essence called the Soul—a child
Fresh sprung from heaven in raiment undefiled
Of sensual taint, and therefore called Salaman.
And who Absal ? The lust-adoring body,
Slave to the blood and sense, through whom the soul,
Although the body's very life it be,
Does yet imbibe the knowledge and desire
Of things of sense ; and these, united thus
By such a tie, God only can unloose ;
Body and soul are lovers each of other.

What is the sea on which they sailed ? The sea
Of animal desire-the sensual abyss
Under whose waters lies a world of being
Swept far from God in that submersion.
And wherefore was it Absal in that isle
Deceived in her delight, and that Salaman
Fell short of his desire ? That was to show
How passion tires, and how with time begins
The folding of the carpet of desire.
And what the turning of Salaman's heart
Back to the Shah, and looking to the throne
Of pomp and glory ? What but the return
Of the lost soul to its true parentage,
And back from carnal error looking up
Repentant to its intellectual throne ?
What is the Fire ? Ascetic discipline,
That burns away the animal alloy
Till all the dross of matter be consumed,
And the essential soul, its raiment clean
Of mortal taint, be left. But forasmuch
As any lifelong habit so consumed
May well recur a pang for what is lost,
Therefore the Sage set in Salaman's eyes
A soothing phantom of the past, but still
Told of a better Venus, till his soul
She filled and blotted out his mortal love.
For what is Zuhrah ?* That divine perfection
Wherewith the soul, inspired and all arrayed
In intellectual light, is royal blest,
And mounts the throne, and wears the crown, and reigns Lord of the empire of humanity."

(*Translated by* **Fitzgerald.**)

In his "Yusuf and Zuleikha" (Joseph and Potiphar's Wife) Jami has handled a theme which has always been a favourite one with Persian poets. The Koran calls the history of Joseph "the most beautiful of stories," which may be one reason for its popularity in the East. The plot of Jami's poem is as follows: Zuleikha, daughter of

* The Persian name of the planet Venus.

Taimaous, King of Africa, sees in a dream the vision of an unknown youth whose beauty inspires her with an ardent passion ; he informs her that he returns her love, and that he is Vizier in Egypt. After this, when Potiphar, Pharaoh's chief officer, makes a proposal for her, Zuleikha, who, like Eastern brides, does not see her husband till the wedding, hopes that he is the object of her dream, but only to be disappointed. Joseph is then sold into Egypt, and purchased by Potiphar. Zuleikha tempts him in vain, and Joseph after his imprisonment becomes Grand Vizier. Potiphar is deposed from his position, and dies in disgrace ; Zuleikha, reduced to poverty, becomes blind by weeping, and having lost her beauty, breaks her idols, and is converted to Islam. Joseph finds her, and, moved with compassion, prays God that she may recover her sight and her beauty. The prayer is granted, and Joseph marries her by the order of the angel Gabriel. After forty years of uninterrupted happiness, Joseph dies, and Zuleikha, over-whelmed with grief, does not long survive his loss.

The following extracts from the poem were translated by Sir W. Jones:

1

"Come, O Love, with all your fascinations and deceitful charms,
You who are the promoter of concord and of strife ;
At one time you make the wise man silly,
And at another time you inspire wisdom into the fool.
When you place your snare in the ringlets of beautiful damsels,
The wisest man falls into the fetters of insanity ;
But if you should loose this snare from the fair one's ringlets,
The lamp of reason will resume its light.
Zuleikha, one night, impatient and distracted, the twin-sister of affliction, and to whom sorrow was as a familiar friend,
Drank to the very dregs of the cup of wretchedness,
And from the burning anguish of passion passed the night without repose."

2

"In the morning, when the raven of night had flown away,
The bird of dawn began to sing;
The nightingales warbled their enchanting notes,
And rent the thin veils of the rosebud and the rose;
The jasmin stood bathed in dew,
And the violet also sprinkled his fragrant locks.
At this time Zuleikha was sunk in pleasing slumber;
Her heat was turned towards the altar of her sacred vision.
It was not sleep : it was rather a confused idea :
It was a kind of frenzy caused by her nightly melancholy.

Her damsels touched her feet with their faces,

Her maidens approached and kissed her hand.

Then she removed the veil from her cheek, like a tulip besprinkled with dew ;
She opened her eyes, yet dim with sleep ;

From the border of her mantle the sun and moon arose ;

She raised her head from the couch and looked round on every side."

Jami's other works are too numerous to be mentioned in detail. Rosenzweig, the German translator of "Yusuf and Zuleikha," gives a list of forty-four. Chief among them are, the "Majnun and Leila," a theme, as we have seen already treated by Nizami (to whom Jami pays an eloquent tribute), and his Diwans, or collections of odes. His " Nafahat-ul-uns " is a collection of lives of the Sufi saints, and his " Tuhfat-ul-ahrar " and " Lawaiih " (Flashes) are also treatises on Sufism. The latter has been recently translated by Mr. Whinfield for the Oriental Translation Fund. Many anecdotes are related of Jami's ready wit, of which the following are specimens :

" You " (*i.e.*, the Deity), says Jami in one of his verses, " so occupy my whole thoughts and vision that whatsoever comes into view from afar appears to me to be You." "What," said a sharp questioner, " if a jackass were to come into view ?" " It would appear to me to be *you*," was Jami's ready reply.

On another occasion a poetaster was boasting to Jami that he had composed a poem from which he had managed to omit entirely the letter Alif (a). " It is a pity you did not omit all the other letters," Jami crushingly retorted. Mr. W. Nassau Lees has preserved the following account of the poet as the defendant in a trial for heresy, which throws a curious light on the method of conducting theological controversy at that period.

One of Jami's countrymen who had accompanied him to Bagdad during a pilgrimage to Mecca, having a grudge against the poet, took one of his works, the "Silsila-ud-Dhahab" (Chain of Gold), and, mutilating a passage, showed it to some of the Shiahs who abounded in Bagdad. As it seemed to cast a reflection upon Ali, the idol of the Shiahs, large numbers of fanatics of that sect assembled and began abusing Jami and his companions. The latter retorted vigorously, and the matter proceeded so far that a public meeting was called in the great Madrasa, or school, of the city. At this Jami attended. Seated on either side of him were the Qazis of the Hanifa and Shafi sects, and in front the Governor and his suite. A great crowd assembled, and when all were seated, the "Silsila-ud-Dhahab" was produced and opened. But when the garbled extract was compared with the original, the fraud became clear, and it was proved not only that Jami had not spoken disparagingly of Ali, but had actually praised him to the skies.

" I assure you," he said jokingly, "that if I had any fears at all in writing this book, they were that the people of Khorassan might accuse me of having Shiah tendencies, but it certainly never entered into my mind to suppose that on account of it I should fall into trouble at the hands of the Shiahs."

On the matter being seen in its true light, a reaction immediately took place in Jami's favour. With one accord the Shiahs exclaimed that Ali and his descendants had never been more suitably praised, and the Qazis on the spot fixed their signatures to the autograph copy of the work, in token of their approval of it.

It was now Jami's turn, and, seeing his opportunity, he called upon his traducer, one Niamat-i-Haidari, to state whether the objections he had against him were on points of theology or philosophy.

"On both," he replied.

"First, then," said Jami, "fulfil yourself the requirements of the law and clip your moustachios, which, since their first growth, do not seem to have been touched by a razor."

The words were hardly uttered when a party of Jami's admirers from Shirwan sprang to their feet, and, seizing hold of Niamat-i-Haidari, placed the hair of his upper lip on a staff, and ere a pair of scissors could be brought, cut half of it off.:

"Now," said Jami "since you have been proved an offender against the law, it is no longer lawful for you to assume the garb of the pious. It will be necessary for you to recommend yourself to some holy man, who may yet put you in the right way."

Niamat-i-Haidari's brother, who had made himself conspicuous in this affair, was then brought forward, and having been severely censured by the assembly, a fool's cap was placed on his head, and, mounted on a donkey, with his face towards the animal's tail, he was led through the streets and bazaars of Bagdad, amid the jeers and scoffs of the townspeople.

Jami then proceeded on his pilgrimage to Mecca. On his return he was received with great honour in the towns he passed through, especially Damascus and Aleppo. Sultan Muhammad II, sent messengers with a present of five thousand pieces of gold to Damascus to invite Jami to come to Constantinople. The poet, however, who loved retirement, hurried home by way of Tabriz, to avoid them. He occupied the rest of his life in poetic composition, meditation, and the instruction of his disciples. One of them was his own nephew, Hatifi, who was ambitious to excel as a poet. Jami at first endeavoured to dissuade, but finding the young man persistent, he gave him, as a test of his poetic powers, the task of imitating Firdausi's satire on Mahmud of Ghazni, part of which we quoted in Chapter III. The young man accepted the test, and composed the following verses:

"Were you to set the egg of a raven, whose nature is gloomy as chaos, under the peahen of the garden of Eden, and during the time she sat on that egg, were you to feed' her with the pulp of the fig of paradise, and give her drink from the celestial fountain-nay, were the angel Gabriel to inspire her with the spirit of life, still that egg of a raven could but produce a raven, and that labour of the peahen would come to a fruitless conclusion."

This parody met with Jami's approval. Accordingly Hatifi devoted himself to poetry, taking Nizami as his model. Later on he was patronized by Shah Ismail Safavi, the first monarch of the Safavi dynasty.

Jami himself died in 1492, at the great age of eighty-one, and was mourned by 'the whole city of Herat. The Sultan of Herat, as a token of respect to the poet, paid his funeral expenses, a great crowd of nobles accompanying his body to the tomb.

As a specimen of his lyrical poetry we may quote the two following odes from his Diwan, translated by Professor Cowell :

Jami

1

"Long ere that day when heaven first kneaded the dust of man
In my water and clay* love sowed the seed of thy desire.
All beauty art thou from head to foot; one would say the eternal Artist
Had moulded thy form, not of water and clay, but of pure soul and heart.
Oh, reveal thy face, that toward the arch of thy brow may turn their eyes
The worshippers from the mosque, the devotees from the idol temple.
No belief we win from thee, howsoever our eyes, with tears of blood,
Write on the door and wall of thy street the story of our love.
If thou wert not my murderer, O would that after my death
They might make bricks of my dust to build the tombs of thy victims.
Rise thou and shed my blood, spread the crimson mat beneath my feet,
For fate has at length resolved to fold up the carpet of my life.
On the future reversion of paradise have others fixed their hearts,
But Jami's paradise is at once paid to the full, wherever thou art seen."

2.

" Yon teacher—what aileth him, that, creeping into his cell,
He renounces fellowship with the world to bind it but closer with himself?
Each thread of sympathy which he severs from other men
He only winds tight round himself, as the silkworm its cocoon.
He himself is the world, and he asks to be free from the world.
How shall *he* be free from the world, who is not yet free from himself?
Let him talk as he will of the Ka'ba, and the pilgrims who toil to its gate,
His ear hath ne'er heard the sound of that caravan's camel-bell.
He has left the pursuit of knowledge, and is frantic after tinsel ;
He has squandered his pearls of price, and has bought only children's beads.
O Jami, ask not from him the qualities of the wine of love;
Never hath he seen that cup, and never tasted that wine."

---

* *I.e.*, the body.

12

FOLK-SONGS AND DRAMA

For our scanty knowledge of the popular poetry of Persia, we are indebted to M. Alexander Chodzko, who collected specimens of the unwritten poetry of the inhabitants of Northern Persia and the coasts of the Caspian, during a sojourn of eleven years in those countries, from oral communications with the lower classes, who could neither read nor write.

The principal piece in the collection consists of the adventures and improvisations of Kurroglu, the " Bandit Minstrel " of Northern Persia, which are current in the Perso-Turkish dialect. This personage was an heroic freebooter, who subsisted and rendered himself famous by plundering the caravans on the great commercial road from Persia to Turkey, between the city of Khoi and Erzerum. His poetry and the memory of his heroic feats are carefully preserved by the wandering tribes of Ilyats, who repeat his love-songs at their festivals and his war-odes in their frays."If the average popularity of poets can be calculated by the number of voices repeating their poetry," observes M. Chodzko, " even Firdausi himself must yield precedence to Kurroglu."

The poetical improvisations of Kurroglu, it appears, are connected together by a narrative which is recited by professional tale-tellers, named "Ausheks," from memory. They sing the poetical passages to the accompaniment of a three-stringed guitar, the favourite instrument of Kurroglu. The adventures are, for the convenience of hearers as well as relaters, divided into " Majlis's," or meetings, of only one of which-namely, "The Expedition of Kurroglu into Syria "—was M. Chodzko unable to obtain a correct report.

The "Bandit Minstrel" was a Turkoman of the Tuka tribe, whose real name was Rushan. His father was master of the horse to the ruler of one of the provinces of Turkestan, who put out his eyes, an act of cruelty which was amply revenged by his son. The old man, being an astrologer, prophesied the future greatness of his son, who on his father's death assumed the name of Kurroglu, or " Son of the Blind," and set forth in quest of adventures.

For this chapter *cf.*, *The Asiatic Journal,* vol. xxxix., and Matthew Arnold, "The Persian Passion Play" ("Essays in Criticism").

His first was a contest with a terrible robber named Hassan, who attacked him with his whole band. Kurroglu, who was alone, killed twenty; the rest fled, leaving Hassan to his mercy; he was easily vanquished, and became one of the bandit's most faithful adherents. Soon after he erected a fortress in the Valley of Salmas (province of Azerbeijan), the ruins of which still remain, whither all who heard of his liberality and valour hastened to join his band. From this stronghold the-robber and his gang, always consisting of the mystical number of seven hundred and seventy-seven, carried on their forays ; thither they conveyed their plunder, till the exhausted state of their cellar and pantry drove them out to new predatory expeditions, or the proximity of some rich caravan tempted their cupidity. Some of the excursions of Kurroglu were of an amorous character, in order to carry off the daughter of some Pasha or potentate, whose affections he had won by the renown of his valour. Like a true knight-errant, he was ready to exert his prowess on behalf of those who had hard-hearted mistresses, or whose mistresses had cruel fathers. One of his most perilous enterprises was at Constantinople itself, where he succeeded in bringing away the daughter of a Pasha to oblige a friend. In obedience to an injunction of his father, Kurroglu never took up arms against the Shah of Persia.

Most of these exploits are performed with a wonderful degree of facility. Armies are routed almost by the hero's single arm or by the supernatural qualities of his horse, who, when necessary, acts the warrior, besides scaling precipices and leaping over yawning gulfs. Chiefs were terrified by the gigantic proportions of Kurroglu, by his formidable moustaches, that reached above his ears, and by the terrible voice in which he shouted forth his improvisations and threats. If a leader was hardy enough to try a personal conflict with him, the latter, after singing to him for some time, would with his Egyptian scimitar cleave his enemy in twain, the weapon burying itself in the earth. The following is a specimen of Kurroglu's mode of proceeding and of his poetical effusions. He had sent his adopted son Ayaz to carry off some game from the Pasha of Tokat, to make *kababs* (roast meat), merely in order to gratify the whim of a guest. The Pasha, however, captured Ayaz and his brother-brigands :

"Listen now to the news of Kurroglu. Four days elapsed before he became sober and returned to his senses after his excessive drinking. All the banditti and servants had hidden themselves in the darkest holes and corners, being afraid lest Kurroglu should punish them, because they had allowed Ayaz to go to Tokat in search of such trifles as the game of the Pasha. Hassan alone went to him; and having made a low obeisance, remained standing without saying one word. Kurroglu told him to call Ayaz to him.

"'I have a headache; I wish he would give me a few glasses of wine; that would refresh me.'

" 'My lord, art thou only laughing at me or dost thou speak in earnest ?'

"'What means this question, thou insolent cur?'

" 'Oh, my benefactor, this is the fourth day since thou hast despatched him to Tokat to fetch some birds from the Pasha's park, to cook a *kabab* for thee.'

"Is it possible?'

"Hassan swore by his master's head that it was true, and added that such and such men went with them on that journey.

" 'Woe to me !' exclaimed Kurroglu. 'I am confident something bad will befall my son.' He then seized the guitar and sang as follows:

" ' I have sent him to fetch some game, but he stays away and does not come back. O my God, in case of need, whom wilt Thou send to his assistance ? He stays away, and does not come back. I heard the firing of guns and muskets ; defeat follows after defeat. My poor boy must have fallen into a stranger's hands, for he stays away, and does not come back.'

" Kurroglu, while singing the above song, was foaming from his mouth like a male camel. He then roared to Hassan :

"'Let Kyrat be saddled.' He sang again:

" 'I have sent Ayaz to Syria. O may my heart be overflowed with a rain of blood. He promised to return the same night. He stays away, and does not come back.'

"He ordered his armour to be brought him, and during the interval sang as follows:

" 'The roses are budding in the garden. The enamoured nightingales have commenced their songs. Thou alone, Kurroglu, must throw ashes upon thy head. Thy son, thy brother, stays away, and does not come back.'

"He put on his armour, took his weapons, mounted upon Kyrat, and rode to the mountains upon which his outposts were stationed. He examined the country all round, but the roads were empty ; there was but one horseman to be seen in the direction of Tokat, galloping towards Chamli (Kurroglu's stronghold) like a shooting star. Kurroglu thought, 'No doubt this is a courier with some news.' He then descended into the valley and advanced towards the horseman, who recognized him, and was sorely frightened, for he was not ignorant of Kurroglu's habit or putting to death all those who happened to bring him any bad news. He therefore advanced a few hundred paces, tied the letter in a handkerchief, and then, throwing it towards Kurroglu, ran away as quickly as he could.

"As soon as Kurroglu had read Ayaz's letter, the world grew confused and dim before his eyes. Taking one of his feet out of the stirrup, he threw it over the knob on the fore-part of his saddle, and taking his guitar, tuned it, and began to sing. His voice was so powerful that the warriors in Chamli could hear every one of his words. Each of Kurroglu's men, as soon as he heard his summons, hastened to arm himself, and, mounting his horse, ran to join his lord. He sang on:

"' My armour and my coat are both adamantine. I can chew steel between my teeth, and then spit it toward heaven. I shall be your advanced guard myself ; I shall go before to scour the country.'

" All his men requested to be led to Tokat without delay, being anxious to avenge before his very eyes the fate of their comrades. Having ended his song, Kurroglu proceeded to Tokat with all his force."

This expedition was, like every other, successful, and the Pasha and most of his subjects glutted the rage of Kurroglu's men, who found "the battle their banquet." The narrative is a tissue of extraordinary feats bordering upon the supernatural, though, contrary to the general run of Eastern romances, there is an entire absence of positively supernatural machinery. At length Korruglu, when he grew old, allowed himself to be taken prisoner by two Persian traitors, who cut off his head, flayed the skull, and, stuffing it with straw, carried it to Ispahan, hoping for a reward. But the Shah, Abbas II. (A.D. 1641-1666), gave the miscreants up to the banditti at Chamli, who cut them in pieces.

The qualities of this model hero of the nomad Persians are great physical strength; a vast capacity for eating and drinking, in which he far excels the heroes of Homer; violent passions, which he never sought to restrain ; rapacity, prodigality, boasting, lying, gallantry, and a devoted attachment to his horse.

Besides the folk-songs relating to Kurroglu, M. Chodzko collected Tartar, Calmuc, and Turcoman songs. The following is a Tartar song in praise of a strong character:

"Let the waves beat as much as they can against a vessel strongly covered with boards, what can they do ? When a fat wild-boar is hit by an arrow, let him gnash his teeth, what can he do ?

When a brown wide-breasted wolf gets an arrow into his heart, let him foam from the mouth, what can he do ? If a man earns a good name, let his enemies plot against him, what can they do ?"

A Turcoman lover expresses his emotion thus:

"Let the whole world rise against me, I shall not part with you, my girl ! Let the doomsday come upon the earth, my girl, I will not part with you ! From the snowy tops of a mountain the Prophet may send his orders with thunder : Ferhad may part with Shirin, I shall not part with you, my girl ! Sugar pours from your lips ; let the nightingale part with his beloved rose, but oh, my girl, I shall not part with you! "I get up early from my bed ; I implore the aid of the Saints. Karajoglan [the speaker] says, 'God grant that my vows may be fulfilled.' Faith, I swear, my girl, that I will never part with you."

THE PERSIAN DRAMA.

It is a singular fact that long after Persian lyrical poetry had decayed, and the so-called poetry had degenerated into artificial and stilted compositions by Court versifiers, the Persian drama rose. It had its origin in the legends yearly recited during the Feast of Muharram regarding the martyred family of Ali, the national hero of Persia. The chief figure in these plays is Hussein, the younger of the sons of Ali and Fatima, the daughter of Muhammad, and the chief event which they celebrate is his death at the battle of Kerbela. His elder brother, Hassan, had renounced his rights to the Caliphate in favour of Mu'awia, the first. Ommiad Caliph. Hussein refused to take the oath of allegiance to Yezid, the son of Mu'awia, when he was declared heir by his father, and in A.D. 680 he headed an insurrection at the instigation of the inhabitants of Kufa, who promised to recognize him as Caliph and to supply him with an army of thirty thousand men. Hussein left Mecca, where he had taken refuge, and departed, at the head of a small company of sixty-two, to join his partisans. When he had arrived at Kerbela, near the banks of the Euphrates, he was surrounded by an army of four thousand men, commanded by Omar Ben Saad, and confronted with the choice of captivity or death. On his refusal to surrender, "the surrounding multitudes galled them from a distance with a cloud of arrows, and the battle at length expired by the death of the last of the companions of Hussein. Alone, weary and wounded, the son of Ali seated himself at the door of his tent. As he tasted a drop of water he was pierced in the mouth with a dart, and his son and nephew, two beautiful youths, were killed in his arms. He lifted his, hands to heaven-they were full of blood-and he uttered a funeral prayer for the living and the dead. In a transport of despair his sister issued from the tent, and adjured the General of the Kufians that he would not suffer Hussein to be murdered before his eyes; a tear trickled down his venerable beard, and the boldest of his soldiers fell back on every side as the dying hero threw himself among them. The remorseless Shimr, a name detested by the faithful, reproached their cowardice, and the grandson of Muhammad was slain with three-and-thirty strokes of lances and swords. After they had trampled on his body, they carried his head to the Castle of Kufa, and the inhuman Obeidullah, the Governor, struck it on the mouth with a cane. "Alas!" exclaimed an aged Mussalman, "on these lips have I seen the lips of the Apostle of God."

This is the event which, dramatized year by year, rouses the Shiites of Persia to a frenzy of grief and indignation. In witnessing it they recall the wrongs which Persia has suffered at the hands of the Arab Sunnis, and it fares ill with any Sunni who may chance to fall in their way. Even the actors who play the parts of the murderers of Hussein are in considerable danger, being sometimes pelted with stones, so that imprisoned criminals are sometimes brought out and obliged to take these parts. In brief, it may be described as an Oriental Ober-Ammergau. An eyewitness has thus depicted the scene at one of these performances, which are sometimes prolonged for ten days :

"As we push our way onward, at some risk of a mischief from the bands of savage fellows who parade the streets, bareheaded, stained with their own blood, brandishing clubs, and shouting, 'O Hussein ! O king of martyrs !' we come to the great open court of a palace, whence issue dolorous cries. We enter a square enclosure tented over, and see a plain raised platform, whereon a few men and children stand gesticulating and reciting. Around are all the people of the place, crowded together in dense lines from wall to platform, from the nobles in the shut-off boxes at the wall to the street urchins crushed against the platform. Women are there, apart, seated each on a little bench. The men are all squatted cross-legged on the ground. A vast amphitheatre of faces, all bent eagerly on the group in the centre, and all showing the marks of grief and intense sympathy with what is going on. Every now and then someone in the crowd lifts up his voice and groans aloud ; then the rest take up the sound, and the whole place rings with cries of 'Ya Hassan ! Ya Hussein ! Ey Hussein Shah!' till the groanings and the shouts fall away into silence as suddenly as they arose. At last there comes a pause; the group in the midst have relaxed their efforts, the people's paroxysms of grief are hushed; young men go round with water-skins to moisten the dried throats ; and we can turn and ask what this strange thing may mean."

The following are specimens of the dialogues in these plays:

IBN SAD [the General conducting the captives across the plain of Kerbela after the death of Hussein]. Comrades, our halting-place to-day is still far, and the heat of the sun is insupportable. It will be better to dismount here to drink fresh water and to rest. Pitch your tents ; we will bivouac here for the night.

SHIMR [the second in command, and murderer of Hussein]. We obey, O Emir. Halt, soldiers ! Pitch your tents and rest. But let the prisoners remain without a shelter, exposed to the sun.

ZAIN-AL-ABIDIN [Hussein's son, still a child, speaking to his Aunt Zeinab, Hussein's sister]. Alas, aunt, I can go no farther ! Burning fever consumes me. Can't you help me, dear aunt?

ZEINAB. What can I do, dear child? Trust in God, and pray. He will relieve you.

SAKINA [daughter of Hussein, still a child]. Aunt, I am choked with heat and thirst; can't we get a drop of water in this desert?

ZEINAB. Come, rest on my bosom, my child. Dry thy tears ; I cannot bear to see them. Alas! tears are all the water I can offer thee.

SAKINA. What would I not give for a drop of water ! O Aunt, when my father was on his way to martyrdom, with how many tears and prayers he confided me to thy care! Dear father! he is gone, and I have only thee ; I pray thee give me something to drink.

ZEINAB. Unhappy child! I cannot see thee suffer thus. For thee I will do what I would do for no one else. I will humiliate myself; I will go to Ibn Sad. God will not desert us ; He will give us water and shade. (*She enters the tent of Ibn Sad.*) Hear me, Ibn Sad! Respect for at least a moment the sacred rights of the family of Muhammad. We are his descendants. Thou art not an Arab. Where is thine honour, thy loyalty? But now be an Arab, and show us a little kindness.

IBN SAD (ironically). What dost thou want, then, noble Zeinab ? What procures me the honour of a visit from a Princess ? What service can I render thee ? What dost thou need ?

ZEINAB. I need pity. We are thirsty, without shade, without water, exposed to the heat of the sun. See these poor children in rags ; they have fever and are dying.

IBN SAD. Sister of the rebellious Imam, know that thou wilt never receive anything but ignominy and enmity from me. Burn in the sun, howl and weep thy fill !

ZEINAB. Cursed miscreant! I ask thee nothing for myself, but have some compassion on these poor orphans.

IBN SAD. A truce to talk! Go out of my tent! Go and sit in the sun! There is thy place!

Zeinab departs heart-broken. A courier arrives. He informs the General that there are partisans of Hussein in the neighbourhood, and that they intend to make a sudden night-attack upon the camp, and to liberate the prisoners. The General summons Shimr and asks his advice. " Don't be anxious, General," he answers ; " on the other side of this mountain there is a fortified Christian convent ; we will pass the night there."

They arrive at the convent, and are admitted. The heads of the slain rebels are committed to the custody of the Prior of the convent.

THE PRIOR (*taking Hussein's head* off *the spear*). Great God ! This beautiful head looks like a freshly-opened tulip ! To whom did it belong ?

THE HEAD OF HUSSEIN speaks the following verse in Arabic from the Koran: " Believe not that God overlooks the injustice of the wicked."

THE PRIOR. Ah, my God! What did I hear ? Whence comes this voice, whose vibrant tones penetrate heaven and earth ? Am I dreaming ? No, I am awake.

THE HEAD OF HUSSEIN. Those who do evil shall one day know what lot is reserved for them.

THE PRIOR. Brothers, run! Come! Tell me, have you heard this voice ? This plaintive melody, whence comes it ? Is it from heaven ?

A MONK. No, venerable Prior; it comes from the mouth of this decapitated head. Its lips move; they explain to us the hidden mysteries of the Gospel—but no ! they are the verses of the Koran.

THE PRIOR. For the love of God, answer me, O head! To whom didst thou belong ? O Faded Rose, from whose garden hast thou been plucked ? The light of salvation beams from thee. Art thou a miracle of Moses or of Jesus ?

THE HEAD. I am the martyr of Kerbela. My name is Hussein. The best of women gave me birth. My father is All ; my grandfather Muhammad ; my native place is Medina ; my burial-place the sands of Kerbela. On this there come on the stage prophets and prophetesses, saints and sainted women, among them Fatima and the Virgin Mary. Each has a word of homage and pity for the martyr, and - many of them also curse his assassins. The effect on the Prior is tremendous. " Hear my humble prayer," he cries, " O martyr fallen under the assassin's steel ! I lay aside the stole of the Christian priest ; I am converted to thy religion." At the Head's dictation he repeats the Moslem formula: " There is no God but God, and Muhammad is the Apostle of God, and Ali is the Friend of God."

A cold-blooded Western critic might stigmatize such scenes as "wallowing naked in the pathetic." Matthew Arnold, who was a poet as well as a critic, has well pointed out the real significance of this apotheosis of passive suffering in the heart of stern and militant Islam:

"Could we ask for a stronger testimony to Christianity ? Could we wish for any sign more convincing that Jesus Christ was indeed what Christians call him, the Desire of all nations' ? So salutary, so necessary is what Christianity contains that a religion-a great, powerful, successful religion-arises without it, and the missing virtue forces its way in. Christianity may say to these Persian Muhammadans, with their gaze fondly turned towards the martyred Imams, what in our Bible God says by Isaiah to Cyrus, their great ancestor: ' I girded thee, though thou hast not known Me.' It is a long way from Kerbela to Calvary ; but the sufferers of Kerbela hold aloft to the eyes of millions of our race the lesson so loved by the Sufferer of Calvary."*

* Matthew Arnold, " Essays in Criticism," vol. i., p. 26.

13

PROSE ROMANCES

PERSIAN prose romances generally take the form of legends woven round some famous hero, such as Hatim Tai or Bahram Gur, or they consist of fables and apologues, a form often adopted in the East in order to give advice to despots whom it is dangerous to admonish directly.

The romance of Hatim Tai, an Arab chieftain famed for his generosity, has been translated by Mr. Duncan Forbes, and its main outlines are as follows: A beautiful damsel of unlimited wealth was wooed by a Prince Munir of Syria. At the instigation of her nurse she proposed seven enigmas which he had to solve before he could hope to win her hand. He was to find examples of the following four sayings :

1. What I saw once I long for a second time.
2. Do good, and cast it upon the waters.
3. Do no evil; if you do, such shall you meet with.
4. He who speaks the truth is always tranquil.
5. To bring an account of the mountain of Nida.
6. To produce a pearl of the size of a duck's egg.
7. To bring an account of the bath of Bad-gard.

Prince Munir set about the task proposed to the best of his ability, but having no clue whatever to guide him, he wandered in vain over mountains and deserts, until his good fortune conducted him to the borders of Yemen, where he sat down under a tree and gave vent to his tears. Hatim Tai, happening to pass that way on a hunting excursion, beheld the young Prince, and having learned from him the cause of his grief, resolved generously to undertake the labours which had been assigned to the lover. Trusting to Providence, he forthwith set out for the wilderness to find the man who constantly exclaimed, " What I saw once I long for a second time."

Before he proceeded far upon his journey, he espied a wolf pursuing a milch doe, and his heart being touched with kindness towards the young to whom the milk belonged, he entreated the wolf to desist from the chase, and to accept a slice from his own thigh instead. The wolf agreed, and having finished his repast, informed Hatim that the man of whom he was in search dwelt in the desert of Hawaida, and pointed out the way which he was to go.

Hatim soon afterwards found himself in the kingdom of the bears, by whom he was received with the greatest politeness and hospitality. He had, however, the misfortune to attract the particular regard of the King, who insisted that the hero should marry his daughter. This proposal he respectfully declined, saying that he was then engaged in a particular service which he could not think of interrupting. The bear-King threatened to commit him to a dungeon, and Hatim, persisting in his refusal, was sent to prison. But sleep came to his aid, and in his dreams an old man appeared to him and recommended that he should acquiesce in the King's proposal. Having acted upon this suggestion, he was introduced to his bride, whom he was astonished to find as beautiful as the moon in her fourteenth night, and seated on a splendid throne arrayed in gold and jewels. Seeing her thus, to his great surprise, one of his own species, he accepted her hand, and took up his abode in her palace. When six months were elapsed, Hatim obtained, through his wife, leave of absence, that he might accomplish his enterprise. He once more found himself in the desert, where there was no sign of human habitation. But, still trusting in Providence, he courageously proceeded. Every evening a mysterious man with a tattered garment brought him a loaf and a jug full of water ; but while he was thus cheerfully making progress he suddenly beheld an immense dragon, who, raising his head aloft, stooped and devoured him at one fell swoop. Fortunately, his wife had fixed a talismanic pearl in his turban before his departure, which prevented his being digested by the dragon, who, sfinding him inconvenient, ejected him on the third day. Hatim, as soon as his clothes were dried in the sun, resumed his journey.

Arriving on the banks of a river, he sat down to refresh himself, and seeing great numbers of fish in the water, he was congratulating himself, while washing his clothes, upon the abundant supply of food he was about to obtain, when a mermaid captured him and took him to her abode in the ocean, very much against his will. Her cavern, though splendidly furnished, did not reconcile him to such a fate, and after much entreaty he was restored to the spot whence he was taken. He then finished the washing of his clothes, which had been so unexpectedly interrupted, and again went on his way.

A lofty mountain soon appeared in sight, covered to the summit with trees. Hatim ascended these shady groves, through which flowed rivulets of pure water, and cooling breezes wafted a delicious fragrance. Here he met a man who warned him that the confines of the Desert of Hawaida were peopled by damsels of surpassing beauty. One of them especially it would require the greatest fortitude to resist ; if he yielded, he was lost for ever ; but if he grasped her hand firmly, she would be compelled to forward him to his destination. This advice sank deep in Hatim's soul, and he was resolved to pursue it.

The next day he reached the borders of a lake, from the bosom of which a nymph of surprising loveliness arose, and seizing Hatim, hurried him into the deep. But he remembered the advice that had been given him, and held firmly to his purpose, saying to himself, "This is all enchantment." He was conveyed to a palace formed entirely of precious stones, and decorated with numberless paintings. Seeing the throne vacant, he thought that he might seat himself upon it ; but when he placed his foot on the step of the throne, a tremendous crash of thunder was heard, which startled him for the moment, but did not deter him from mounting it. When he sat down upon it, another peal seemed to shatter the whole building ; but when it passed away, the damsel, against whom he had been forewarned, approached, clothed in costly gold and jewels, her face veiled. Hatim was strongly tempted to remove the veil, but he forbore, after a moment's reflection, to expose himself to so great a temptation. Wishing, however, to see something more of this enchanted palace, he remained three days and three nights seated upon the throne. The darkness of the night was dispelled by magic lamps, and his ears were delighted with melodious music. Fantastic groups in endless variety danced before him ; but all the while the damsel of surpassing beauty stood by the throne, sweetly smiling in his face. They presented him with foods and fruits of every description in costly dishes, but although Hatim ate most heartily, his hunger was not in the least appeased. Wondering in his mind, he said to himself: " Though I am constantly eating, I am never satiated ; how is this to be accounted for ?" In this manner three days elapsed, and on the fourth he said to himself: " O Hatim were you to look for a hundred years at these delusive appearances, still you would not have tired of them. At the same time, you have left behind you a helpless youth, whose expectations are fixed on your exertions ; if you waste the time, what will you have to answer before God ?"

Upon this Hatim, grasping firmly the hand of the beauteous damsel, was at the same moment struck by some invisible power from the throne to the ground. But lo ! on recovering from the stupor which had seized him, he saw not a trace of the enchanted gardens or their fair inhabitants. He found himself in the Desert of Hawaida, and commenced his search for the man who was constantly repeating the words, "What I saw once I long for a second time." At length he found him, and learnt that his longing was produced by the sight of the matchless nymph whose charms Hatim had resisted.

In this manner, and after undergoing a variety of adventures in which the imagination is allowed full play, Hatim succeeds in satisfying the damsel's curiosity upon every point, and she finally consents to surrender her hand to the young Prince of Syria.

Similar in style are the romances of Bahram-Gor and the Fairy Peri-Banou, the Sindibad-Nama, the Bakhtyar-Nama, and many others. The reader can hardly fail to be reminded in certain passages of the " Arabian Nights," many of which are doubtless of Persian origin. For this we have the authority of the " Fihrist," the most ancient record of Arabian literature, by Muhammad-ben-Ishak-en-Nedim, in the eighth book of which the author says that the first who composed tales were the Kings of the Kaianian, or first dynasty of the Persians. These tales were augmented and amplified by the Sassanides, or fourth dynasty. The Arabs, he then proceeds to say, translated them into their tongue, composing others like them. The first book of this kind was the " Hazar Afsanah," or Thousand Tales. "It is said," continues the author, " that this book was composed by Hoomay, the daughter of Behman. The truth is that the first who had these tales told him at night was Alexander, in order that he might keep awake and be on his guard. The Kings who came after him made use for the same purpose of the Thousand Tales, which were related in a number of nights." Turning to the other branch of Persian Prose Romance, the Apologue and Fable, we have, after the " Marzuban-Nama," a collection of fables translated from Pehlevi into Persian in the thirteenth century, the celebrated collection called the " An-war-i-Suheili" (The

Lights of Canopus), of which two complete translations exist in English by Mr. Eastwick and Sir Arthur Wollaston. This is the work of Husain Vaiz Kashifi, who died A.D. 1505. The Amir Sheikh Ahmed-es-Suheili, a noble at the Court of Sultan Hussein Mirza, persuaded the author to undertake this work, which was in consequence dedicated to him. It is a collection of fables well known in Europe under the name of the "Fables of Pilpay." In his preface Husain Vaiz gives the following account of its origin :

"An enlightened sage called Bidpai the Brahmin wrote this book originally in Sanskrit and dedicated it to King Dabshelim, who reigned over part of Hindustan. His design was to throw together such maxims and precepts under this disguise as might be a guide to Princes in governing their people and in the exercise of justice and clemency among them. Dabshelim preserved it as a precious treasure, which it was prudent to conceal from the view of others, and his family also followed his example through successive generations. But, notwithstanding these precautions, its merits became known and its fame was carried even into distant countries, so that in the time of Noushirvan the Just, King of Persia, it was the subject of general discourse in that country. The curiosity of that Prince was much excited by what was said in its praise, and he prevailed on Barzuiyah, a learned physician of his Court, to take a journey into India to obtain this celebrated book. Barzuiyah, after a long stay in that country and using various stratagems to effect his purpose, at length obtained a copy of the book, and having made a version of it into Pehlevi, presented the original and the translation to Noushirvan, who raised him to great honours in consequence."

Husain Vaiz then proceeds to say that his patron, Ahmed-es-Suheili, had desired him to make a new version better suited to the taste of that age. Husain's translation is written in a very florid style of Persian, interspersed with his own verses and those of other poets, and with texts from the Koran. It consists of fourteen chapters, in which various moral themes—*e.g.*, "the fatal effects of precipitation "-are illustrated by stories and fables. The following story, translated by Sir John Malcolm, may be given as a specimen of one of these:

" In former days there was an old woman who lived in a hut more confined than the minds of the ignorant and more dark than the tombs of misers. Her companion was a cat, from the mirror of whose imagination the appearance of bread had never been reflected, nor had she from friends or strangers ever heard its name. It was enough that she now and then scented a mouse or observed the print of its feet on the floor ; when, blessed by favouring stars, one fell into her claws.

"She became like a beggar who discovers a treasure of gold. Her cheeks glowed with rapture and past grief was consumed by present joy.

"This feast would last for a week or more ; and while enjoying it, she was wont to exclaim:

" 'Am I, O God, when I contemplate this, in a dream or awake ? Am I to experience such prosperity after such adversity ?'

" But as the dwelling of the old woman was in general the mansion of famine to this cat, she was always complaining and forming extravagant and fanciful schemes. One day, when reduced to extreme weakness, she with much exertion reached the top of the hut. When there, she observed a cat stalking on the wall of a neighbours' house, which, like a fierce tiger, advanced with measured steps, and was so loaded with flesh that she could hardly raise her feet. The old woman's friend was amazed to see one of her own species so fat and sleek, and broke out into the following exclamation :

" 'Your stately strides have brought you here at last; pray tell me from whence you come? From whence have you arrived with so lovely an appearance? You look as if from the banquet of the Khan of Khatai. Where have you acquired such a comeliness? and how came you by that glorious strength ?'

" The other answered : 'I am the Sultan's crumb-eater. Each morning when they spread the convivial table I attend at the palace, and there exhibit my address and courage. From among the rich meats and wheat-cakes I cull a few choice morsels ; I then retire and pass my time till next day in delightful indolence.'

"The old dame's cat requested to know what rich meat was, and what taste wheat-cakes had.

" 'As for me,' she added in a melancholy tone, 'during my life I have neither ate nor seen anything but the old woman's gruel and the flesh of mice.'

"The other, smiling, said: 'This accounts for the difficulty I find in distinguishing you from a spider. Your shape and stature is such as must make the whole generation of cats blush; and we must ever feel ashamed while you carry so miserable an appearance abroad.

"'You certainly have the ears and tail of a cat,

But in other respects you are a complete spider.

" 'Were you to see the Sultan's palace and to smell his delicious viands, most undoubtedly those withered bones would be restored ; you would pass from behind the curtain of invisibility into the plain of observation.

" 'When the perfume of his beloved passes over the tomb of a lover,

Is it wonderful that his putrid bones should be reanimated ?'

"The old woman's cat addressed the other in the most supplicating manner.

" 'O my sister !' she exclaimed, ' have I not the sacred claims of a neighbour upon you? Are we not linked in the ties of kindred ? What prevents your giving a proof of friendship by taking me with you when next you visit the palace? Perhaps from your favour plenty may flow to me, and from your patronage I may attain dignity and honour.

" 'Withdraw not from the friendship of the honourable ; Abandon not the support of the elect.'

"The heart of the Sultan's crumb-eater was melted by this pathetic address ; she promised that her new friend should accompany her on the next visit to the palace. The latter, overjoyed, went down immediately from the terrace and communicated every particular to the old woman, who addressed her with the following counsel:

"' Be not deceived, my dearest friend, with the worldly counsel you have listened to ; abandon not your corner of content; for the cup of the covetous is only to be filled by the dust of the grave, and the, eye of cupidity and hope can only be closed by the needle of mortality and the thread of fate.

" 'It is content that makes men rich.

Mark this, ye avaricious, who traverse the world :

He neither knows nor pays adoration to his God

Who is dissatisfied with his condition and fortune.'

"But the expected feast had taken such hold of poor puss's imagination that the salutary counsel of the old woman was thrown away.

" 'The good advice of all the world is like' wind in a cage

Or water in a sieve when bestowed on the headstrong.'

" To conclude, Next day, accompanied by her companion, the half-starved cat hobbled to the Sultan's palace. Before this unfortunate wretch came, as it is decreed that the covetous shall be disappointed, an extraordinary event had occurred, and, owing to her evil destiny, the water of disappointment was poured on the flame of her immature ambition. The case was this: A whole legion of cats had, the day before, surrounded the feast, and made so much noise that they disturbed the guests, and in consequence the Sultan had ordered that some archers, armed with bows from Tartary, should on this day be concealed, and that whatever cat advanced unto the field of valour should, on eating the first morsel, be over taken with their arrows. The old dame's cat was not aware of this order. The moment the odour of the viands reached her, she flew like an eagle on her prey.

"Scarcely had the weight of a mouthful been placed in the scale to balance her hunger, when a heart-dividing arrow pierced her breast.

" 'A stream of blood rushed from the wound ;

She fled, in dread of death, after having exclaimed,

"Should I escape from this terrific archer,

I will be satisfied with my mouse and the miserable hut of my old mistress.

My soul rejects the honey accompanied by the sting;.

Content, with the most frugal fare; is preferable.,'"

This is evidently an Eastern version, told in the elaborate Persian style, of "The Town Mouse and the Country Mouse."

The "Fables of Bidpai," in one form or another, have had a larger circulation than any other Eastern work of fiction, except the "Arabian Nights." They have been translated into several other Eastern tongues—into Arabic, under the title of "Kalilah and Dimnah," by lbnal Muqaffa, in the time of the Caliph Mamoun ; and into Syriac, Hebrew, Pushtu, Hindustani, and other languages of the East. They came also into Europe by two different routes-first from Spain, through direct translations generally made by learned Jews who had been converted to Christianity. Thus, in the thirteenth century a converted Jew, known as " John of Capua," translated into Latin the book of "Kalilah and Dimnah." The second way in which Oriental stories found their way to Europe was through the relations with Syria established by the Crusades.

The son of Husain Vaiz, Ali Safi, is the author of a collection of tales named " Lataif-et-Tawaif." This is merely a series of anecdotes, of which the following two are specimens :

Birds of the Feather.

"A sucking-child had crept to the edge of a water-course, while its mother was otherwise engaged. She could not reach it with her hand, and from the edge of the watercourse to the bottom was twenty yards. She showed her hair and face over the beam to the child, and bared her breast to him, but he would not turn to her. Men came together, but they knew not how they should help her. Suddenly the Emir arrived at that place, heard what was the matter, and saw the distress of the woman. He bade them bring the twin-brother of the child on the beam and hold it before him. The infant turned towards his brother from the impulse of natural affection, and crept upon the beam towards him till he came within reach of the arm of his mother, who put forth her hand and withdrew him from the danger ; and then she kissed the hands and feet of the Emir."

Two Ways of putting It.

" A certain king saw in a dream that all his teeth dropped out. Greatly troubled, he called in the morning a learned man, and told him his dream. He said : ' The children and wives and near relatives of the King will all die in his presence.' The King was greatly displeased at this interpretation, and commanded that the teeth of the interpreter should all be struck out with an axe, and his tongue cut out. After this he called another interpreter, and told him his dream. The second was a man of knowledge and of pleasant disposition. He said: 'O King, this dream shows that the King's life will be long, and its interpretation is this : that your life will be longer than that of all your children and wives and relations.' The King was much pleased with this interpretation, and gave him a horse, and a robe of honour, and a thousand dirhems, saying : 'The substance of these two interpretations is the same, but the one was blown by the wind of his explanation into the whirlwind of destruction, while the other, by reason of his ingenious speaking, raised the banner of prosperity."

Numerous similar collections of tales exist, among which may be mentioned the " Tuti-nama," by Nakhshebi, and the "Ayyar-i-Danish," by Abu'l Fazl, secretary of the Emperor Akbar.

14

HISTORY

Two circumstances have contributed much towards the cultivation of the historical sense among the Persians and Arabs—the custom, which arose very early in Islam, of collecting authentic traditions concerning Muhammad and his companions; and the pride in their ancestors, which both nations felt in an excessive degree. This led to a close study of genealogy. The ambition to prove a royal and noble descent, more powerful among Asiatics than any Europeans, was productive of much research, and opened many channels for historical investigation.

The first Persian historian is Abu Jafar ibn Jarir at-Tabari, who was born A.D. 838 at Amol in Tabaristan, and died in A.D. 922 at Bagdad. He was celebrated for his great learning, and was pre-eminent in the sciences of the interpretation of the Koran, the Traditions, Jurisprudence, and History. His History of the World was orginally composed in Arabic, but was very soon translated into Persian by Abd ullah al Balami. The translation by Balami is curious from a philological point of view, as it is the oldest work extant in modern Persian, being anterior to the " Shah-Namah " of Firdausi. The style is remarkably easy and simple, and words of Semitic origin are but rarely introduced. The following is a specimen of the narrative :

The Death of Abdullah ibn Zubair.

"Hejaj having stationed his troops' before the gates of Mecca, battles daily took place in the holy city, and many men were slain. Hejaj then constructed an engine, and threw stones into the town and at the Ka'ba ; but when one stone fell on the Ka'ba, the sun became dark, and his troops feared and wished to withdraw the engine and to retreat. Hejaj said: 'Fear not; such is the nature of the climate of Hidjaz whenever a thunderstorm occurs ; and if the lightning seek you to-day, to-morrow it will seek them.' His men put no faith in these words, and were retreating, when Hejaj advanced and began to work the engine with his own hand, and exhorted his men to continue the battle with firmness. But the defence was for a long time maintained, till at last the two sons of Abdullah bin Zubair, Habib and Hamza, gave themselves up to Hejaj. Hejaj then knew that no troops remained with Abdullah, and despatched a messenger to him to say: 'Why dost thou thus vainly expose thyself to death, as all the people have left thee, and thy sons have turned their faces from thee ? Come forth, therefore, and demand mercy, and whatever thou mayest desire I will do unto thee.'

"But Abdullah consented not. When Hejaj learnt that the son of Zubair had fixed his heart on death, he ordered that he should be closely invested, and that guards should be placed over the five gates of Mecca. Abdullah, being then deserted by all except five followers, entered his house, and proceeded to his mother, the daughter of Abu Bekr and the sister of Ayesha, a woman of sense and judgment, whom he consulted in every affair; to her he went clothed in his armour, and said: ' O my mother! all the world has turned from me, and has done me greater injury than the men of Iraq did to Hussein ; for his sons remained faithful to him, but mine have sought the protection of my enemies, and Hejaj offers to grant whatever I may demand. My mother, shall I go to him or not?'

"She replied: ' Thou knowest best, my son. If thou believest that thou hast maintained the right, and called men to support the just cause, still adhere to it, and yield not thy right to anyone, but die in its defence in the same manner that thy friends have died ; and give not thy enemies power over thee, nor trust thyself in the hands of the sons of Omeyyah. Recollect how short a space of life remains to thee ; and wouldst thou for a few short days of life disgrace thyself, when thou must die at last ? But fix not a stigma upon thyself, nor yield to thy enemies.'

" Abdullah kissed the head of his mother, and said: 'Such was my intention, and I came, therefore, to bid thee farewell. God knows that I have maintained the right, and that I never acted contrary to it, and that I have never injured nor betrayed my neighbour, and that I have in everything sought to please the Almighty. O Lord ! Thou knowest that I do not exalt myself ; but still, my mother, I mourn for thee.'

" She replied: 'My son, mourn not for me, for I ought to have departed before thee ; and since I remain, God will grant me patience.' Then, raising up her head, she said: ' O God ! Thou knowest that this son of mine has performed every prayer and kept every fast which was required ; let not, then, their efficacy be lost. And Thou knowest that his father and mother were always pleased with him—be Thou also pleased with him ; and give me patience to support me when he is gone, and grant me the reward of the patient.'

" Abdullah, having bade his mother farewell, went and passed the night in the mosque, in company with the few friends who remained with him. The next morning, having finished his prayers, he armed himself, and as each door of the mosque was guarded, he rushed from one of them, and made many attacks on the troops stationed before it, in all of which he slew many men. Thus he continued fighting until the prayers of noon, when, the day being very sultry, he became wearied, and was obliged to stand on one spot, when he was overpowered and fell, and his enemies gathered round him and cut him to pieces."

Another great historical ; work is the " Raudhat-us-Safa," or Garden of Purity, by Mirkhond, born A.D. 1433. His patron was Ali Sher, Vizier of Sultan Husain Mirza of Herat, to whom he dedicated the above work. When his father, Khawend Shah, died, Mirkhond was young, and being compelled by circumstances to abandon his home in Mawarau-n-nahar, he went to Balkh, where he studied literature and science.

Of Mirkhond himself very little is known. When he was only thirteen years of age he accompanied his father on a political embassy, the conductors of which were pillaged by the Turks and deprived of everything they possessed. On another occasion he tells us that he was on a hunting expedition, when, for leaving his post to join in midday prayer, he was reprimanded by some of the King's servants, and was so much alarmed that he fell ill for seven days. " Frightful dreams," he says, "troubled him during the night, and before his departure the humble author of this history took God to witness, and vowed that on no account would he ever be induced to join another hunting expedition."

These adventures seem to have indisposed him towards an active life, and he devoted himself early to literature. His son Khondemir tells us that Mirkhond, having employed his early life in acquiring all that was attainable in Eastern science, in which he soon outstripped all his contemporaries, applied himself with equal assiduity and success to the study of history.

" Through the seductions of a convivial disposition, however, and too unrestrained an intercourse with the votaries of pleasure, it never occurred to him to engage in the labours of composition, until, by the goodness of Providence and the influence of his better destiny, he found means to be introduced to the excellent Ali Sher, from whom he immediately experienced every mark of kindness and encouragement." He assigned to Mirkhond apartments in the Khankah Akhlasia, a building erected by him " to serve as a retreat and asylum to men of merit distinguished by their attainments."

A great portion of the " Raudhat-us-Safa " was composed on a bed of sickness, and the author has himself given a painful account of the circumstances under which he was compelled to write :

" I wrote all, chapter by chapter, lying on my right side, and because of the violent pains I felt in my loins, I was not able to write a single page sitting down. Clever physicians assured me that this occupation would relieve me of the malady, or, at least, prevent its becoming worse. If on any night I happened to neglect my usual labour, and wished to abandon myself to repose, I had troublesome dreams, woke up in affright, or an excessive heat came over me, which prevented my sleeping. If, on the contrary, I set myself to write as usual, I had a good sleep and agreeable dreams."

For a whole year before his death he gave himself up entirely to religious duties, and after a lingering illness he died A.D. 1498, at the age of sixty-six. " There is no Oriental work," says Sir H. M. Eliot, " that stands higher in public estimation than the " Raudhat-us-Safa." The author has availed himself of no less than nineteen Arabic and twenty-two Persian histories, besides others which he occasionally quotes."

The following are specimens of the work:

1. Alexander the Great admonished.

"Alexander, during his circuit in the provinces, happened to pass by a certain village in which the dwellings of the inhabitants were narrow and dark ; and at the door of each he saw a grave prepared. Among them was neither governor nor judge. Alexander having asked the reason of the uniformity observed in the houses, the absence of a governor or ruler, and the excavated graves, they answered : 'A difference in the elevation of the houses would lead to a claim of superiority and pre-eminence over each other, and we are far removed from the influence of emulation ; we have the graves dug ready at our doors, that we may not forget death or feel pride at our ephemeral existence, as pride is necessarily connected with calamity ; and, lastly, as our actions are ruled by equity, what occasion have we for judge or governor ?'

" Alexander asked: 'If I should appoint for your dwelling a more cheerful place, would you remove from your present abode?'

"They answered : 'Our request from the King is that he would drive from us the predestined hour of Fate.'

" To which Alexander replied: 'If the fulfilment of your request had been possible to mortal man, no human being would have been more able than myself to grant it.'

" On this they answered: 'As the King in this matter is as weak as others, our request is that he permit us to remain in our own abode ; for residence in the place of one's birth and growth has a peculiar delight.' "

2. *The Avarice of Sultan Mahmud of Ghazni.*

" For two years before his death he was afflicted with a paralytic affection ; but he continued, notwithstanding the injunctions of his physicians, to ride and move about in his usual manner. It is related that the Sultan, two days before his death, ordered all the bags of silver and gold, the precious gems and valuable rarities which had been collected during his reign, to be brought before him and to be spread out on rich carpets on the floor of the hall ; and that floor appeared to the eyes of the beholder like a garden adorned with flowers of red, and yellow, and purple, and other various hues. The Sultan viewed them with the eye of grief, and wept aloud ; and after much weeping he directed them all to be carried' back to the treasury, without bestowing on those entitled to charity a single dirhem from all that quantity of gold and jewels, although he knew that he must yield up in a few days his cherished soul in a hundred agonies. When Mahmud had contemplated his various treasures, he proceeded to a balcony, where he beheld, as they passed in review before him, the imperial collection of valuable animals, such as Arabian horses, Burdaa camels, and the like. After having cast his eyes over them, he uttered groans and lamentations like a woman ; and, pierced with grief and affliction, returned to his palace.

" Abu'l Hosain ben Ali relates that Sultan Mahmud one day inquired from Abu Taher Samani what quantity of precious gems had been collected by the Samanide Princes. He replied that Amir Nuh had possessed in his treasury the weight of seven ratls. Mahmud, immediately bending his head towards the ground, said : 'Praise be to God that the Almighty has bestowed on me more than one hundred ratls of jewels!' [The ratl is about one pound avoirdupois.]

"Abu Bekr Ali observes that Mahmud was a man most zealous in his sect and religion, and that his principal fault was the extreme avarice with which he seized the property of the people. It once came to his knowledge that there was in Shahpur a man possessed of great wealth. He sent for that man to Ghazni, and said to him:

" ` It appears that thou art a heretic.'

" The rich man replied : 'I am not a heretic ; but the Almighty has enriched me with the wealth of this world. Take all that I possess, but do not stigmatize me with the name of heretic.' The Sultan accordingly took all his property, and gave him in return a certificate of his orthodoxy."

Mirkhond's son, Khondemir, born about A.D. 1475, is also a celebrated historian. From his early youth he showed a predilection for history, and, guided by the example and advice of his father, he prepared himself for the composition of some work by which he might attain equal celebrity. In this purpose he was assisted by the Vizier, Ali Sher, who, having collected a valuable library, placed him in charge of it. About A.D. 1498 Khondemir completed his first work, the " Khulasat-ul-Akhbar," and at the close of it he gratefully acknowledges that, had it not been for Ali Sher's kindness in placing him in charge of the library, he could not have completed in six years a tenth part of what he had concluded in as many months, and to him he dedicated the work. His native country, Khorassan, being in a disturbed state owing to the incursions of the Uzbeks, Khondemir quitted Persia, and betook himself to the Emperor Baber at Agra. At the conclusion of the " Habib-us-Siyar," another of his works, he tells us :

" Under the unavoidable law of destiny, the writer was compelled to leave Herat and bend his steps towards Candahar. " Thence he undertook a hazardous journey to Hindustan, which, in consequence of the great distance, the heat of the weather, the setting in of the rainy season, and the broad and rapid rivers which intervened, occupied seven months. Finally, he reached the metropolis of Agra, and on that day had the good fortune to strengthen his weak eyes with the dust of the high threshold of the Emperor, the mention of whose name in 'so humble a page as this would not be respectful. He was allowed without delay to kiss the celestial throne, which circumstance exalted him so much that it placed the very foot of his dignity over the heads of the Great and Little Bears in the heavens."

He accompained Baber on his expedition to Bengal, and upon his death attached himself to Humayun. He accompanied the latter of Guzerat, and died in his camp A.D. 1535.

FROM THE "KHULASAT-UL-AKHBAR" OF KHONDEMIR

I. *Luqman and his Master.*

"He was contemporary with David, and frequented the Court of that monarch. Many historians agree that he was at first a slave to an Israelite, and they assign various causes for his emancipation. Fearful of running into prolixity in this place, I shall content myself with one tradition. It is said that once Luqman's master ordered him to sow barley in a certain field, and he sowed it with millet. "His master having come to the spot when it was green, and seeing what was sprung up, said: `I ordered you to sow barley in this field. Why have you sown millet ?'

" Luqman answered : 'In hope that the millet-seed would produce barley.'

"The master reproached him, and said: `What an impossible idea this is !'

" Luqman replied : 'Since you in the field of the world always sow the seed of sin, and expect that at the day of retribution, which is the time of harvest, you shall be blessed with good fruit, I also conjectured that this millet-seed would produce barley.'

"The Israelite was ashamed at hearing these words, and gave Luqman his liberty."

2. *Nimrod's Flying-Machine.*

" When Nimrod had repeatedly seen the power of God in respect to Abraham, he wanted to go up to heaven that he might war with the Almighty. He therefore built a tower of an immense height, and, having ascended to the top of it, he there beheld the sky just the same as it appeared from the earth. He descended, greatly ashamed, and as soon as he alighted at the bottom of the tower, it fell down, and a loud noise was heard by the people of Babylon. Nimrod, having another time thought of ascending to heaven, ordered four young vultures to be trained up. When the vultures were full grown, he constructed a machine sufficiently large to contain two persons, and to which there were two doors. Having kept the vultures without food for some days, he placed himself in the machine with one of his nobles ; and fastening four pieces of flesh to the upper corners of the machine, he tied the vultures to the four feet thereof. The vultures, seeing the flesh over their heads, supported the machine with all their strength, and flew upwards. After they had kept ascending for the space of three days and three nights, Nimrod looked out of the machine towards heaven, and beheld the sky just the same as it appeared from the earth ; and upon looking down towards the earth, he saw nothing but darkness. Therefore, being doubtful, he ordered his companion to remove the flesh to the lower part of the machine. The courtier having done as he was commanded, the vultures descended, and Nimrod alighted on the earth with shame and confusion."

The best known of the Persian historians is Muhammad Kasim Firishta, born about A.D. 1570 at Astrabad, on the shores of the Caspian Sea. His father's name was Ghulam Ali Hindu Shah, and at the age of twelve years he accompanied him on his journey to India. They reached Ahmednuggur in the Deccan, where Murtaza Nizam Shah was then reigning, about A.D. 1582. Ghulam Ali was shortly after appointed private tutor to the Prince Meeran Hosein, whom he educated with Firishta. The latter was a great favourite with the King, and on his father's death received a commission in the King's guard. While he was in this situation the violent conduct of the King (who was insane) towards his son brought about a revolution, which ended by the King being suffocated in a bath, when the tide of affairs had turned in his son's favour, and led to the departure of Firishta from Ahmednuggur to Bijapur. In a war which ensued between the States of Ahmednuggur and Bijapur, Firishta took part, and was severely wounded. Firishta afterwards attended the daughter of the King of Bijapur on the occasion of her marriage to Prince - Damel, son of the Emperor Akbar. Two years later he was sent on an embassy to the Emperor Jehangir, the precise nature of which is not known. The date of his death is unknown, some biographers placing it in A.D. 1612, and others in A. D. 1623. His work is named "Gulshan-i-Ibra-himi," after Ibrahim Adil Shah, the Sovereign of Bijapur. The whole of it has been translated into English by General Briggs.

FROM FIRISHTA'S HISTORY.

Mahmud of Ghazni in India.

" Mahmud having thus settled his affairs in India, returned in the autumn to Ghazni, where he remained during the winter. In the spring of the year A.D. 1008 he determined again to attack Anandpal, Rajah of Lahore. Anandpal, hearing of his intentions, sent ambassadors on all sides, inviting the assistance of the other Princes of Hindustan, who now considered the expulsion of the Muhammadans from India as a sacred duty. Accordingly, the Rajahs of Ujjein, Gwalior, Kalunjar, Canauj, Delhi, and Ajmir, entered into a confederacy, and, collecting their forces, advanced towards the Panjab with the greatest army that had yet taken the field. The Hindus and

Muhammadans arrived in sight of each other on a plain on the confines of the province of Peshawar, where they remained encamped forty days without coming to action. The troops of the idolaters daily increased in number. The Hindu females on this occasion sold their jewels and melted down their gold ornaments to furnish resources for the war ; and the Gukkurs and other warlike tribes, joining the army, surrounded the Muhammadans, who were obliged to entrench their camp. Mahmud having thus secured himself, ordered six thousand archers to the front to endeavour to provoke the enemy to attack his entrenchments. The archers were opposed by the Gukkurs, who, in spite of the King's efforts and presence, repulsed his light troops, and followed them so closely that no less than thirty thousand Gukkurs, with their heads and feet bare and armed with various weapons, penetrated into the Muhammadan lines, where a dreadful carnage ensued, and five thousand Muhammadans were slain in a few minutes. The enemy were at length checked, and being cut off as fast as they advanced, the attacks became fainter and fainter, till, on a sudden, the-elephant upon which the Prince who commanded the Hindus rode, becoming unruly from the effects of the naphtha balls and the flights of arrows, turned and fled. This circumstance produced a panic among the Hindus, who, seeing themselves deserted by their General, gave way and fled also."

" It is said that when Mahmud was proceeding to Multan through the deserts of Scinde, he gave orders to procure a guide to conduct him on his journey. A Hindu offered his services, but treacherously led the army through a path which brought them to a place where no water could be procured. When the army had passed on for a whole day and night, and found no water at any place, they were sore bested, and everything wore the appearance of the horrors of the day of judgment. The Sultan then asked his guide the reason why he had brought them to such a fearful pass; the Hindu replied that he was a worshipper of Somnath, and had conducted the King and his army to the desert with a view to their destruction. The Sultan, being exceeding wrath, ordered his men to put the Hindu to death.

" On that very night the Sultan retired from his camp to a neighbouring spot, and prostrating himself on the earth, offered up prayers, mingled with lamentations, to Almighty God, imploring deliverance from the danger in which he was placed. After the first watch of the night had elapsed a light was seen towards the north. The army, according to the Sultan's command, directed their march toward the light, and by the morning found themselves in safety on the borders of a lake. Thus the piety of the Sultan rescued him from the brink of destruction."

"When the Sultan on one occasion saw an idol in a Hindu temple poised in the air without any support, he was much surprised at the sight, and inquired of the philosophers of the time the cause of the phenomenon. They answered that the roof and walls of the building were entirely made of magnetic stone, and that the idol, which was made of iron, being equally attracted from the different points of the magnetic edifice, was thus naturally suspended in the middle of it. On one of the walls being destroyed by order of the Sultan, the idol fell to the ground."pointed out the way which he was to go.

15

BIOGRAPHY AND MISCELLANEOUS PROSE WORKS

PERSIAN prose, literature is especially rich in collections of lives of the poets, called Tazkiras. Chief among these is that by Daulat Shah of Samarcand, written in A.D. 1486, and dedicated to Ali Sher, the Prime Minister of Sultan Husain of Herat. It is a curious and entertaining work, interspersed with biographical sketches and anecdotes of the different Princes under whom the poets whose lives he describes flourished. In his preface Daulat Shah observes:

"Poets have at all times been honoured by Kings and nobles, and admitted into their society, and, among the poets of Persia, Rudaki received from Amir Ahmad Samani a present of eighty thousand dirhems for his translation of the `Kalilah-wa-Dimnah,' and Unsari was raised to the rank of nobility by Mahmud of Ghazni, and Amir Mazzi was honoured by being selected as one of the confidential courtiers of Malek Shah. But nowadays no respect is paid to this class of men, and they are degraded from all the honours they formerly enjoyed."

This complaint was well founded, as Daulat Shah lived at a time when the divided and distracted state of Persia prevented the encouragement of poetry or learning. Daulat Shah gives one hundred and forty memoirs of Persian and ten of Arabic poets. The following anecdote which he relates throws an interesting light on the beginnings of Persian literature :

" One day, when Amir Abdullah Tahir, the Governor of Khorassan, under the Abbasside Caliphs, was giving audience, a person laid before him a book as a rare and valuable present.

" He asked : 'What book is this ?'

"The man replied: 'It is the story of Wamik and Azra, a singular and wonderful tale, which was composed by learned men for the Emperor Naushirvan, who was renowned in every country for his equity and justice.'

" The Amir observed : 'We are readers of the Holy Koran, and we read nothing except that sacred volume and the traditions of the Prophet, and such accounts as relate to him, and we have therefore no use for this kind of book. They are, besides, the compositions of infidels and the productions of worshippers of fire, and are therefore to be rejected and contemned by us.' He then ordered the book to be thrown into the water, and issued a command that whatever books could be found in the kingdom which were the composition of the infidels of Persia should be immediately burnt."

Daulatshah's remarks on poetry in his preface deserve quotation :

"Among the various kinds of eloquence," he says, " wise men and connoisseurs have always given the palm to poetry. They compare prose to the natural attractions of a young bride, and poetry to the jewels which set them off. By poetic genius ideas are summoned from the void and beautified by the rhythm of verse. Since Adam's fall, each age has been distinguished by a special form of knowledge to which men have devoted themselves, and preeminence in this form of knowledge distinguished the prophet of each age. Thus Moses, who lived in an age when magic was much sought after, wrought the greatest wonders by means of his staff ; and Jesus, born in an age when the art of healing was much cultivated, worked the most surprising cures, giving sight to the blind, health to lepers, and life to the dead. These miracles were the proof of the divine mission of these two prophets.

" In the same way Muhammad, sent by Heaven at a time when eloquence was held in high esteem by the Arabs, and those who excelled in it were regarded as prophets, received as a testimony to his divine mission the Koran, which is in truth a prodigy of eloquence, which men and genii united might strive in vain to emulate. Before the sublime eloquence of the Koran all the skill of the most celebrated orators of Arabia was confounded and eclipsed like the light of the moon before the rays of the sun. Muhammad himself set great store by those poets who became his disciples. He called poets the 'fountainhead of wisdom,' and kept a great number round him, who celebrated his praises and received numerous rewards from him.

" In the times before Muhammad poetry was carefully cultivated by the Arabs, and he who excelled in this art was usually called to the dignity of Amir of his tribe. Thus Amr-ul-kais, one of the most celebrated Arab poets, reigned in Yemama. The author of the book `Sherif-ul-nabi' relates that Muhammad kept continually by him the poet Hassan ben Tabeth, and used to employ him to reply to the attacks of the idolatrous poets. Moreover, the King of Syria having sent as a present to the prophet Mary the Copt and her sister Shirin, the prophet married Mary and gave Shirin to the poet Hassan as a reward for his verses on the Battle of the Trench.

"The Caliph Ali successfully cultivated poetry, and his example has been imitated by the most distinguished Muhammadan Princes. We are informed by historians that when Sultan Mahmud of Ghazni had once struck anyone, no one else was allowed to raise a hand against them. Similarly may we not say that an art which has actually dared to rival the divine Koran, and been conquered by it, should not recognize any other art as its superior ?"

Daulatshah proceeds in a somewhat naive fashion to give his reasons for composing this work :

" After having spent the first fifty years of my life in a useless manner, and in seeking the pleasures of the present world, I began to reflect on my past life, and finding that I had never spent a single moment in the acquisition of knowledge and virtue, I was struck with keen remorse. I felt that it was impossible to recall time misspent, and that I must give all my care to the proper use of the time I had remaining. I resolved, therefore, to begin something before death came to cut the thread of my life; but I perceived that knowledge can only be properly acquired in youth, and being only an infant in knowledge, the thought of the years I had wasted made me despair of reaching the goal. Convinced also that it would be a vain attempt to follow the example of my ancestors and adopt the life of a courtier, in which I had no experience, I withdrew to a life of solitude.

" Want of occupation soon produced weariness, till I discovered a treasure in my pen. The history of prophets and Kings had already been treated of by a large number of writers ; many had composed treatises on geography and other useful subjects ; but no one had yet thought of compiling a history of poets, doubtless because the subject appeared to them to have little importance. I seized on this idea, and collected together in a single work a large number of scattered facts from the time of the establishment of Islam to the present."

Many other Tazkirahs, or collections of lives of the poets, were composed, among which we may mention that by Sam Mirza, one of the sons of Ismail Shah, the first of the Safavi dynasty (circa 1550), and another by Lutf Ali Beg, entitled "Atish Kedah ," or the Fire-Temple (circa A.D. 1770), a strange title for a Muhammadan work. This work is more copious than Daulat Shah's, and treats of the poets under geographical divisions. While he was engaged in this work, the author says, "a young poetaster of his acquaintance, unripe in judgment, as he was immature in years, proposed that some of his own composition also should be inserted." This Lutf All refused, telling him that this "was truly a fire-temple, in whose furnace thorns would be consumed, but roses turn to delicious attar to rejoice the senses."

The following is his account of Ispahan, of which, as a native, he speaks with enthusiasm :

"It was founded by Tahmuras the Pishdadian, and Jamshid and Iskender. Kai Kobad, the first of the Kaianaina Kings, made it his seat of government, and added some fine buildings. By degrees it became of such great extent that it was styled ' Isfahan, the half of the world.' The temperature of the air is perfection. The climate is remarkably salubrious, so that they say a dead body, if buried, will be preserved in the soil thirty years without decay ; and whatever grain is sown in it is never lost. Besides pomegranates and grapes, all kinds of fruit in great abundance and of excellent quality are produced in that happy district. It is recorded in the annals of Ispahan that this city, in compliance with the prayer of Ibrahim Khalil, is always blest with thirty saints, in memory of its thirty inhabitants who, regardless of the violence of the tyrant Nimrud, declared their faith in the true God in confirmation of the faith of Abraham." The inhabitants of Ispahan were renowned of old for bravery. Kawah, the blacksmith, who raised the standard of revolt against the tyrant Zohak, is a well-known proof of this assertion. In fine, without incurring the slightest suspicion of partiality, one may fairly call it the most excellent of cities."

Among the poets mentioned by Lutf Ali is Sheikh Muhammad Ali Hazin, who has written an autobiography. In it he informs us that he was born at Ispahan in 1692, that his father was an eminent scholar, and descended from a line of learned men. His erudition, his piety, and his rigid obedience to the precepts of the Koran are

* In the Koran Nimrud is said to have cast Abraham into a furnace, which forthwith turned into a bed of roses.

commemorated by his son. Muhammad Ali relates the course of his education ; he tells us that before he was eight years old he had a great liking for logic and poetry, but practised the last by stealth, being forbidden to write verses by his father, till the latter found that his son's propensity was too strong to be subdued. He then encouraged it, and one day, when a party of learned men had assembled at his house, he asked the young poet, if he had composed any verses, to recite to them. Muhammad Ali thereupon repeated some verses of his composition, and the company, he tells us, moved from their- places and burst into applause.

When he grew up he spent most of his time at Shiraz, writing treatises and commentaries, until the death of his father, when he represents himself as " horror-struck " with the world, his constant desire being to put on the dress of a Dervish and retire into seclusion. The disorders in the province of Gilan, invaded by a Russian army, robbed him of most of his possessions and reduced him to poverty. He then describes the Afghan invasion and the Siege of Ispahan, during the famine in which place the price of a loaf of bread rose to four or five ashrafis (about £ 8 or £ 10). "Everything," he says, "that the hand of my ability could reach to I expended, and except my library scarcely anything remained unsold in my house. I distributed nearly two thousand volumes of my books ; the remainder of my collection became the plunder of the Afghans."

After many varied experiences, including a pilgrimage to Mecca, he determined to quit Persia for Hindustan.

A European, he says, dissuaded him from going, " enumerating some of the deformities in the qualities of that Empire," and advised him to go to Europe ; but he declined, and proceeded to Tatta in Scinde, where he remained, enduring the pain of being alone and without friends, his "body and soul worn out " with the visits and conversation of " worldly persons " who frequented his house. He repented his resolution not to sail to Europe, and determined to go back to Persia, but was prevented by the " imperious decree of fate," and proceeded to Delhi, in a retired corner of which he penned these memoirs.

A much more important author is Ibn Khalliqan, whose " Wafyat ul Ayan," or Biographies of Eminent Persons, has been highly praised by Orientalists, and was translated into English by De Slane. Sir William Jones characterized its author as "more copious than Cornelius Nepos, more elegant than Plutarch, and more pleasing than Diogenes Laertius." "Before him," observes De Slane, " none ever thought of combining in one treatise and in alphabetical order the lives of the most remarkable men of Islam. There existed, it is true, a great number of biographical dictionaries, composed before his, and some of them dating from a remote period; but they were works of a special cast, and limited in their subject."

Ibn Khalliqan was of a family of Balkh, said to be connected with the famous Barmecides. He passed his early years at Arbela, and then proceeded to Mosul, where he studied jurisprudence. Whilst in the prime of life he went to Damascus, and after a short residence there he travelled to Egypt, where he acquired a complete knowledge of all the sciences, and attained pre-eminence as a jurisconsult, theologian, and grammarian. He quitted Cairo, being appointed Cadi of Damascus, at the age of fifty, and died in the seventy-second year of his age.

The following is a specimen of one of the shorter biographies in his great work the " Wafyat " : " Abu'l Fadhl al Hamadani is the author of some beautiful epistles and excellent Makamas, which Al Hariri took as a model in the composition of his, framing them on the same plan, and imitating the manner of their author, in whose footsteps he walked. In his preface Al Hariri acknowledges the merits of his predecessor, and admits that he was guided by his example in the path he followed. Al Hamadani dwelt at Herat, a city in the province of Khorassan."

The following is a specimen of his epistolary style : "To him, whose honourable presence is a point of union for the needy, not to say the Ka'ba of pilgrims ; the station of honour, not to say the station of sanctity to him let this be a consolation : Death is awful till it comes, and it then it is found light. Its touch grating till felt, and then it is smooth. The world is so hostile, and its injustice so great, that death is the lightest of its inflictions, the least of its wrongs. Look, then, to the right. Do you see aught but affliction ? Look to the left. Do you see aught but woe ?"

The lines which follow are taken from a long poem of his composition :

"The gush of the fertilizing shower were like thee, did it in smiling pour forth gold. Fortune were like thee, did it not deceive ; the sun, did he speak ; the lion, were he not hunted ; the sea, were its waters fresh."

His prose and verse abound in beauties of every kind. He died of poison at Herat in the year of the Flight of Muhammad, A.D. 1282. I have since found, however, the following note written at the endof his epistles, which have been collected by the Hakim Abu Said : " End of the epistles". The author died at Herat in the year of the Flight, 681."

On this the Hakim observes : " I have been assured by persons of good authority that he fell into a lethargy and was buried with precipitation. He recovered when shut up in the tomb, and, his cries having been heard, that night his grave was opened, and he was found dead from fright, with his hand grasping his beard."

Among miscellaneous prose works may be mentioned the Kitabi Kulzum Nameh, which has been translated into English by Mr. James Atkinson. This is *a jeu d'esprit,* laying down with mock solemnity the rules to be observed by women in their conduct at home and abroad. The work gives many interesting glimpses into the domestic life of the Persians. In the chapter on the mutual conduct of wives and husbands we have rules respecting the liberty to be allowed the former. The husband is to allow his better half plenty of cash, that she may enjoy feasts, and excursions, and the bath, and every other kind of recreation. If he stint her in these matters he will assuredly be punished for all his sins and omissions on the day of resurrection. The woman should invariably assume that her husband's mother and other relations are at heart her enemies. She will therefore find it necessary at once to establish her authority over them by at least once a day giving them physical proof of her resolution. The husband is to be conquered in a different manner. She must on all occasions ring in his ears the threat of a divorce.

"If he still resists, she must redouble all the vexations which she knows from experience irritate his mind, and day and night add to the bitterness and misery of his condition. She must never, whether by day or by night, for a moment relax. For instance, if he condescends to hand her the loaf, she must throw it from her or at him with indignation and contempt. She must make his shoe too tight for him, and his pillow a pillow of stone, so that at last he becomes weary of life, and is glad to acknowledge her authority. On the other hand, should these resources fail, the wife may privately convey from her husband's house everything valuable that she can lay her hands upon, and then go to the Qazi and complain that her husband has beaten her with his shoe, and pretend to show the bruises on her skin. She must state such facts in favour of her case as she knows cannot be refuted by evidence, and pursue every possible plan to escape from the thraldom she endures. For that purpose every effort of every description is perfectly justifiable and according to law."

The above gives a different view of the Eastern woman to that usually prevalent in Europe. There is a doubtless a germ of truth in it—*e.g.*, it is related that even the redoubtable Haroun-al Raschid was considerably henpecked by his wife, Zobeidah.

The following are a few more of the precepts laid down in this curious work :

"Among the things forbidden to women is allowing their features to be seen by men not wearing turbans—unless, indeed, they are handsome, and have soft and captivating manners. In that case their veils may be drawn aside without the apprehension of incurring blame or in any degree exceeding the discretionary power with which they are traditionally invested. But they must scrupulously and religiously abstain from all such liberties with Mullahs and Jews, since respecting them the prohibition is imperative. It is not necessary, however, to be very particular in the presence of common people. There is nothing criminal in being seen by singers, musicians, servants of the bath, and such persons as go about the streets to sell their wares and trinkets.

"On the very day a woman goes to the house of her husband upon being married, it is necessary that everything of importance relating to her own interest and advantage should be first settled, all arrangements made to secure her own comfort and the uninterrupted exercise of her own will, so that she may be exonerated from the responsibility which might otherwise attach to her; for it is right that all blame should invariably be laid upon the back of her husband. It is not to be conceived that a woman can live all her life with one husband in one house. Why should he deprive her of the full enjoyment of this world's comforts ? Days and years roll on and are renewed, whilst a woman continues the same melancholy inmate in the same melancholy house of her husband. She has no renewal of happiness—none.

" 'The seasons change, and spring
Renews the bloom of fruit and flower ;
And birds with fluttering wing
Give life again to dell and bower.

But what is woman's lot ?
No change her anxious heart to cheer,
Confined to one dull spot
And one dull husband all the year:

" For a woman to be without familiar friends of her own is reckoned a heavy misfortune, and there is no one so poor who does not struggle hard to avoid so great a curse. A woman dying without friends or gossips has no chance of going to heaven; whereas happy is that woman whose whole life is passed in constant intercourse with kind associates, for she will assuredly go to heaven. What can equal the felicity of that woman whose daily employment is sauntering hand-in-hand with friends amidst rose-bowers and aromatic groves, and visiting every place calculated to expand and exhilarate the heart ? That woman at the day of resurrection will be seen dancing with her old companions in the region of bliss. The very circumstance of living in such a state of social freedom and harmony always produces a forgiveness of sins. If a damsel dies before she has established a circle of intimates to whom she can communicate her secret thoughts and actions, the other world can never be to her a scene of happiness and joy. But if she is more favourably circumstanced, every supplication for pardon will have the effect of angel-prayers ; and this is the reward of those who in this life cultivate social connections and are bound in the endearing ties of friendship."

A kind of compendium of miscellaneous knowledge, entitled the " Ajaib-ul-Makhluqat," or The Wonders of the Creation, was composed by Zakaria bin Muhammad al Qazwini, a native of Qazwin. He divides all things into the " high" and the "low," or the celestial and the terrestrial. Under the first head are comprehended the heavens, the angels, the times and seasons; under the second the four elements-fire, air, earth, and water: their properties, divisions, and inhabitants. The description of the angels called " the bearers of the throne " is one of the many instances of plagiarism from the Jewish Scriptures which occur in Muhammadan writings :

"Among the angels are the bearers of the throne of God, and they are the highest in dignity and honour of all the angels, and all the other celestial inhabitants seek access unto them and salute them, on account of their near approach to Almighty God. And they chant the praises of their God, and believe in Him, and intercede with Him for mercy for the believers ; and it is on record that one of them is in the shape of a man, and one of them is in the shape of a bull, and a third in the shape of an eagle, and a fourth in the shape of a lion. When the Prophet heard the word of Ommiah Ben Abuasalb he wondered whence he had taken it, for they were all four mentioned in his verse, and yet he lived in the time of ignorance [*i.e.*, before Islam]. His verse was :

" 'A man and a bull under the right hand of his throne, On the left an eagle and a full-grown lion."'

This is their shape. Ibn Abbas says of them :

"God created the bearers of His throne, who are four in number now ; but when the day of resurrection comes He will give them four others to help them, for this is the word of the Most High : 'And in that day eight shall bear the throne of thy Lord upon them, and they are of a size indescribable.' Some there are of them in the human shape, in pity to the sons of Adam ; and some of them are in the shape of a calf, in pity to the brutes in like manner; and some of them in the shape of an eagle, for the sake of the birds ; and some of them in the shape of a lion, for the sake of the beasts of prey."

Descending from celestial to sublunary subjects, Qazwini gives a section on the climates of the earth, in which he mentions the half-yearly nights at the Pole :

" Near the North, under the constellation of the Benat al Naash, the cold is intense ; for six months of winter there is perpetual night, and the air is dark with a tremendous darkness, and the animals take to the water from the extreme coldness of the air, and plants Wither and animals droop. And opposite to this is the place near the South under the constellation of Sohail.

" There are six months of summer, perpetual day; and the air is hot and becomes like poisoned fire; and plants and animals are burnt up from intense heat, and there are no inhabitants there. And on the side of the West the ocean hinders travelling, from the dashing of the waves and the thick darkness. And in the neighbourhood of the East travelling is impossible, from high mountains. And when I have pondered on this subject I have found that men were shut up in the seven climates as in a fortification, and they know nothing of the rest of the world. Let us ask the Most High God that He will give us protection and confirmation, and that He will enable us to travel in the right path : for He is liberal and merciful."

In the serious way in which he describes certain fabulous animals Qazwini resembles the credulous but honest Herodotus. The following is his description of the Anka or Simorg, the Eastern analogue, if not the prototype, of the phoenix of the West :

"The Anka is called in Persian the Simorg, and it is the greatest of birds. They say it carries away buffaloes and elephants as a crow would carry away a mouse. In former days it lived among men, but as its perfidies were many, men prayed to be delivered from it. At length, on a certain occasion, it carried away "a bride treacherously, and Handalah the prophet prayed against it and it disappeared from mankind. They say that the Creator took away the Anka from amongst men to a certain island under the equinoctial line where men do not come ; and in that island are many animals, as elephants, and buffaloes, and rhinoceroses, and leopards, and lions, and birds of prey. The Anka does not prey on these, for they are subject to him and under his dominion, but he preys on huge fishes. He eats of these as much as he wants, and leaves the rest for the ravening beasts and cattle and birds who are under his dominion, and he sits on high and amuses himself with watching their feeding. And when he flies away there is a rushing sound like the blowing of a stormy wind, so that trees fall down with a heavy crash. They say that if anyone loses his way in the sea, the Anka will set him in the right way again. A certain merchant relates : `We were lost in the sea, when suddenly we saw a huge black figure like a cloud. The sailors said, " It is the Simorg," and they strove with all their might to get under that dark object, and prayed to it ; and the Simorg came, and we sailed under its shadow till we found the right way again.' They say that the Anka lives to the age of one thousand five hundred years ; and when it has come to the age of five hundred years it begins to sing ; and when the time for the female to lay its egg is come, the male Anka comes with his beak full of sea-water, and sprinkles her till the egg is laid ; and when it is laid, he sits upon it, while the female goes out for food. In one hundred and twenty-five years the young bird is hatched; and when it is grown up, if it be a female, the female Anka gathers much wood, and the male and female rub their bills together, from which comes a great fire and falls among the wood ; into this the female goes and is burnt, and the young one becomes the mate of the male bird. And if the young is a male, the male Anka goes into the fire, and the young one becomes the mate of the female. Many other things are related of the Anka, but as they rest on no good authority, I have not thought it well to insert them here."

16

MORAL PHILOSOPHY AND THEOLOGY

THIS is not the place for a systematic account of Persian philosophy, of which something has been said in the chapter on Sufism. Here we can only briefly touch on some of the outstanding figures among the philosophers and theologians. Among the earliest of these was Avicenna (whose poetry has already been mentioned), born A.D. 980, at Afshena, a village of Bokhara. By the time he had attained his tenth year he had learned the Koran by heart. After this he was placed under the tuition of a herbalist, who was skilled in the Indian method of keeping accounts, to learn the science of arithmetic. He then entered upon the rudiments of logic, and the first five or six propositions of Euclid were explained to him by a private tutor. He went through the rest of Euclid by himself, consulting the commentaries. He next took up the study of medicine, and, to gain experience, visited patients, being then about sixteen. The following year and a half he employed in reading with incredible industry, and when any difficulty occurred he had recourse to prayer. "Whenever I was puzzled," he says, "about any question, or could not find the middle term in a syllogism, I went to the mosque and humbly poured out my prayers to the Creator of all things, that He would be pleased to make plain to me what appeared abstruse and difficult. Returning home at night, I set a lamp before me, and applied myself to reading and writing. As often as I was overcome by sleep, or found myself faint, I drank a glass of wine to recover strength, and then returned to reading again. If I slept ever so little, I dreamt of those very questions, so that the reasons of many of them were made known to me in my sleep."

Having attained to a thorough knowledge of logic, natural philosophy, and mathematics, he proceeded to theology, and as a proper preparation for this study he wished to master Aristotle's " Metaphysics." But having read the book over forty times, and even got it by heart, without being able to comprehend the author's meaning, he laid it by as unintelligible. One day, however, on a bookstall, he came across Al Farabi's Commentary, which threw light on it. Avicenna was so overjoyed at the discovery that he gave a large sum in alms to the poor. The King of Khorassan, who, having been ill, had sent for Avicenna and been cured by him, kept him near his person and allowed him free access to his large and valuable library. This was soon afterwards burnt, and Avicenna's enemies accused him of having set it on fire, that nobody else might enjoy the same advantage as himself, and that what he had learned there might be taken for his own. When he was twenty-two years old, Avicenna lost his father, whom he succeeded for a short time in the office of Vizier to the Sultan of Bokhara ; but after the downfall of the Samanide dynasty, which happened about the beginning of the eleventh century, he quitted Bokhara. He was for a time attached as physician to the Court of Shams-al-Maali Kabus ben Washmgir, himself a poet, as has been already mentioned. Sultan Mahmud of Ghazni, having heard of Avicenna's fame, sent for him to adorn his Court, but Avicenna, fearing Mahmud's orthodoxy, fled and concealed himself. Mahmud sent descriptions and portraits of him in many directions, but without success.

When Shams-al-Maali was dethroned, about A.D. 1012, Avicenna retired to Jurjan, on the Caspian, where he began to write his celebrated treatise on medicine, known under the name of the "Canon." After various wanderings he became physician to Ala-ed-Dawlah, the Sovereign of Ispahan, and accompanied him on a journey to Hamadan. His health had been previously weakened by too much indulgence in wine and women, and an attack of colic proved fatal shortly after his arrival at Hamadan, A.D. 1037.

In his philosophic writings Avicenna developed the theory of the soul with great care. He distinguishes three species of souls-the vegetative, animal, and human soul. This last presupposes the two former, just as the animal soul presupposes the vegetative soul. The soul is not contained in any special part of the body, nor diffused like a force throughout the whole body ; it is united to it, and in this union one or the other may gain the ascendant. The soul is created for eternity; it is united to the body in order to develop into a spiritual and independent microcosm, in which the good, the true, and the beautiful combine with it in a single essence. During our life on earth we have only an obscure presentiment of this future state ; this presentiment produces in different dispositions a desire more or less intense, and it is precisely on this desire that the thoroughness of our preparation for that future state depends. This preparation is only accomplished by the development of the highest faculties of the soul. Thus prepared, the soul, as soon as it is delivered from the body, which has merely been its instrument, enters on the enjoyment of eternal beatitude by virtue of its now purely spiritual existence. Every soul, being eternal and imperishable, will finally attain the beatitude for which it is created. If it deserves punishment beyond the grave, this punishment will consist in the privation of, or temporary exclusion from, this beatitude.

Speaking generally, the philosophy of Avicenna may be regarded as a spiritual deism, which he seeks to reconcile as far as possible with Islam. This system contains elements derived both from Aristotle and Plato. Among Muhammadans the writings of Avicenna have generally been regarded as heretical ; many of them have been destroyed, and are only preserved in Hebrew translations.

Avicenna's great opponent was Al Ghazzali, surnamed Zainuddin (" Glory of Religion "), born A.D. 1058, at Tus in Khorassan, the birthplace of Firdausi and burial place of Haroun-al-Raschid. The surname of Ghazzali was given to him because his father dealt in , " ghazal," or spun, cotton. Left an orphan at an early age, by the advice of his guardian, a Sufi, he went to Jurjan, with the intention of devoting himself to study and science as a means of support, and became the favourite pupil of Abu Nasr Ismail, an eminent teacher of the time. He afterwards betook himself to Nishapur, where he attended the lectures of the learned Imam-ul-Haramain on law, philosophy, and theology, and remained there till the death of his instructor. The Grand Vizier of Bagdad, Nizam-ul-Mulk, then appointed him to a professorship at the Nizamiya University, which he left four years later, ostensibly in order to perform the pilgrimage to Mecca, but really to give himself to a life of meditation. He visited Jerusalem and Damascus, and remained at the latter place for ten years, leading a studious and ascetic life. He afterwards visited Cairo, Alexandria, and other places in Africa, even teaching and lecturing on religion and science, and returned for a short time to Nishapur ; but finally he went back to Tus, his native place, where he died A.D. 1111, after founding a monastery for Sufis. Of the ninety-nine works written by him (mostly in Arabic, a few in Persian), the most famous is the " Ihya-ul-ulum," (Revival of Religious Sciences), a work so remarkable and exhaustive that it has been said, " If all the books of Islam were lost, and we had only this one left, we should not miss the others." Of this work, which was in Arabic, Ghazzali wrote an epitome in Persian, which he named " The Alchemy of Happiness." The Muhammadan authorities of Spain, however, condemned it as heterodox, and had it publicly burned. It is said that Ghazzali, on hearing of the fate of his work, tore the book which he had in his hands, and, looking to heaven, exclaimed : " May God thus tear the kingdom from the impious All!" (The King of Cordova, who had ordered the destruction of his book.)

Next in importance stands his great work " Tahafat-al-Filasafah " (The Overthrow of the Philosophers), which has survived only in translations. But the most interesting of his works is the " Munqidh-min-ud-dallal " (The Deliverance from Error), in which he recounts his own spiritual experiences with a sincerity and earnestness equal to that of St. Augustine. In the following extract he describes the inner crisis which made him leave Bagdad and his professorship :

"Coming seriously to consider my state, I found myself bound down on all sides by these trammels. Examining my actions, the most fair-seeming of which were my lecturing and professorial occupations, I found to my surprise that I was engrossed in several studies of little value and profitless as regards my salvation. I probed the motives my teaching, and found that, in place of being sincerely consecrated to God, it was only actuated by a vain desire of honour and reputation. I perceived that I was on the edge of an abyss, and that without an immediate conversion I should be doomed to eternal fire. In these reflections I spent a long time. Still a prey to uncertainty, one day I decided to leave Bagdad and to give up everything ; the next day I gave up my resolution. I advanced one step and immediately relapsed. In the morning I was sincerely resolved only to occupy myself with the future life.; in the evening a crowd of carnal thoughts assailed and dispersed my resolutions. On the one side the world kept me bound to my post in the chains of covetousness, on the other side the voice of religion cried to me : ' Up! up! thy life is nearing its end, and thou hast a long journey to make. All thy pretended knowledge is nought but falsehood and vanity. If thou dost not think now of thy salvation, when wilt thou think of it? If thou dost not break thy chains to-day, when wilt thou break them?' Then my resolve was strengthened. I wished to give up all and fly ; but the tempter, returning to the attack, said : 'You are suffering from a transitory feeling ; don't give way to it, for it will soon pass. If you obey it, if you give up this fine position, this honourable post, exempt from trouble and rivalry, you will regret it later on without being able to recover it.'

"Thus I remained, torn asunder by the opposite forces of earthly passions and religious aspirations, for about six months from the month Rajab of the year A.D. 1096. At the close of them my will yielded, and I gave myself up to destiny. God caused an impediment to chain my tongue, and prevented me from lecturing. Vainly I desired, in the interest of my pupils, to go on with my teaching, but my mouth became dumb. The silence to which I was condemned cast me into a violent despair. My stomach became weak; I lost all appetite; I could neither swallow a morsel of bread nor drink a drop of water."

The moral realism of Ghazzali, as shown in the above extract, partly explains the reason why his influence has been much more deep and permanent in Islam than that of merely intellectual philosophers, such as Averroes. Ghazzali's influence gave a decided check to scholastic philosophy in the East, but it encouraged moral philosophy. Several ethical treatises were composed which derived much from him. The most important of these is the "Akhlaq-i-Jalali," by Jalaluddin Asaad Aldawani, which has been ably translated into English by Mr. W. F. Thompson. The "Akhlaq-i-Jalali " itself is partly a translation into Persian from the Arabic, the original of which appeared in the tenth century under the name of " Kitab-ut-Taharat." Two centuries after it was translated into Persian by Abu Nasr, and named "Akhlaq Nasiri," enriched with some important additions from Avicenna. In the fifteenth century it assumed a still further improved form under its present name, the "Akhlaq-i-Jalali." The following are extracts from the work :

Cure for the Fear of Death.

"We are to know that death is not the cessation of human being ; for the reasonable soul is the most tenacious of our endowments, being a ray from the glory of Omnipotence, over whose unbounded permanence extinction cannot pass, and whose essential substance has no connection with the events of space.

He cannot die who lives by love divine ;

His name is in the book that lives for ever.'

"This has been established as a fundamental principle of science by many convincing proofs, of which the following is one : Let a man suppose that one of his members-a finger, for instance—is destroyed : his identity is thereby unaffected. Next, let him in imagination withdraw some other member, and so on, till he has successively supposed every limb wanting ; and he will find his essence to survive through every stage intact."

The Management of a Wife.

"Three things are to be avoided in the management of a wife. The first is excess of affection, for this is gives her the predominance and leads to confusion. When the chief power is overpowered, and the commander commanded, all regularity must infallibly be destroyed. If troubled with excess of affection, let her husband at least conceal it from her. Secondly, let him not consult her on matters of paramount importance ; let him not make her acquainted with his secrets, nor let her know the amount of his property or the stores he possesses, or her weakness of judgment will infallibly cause calamity.

* "Confessions of Ghazzali" ("Wisdom of the East" Series).

" We are told in history that Hajaj, Governor of Iraq, had a chamberlain with whom he was on very familiar terms. In the course of conversation he happened one day to remark that no secrets should be communicated to a woman. The chamberlain observed that he had a very prudent and affectionate wife, in whom he placed the utmost confidence, because by repeated experiment he had tested her conduct, and now considered her the treasurer of all his fortunes.

"'The thing is repugnant to reason,' said Hajaj, (and I will show you that it is) On this he bade them bring him a thousand dinars in a bag, which he sealed up with his own signet, and delivered to the chamberlain, telling him the money was his, but that he was to keep it under lock and key, take it home, and tell his wife he had stolen it for her from the royal treasury. Soon afterwards Hajaj made him a further present of a handmaiden, whom he likewise brought home with him.

"'Pray oblige me,' said his wife, 'by selling this handmaiden.' The chamberlain asked how it was possible for him to sell what the Governor had given. At this his wife grew angry, and coming in the middle of the night to the door of the palace where Hajaj resided, desired that he might be informed that the wife of his chamberlain requested an audience. On obtaining access to the Governor, she represented that, long as her husband had been attached to his household, he had yet been perfidious enough to steal from his master, an offence which her own sense of gratitude would not allow her to conceal. With this she produced the money-bag, saying it was the same her husband had stolen, and there was the Governor's seal to prove it. The chamberlain was summoned, and soon made his appearance.

" 'This prudent, affectionate wife of yours,' said Hajaj, ' has brought me your hidden deposit ; and were I not privy to the fact your head would fly from your shoulders, for the boys to play with and the horses to trample under foot.'

" Thirdly, let the husband allow his wife no musical instruments, no visiting out of doors, nor listening to men's stories, nor any intercourse with women noted for such practices, especially where any previous suspicion has been raised. We have it among the Prophet's dicta that women should be forbidden to read or to listen to the history of Joseph, lest it lead to their swerving from the rule of chastity."

One of the most striking philosophico-religious works in later Persian is the "Dabistan," or History of Religious Sects, by Muhsin Fani. Sir William Jones, who first drew the attention of Orientalists to this work, pronounced it the "most amusing and instructive book " he had read in Persian.

In 1843 the whole work was translated into English by Messrs. Shea and Troyer. In summing up the general merits of the " Dabistan," Mr. Troyer remarks:

" The 'Dabistan' adds, if I am not mistaken, not only a few ideas to our historical knowledge, but also some features to the picture which we hitherto possessed of the Asiatics. May I be permitted to quote a remarkable instance relative to the latter ? We are wont to speak of the inherent apathy and stationary condition of the Muhammadans as an effect of their legislation. Although this general idea of their character and state be not unfounded, yet it is carried to such an exaggerated degree that we think them incapable of progress. We may therefore be astonished to find in the work before us a maxim such as this, ' He who does not proceed, retrogrades,' and a declaration attributed to Muhammad himself, 'He, whose days are alike, is deceived.'

Our author, it is true, interprets it from the particular point of view of an orthodox, Sufi, who thinks that there is a degree of mental perfection beyond which it is impossible to rise. This was, he says the state of Muhammad the Prophet, always the same, from which no ascent or descent was possible ; the perfection of unity with God, higher than whom nothing can be: 'the blackness beyond which no colour can go.' "

The work is divided into twelve chapters, including numerous sections, and professes to treat generally of the religious systems of the Persians, Hindus, Jews, Christians, and Muhammadans, as well as particularly of the various sects and divisions comprehended in each system. The account which Muhsin Fani gives of Christianity (a knowledge of which he appears to have derived from a Portuguese priest, whom he met at Surat) may be taken as an evidence of the general correctness of his statements, and of the impartial love of truth which actuated him. He tells us that some of the Christians declare that—

" When we say that Jesus is seated at the right hand of God His Father, we mean not to say that God has a body and is anything corporal. No! the Divine Being has neither right nor left side. By such a description we intend to be intelligible to the vulgar ; for Jesus, in the abstract sense of being the Son of God, possesses the same greatness and power which His Father has ; and in the "abstract sense of His being a man, he dwells in the most glorious and most excellent place, which is in heaven."

They declare further :

"When we say that Jesus shall come on the last day of the world to judge the dead and the living, and to give their due to all men, we mean not to imply that all men will be then alive ; but by the living we denote the good men, and by the dead the wicked."

The theological discussions held at the Court of Akbar, and the attempts of that Emperor to introduce a new eclectic religion, are given at considerable length in the " Dabistan," which also contains an interesting account of Nanak, the founder of the Sikh religion. In the keen interest which he took in the religions of India, Muhsin Fani resembles Al Biruni, who wrote on India in the reign of Mahmud of Ghazni. The latter, however, though a Persian, wrote in Arabic, and his work belongs to Arabic rather than to Persian literature.

The following are specimens of the work :

1. *Zoroastrian View of the Origin of Evil.*

" It is well known that, according to their (the Zoroastrian) system, the world had two creators-Yazdan (the Lord) and Ahriman ; but the Lord having entertained this evil thought, `Perhaps a antagonist may rise up to oppose Me,' Ahriman was produced from that thought. In some places it is mentioned that Yazdan was alone, and gloom having come over Him, He entertained an evil suspicion, on which Ahriman was produced. They say that Ahriman, who was outside the world, on looking through a small aperture and beholding the Lord surrounded with glory and majesty, bore Him envy, and raised up wickedness and corruption. God then created the angels to be His host, and with them fought against Ahriman ; but as He was unable to destroy him, they made peace with each other on this condition: that Ahriman should remain in the world during a definite period, and that on his departure it should become the abode of unalloyed good."

2. *Tenets of the Sipasis.*

"The insurmountable barrier in the road of approaching God is the slaughter of the Zindibar—that is, those animals which inflict no injury on any person, and slay not other living creatures such as the cow, the sheep, the camel, and the horse. There is assuredly no salvation to the author of cruelty towards such, nor can he obtain final deliverance by austerities or devotions of any description. Should we even behold many miraculous works performed by the slayer of harmless animals, we are not even then to regard him as one redeemed ; the works witnessed in him are only the reward of his devotions, and the result of his perseverance in the practice of religious austerities in the world ; and, as he commits evil, he cannot be perfect in his devout exercises, so that nothing but suffering in another generation can await him when born again. Such an instance of an ascetic endued with miraculous powers is likened in the Shat Dasatir to a vase externally covered with choice perfumes, but filled internally with impurities. They also maintain that in no system of faith is cruelty to innoxious animals sanctioned ; and all human sanction for such acts proceeds from their attending to the apparent import of words without having recourse to profound or earnest consideration. For example, by putting a horse or cow to death is meant the removal or banishing from oneself of animal propensities, and not the slaughtering or devouring, of innoxious creatures. They state that the later historians recorded, without due discrimination, that Rustan used to slay such animals, whereas tradition informs us that the mighty champion pursued in the chase noxious animals only. What they write about his hunting the wild ass implies that the elephant-bodied hero called the lion a wild ass ; or said that ' a lion is no more than a wild ass when compared to my force.'

" In the several passages where he is recorded to have slaughtered harmless wild asses, etc., there is only implied the banishment of animal propensities and passions, as Fariduddin Attar declares:

" 'In the heart of each are found a hundred swine ;

You must slay the hog or bind on the zunar.' "*

The accession of Shah Ismail, the founder of the Safavi dynasty, to the throne of Persia in 1499 gave a powerful impulse to philosophic speculation.

Shah Ismail himself, who came of a Sufi family, held pantheistic views, and for some time seems to have meditated the abrogation of Islam as the State religion altogether. The dangers of such a step, however, appeared too great, and he finally abandoned his purpose. But towards the close of the seventeenth century the philosophic ideas of Avicenna, which had long fallen into neglect, were revived by a; celebrated philosopher named Mullah Sadra. He had, as a young man, renounced the world in order to devote himself entirely to study, and travelled from one place to another as a " talib-i-ilm " (seeker of wisdom), attending the lectures of several teachers. After a time he began to lecture himself, and as he was unrivalled in eloquence of expression and facility of exposition, he attracted large audiences, from among whom several persons became his ardent disciples.

---

* The girdle worn by non-Moslems.

But Mullah Sadra himself was afraid of the orthodox Shiah theologians, always so quick to scent a fresh heresy. Fearing to become an object of persecution, and to miscarry in the revival of philosophy which he designed, he had recourse to the policy of concealment of his real views, technically known among Muhammadan theologians as " ketman." Whenever he arrived in a town he took care to present himself before the leading Mullahs in the aspect of a humble learner. He took the lowest place among their hearers, and rarely opened his lips except to applaud what they said. When questioned regarding his beliefs, he replied in terms consonant with the strictest Shiah theology, and carefully concealed his addiction to philosophy. After some time, seeing him so docile, the Mullahs themselves engaged him to deliver public lectures. Commencing very cautiously with disquisitions on the ordinary rites of Islam—prayers, fasting, ablutions, etc. —he gradually insinuated into his discourses, which were for the most part couched in orthodox language, new philosophic ideas. These worked silently like leaven, till nearly the whole of the lettered classes were permeated by a teaching which strongly resembled that of the early heretic Avicenna.

He was equally cautious in committing his real ideas to writing, so that students of his works, who wish to arrive at what he really taught, must study the oral traditions which have been handed down by a long line of his disciples. These, from, generation to generation, have been the heirs of his thoughts, and possess the only key to his enigmatic expressions. He is not a great original thinker, but a restorer of ideas derived, for the most part, from ancient Iranic systems ; and since his time orthodox theology has been held in check by philosophic speculation. Among the numerous disciples who transmitted the teachings of Mullah Sadra, the most distinguished was Haji Mullah Hadi, of Sabzawar, who composed several commentaries on his master's works. So great was his reputation that students used to flock to Sabzawar from India, Turkey, and Arabia to hear his lectures. He lived a strictly ascetic life, and was distinguished for his charity to the poor.

Another of the later Persian philosophers was Kamran the Aristotelian, of Shiraz, of whom Muhsin Fani gives the following account:

"After having acquired learning, he happened to find himself at the mountain which is near the seaports of the Firangis (Europeans). He took a great liking to their society, and was attracted by the religion of the Nasara (Christians) ; on that account he studied the Gospels and derived great profit from their doctrines. Afterwards he went to India, where he contracted friendship with some Rajahs. He became fond of their religion ; read with learned Brahmins the Shastras of the Hindus-that is, their scientific books-and in these also he became a master of art among the learned of India. He showed great aversion to lying, thieving, and debauchery, and, according to the custom of the wise, forbore from killing animals ; but now and then he indulged in a draught of wine, saying that it is very salutary. He was wont to sing hymns which are in use among the philosophers, in praise of God, the high intelligences and spirits, and the stars. He accepted no gift from anybody ; he was employed in trade, but he contented himself with a competence. In the year of the Hijra 1050 (A.D. 1640) he retired to-solitude at the Serai Fargh ('The Fortunate Palace'), near the town of Akbarabad. He delivered garments into the care of a man, with orders to distribute them among the poor upon the road of Kashmir and Kabul, where the cold is severe. He there caused to be collected forage and provisions, which were given to cows and asses, to travellers and the indigent. He also handed over scientific books to a friend named Hushyar, that he might give them to doctors devoted to science; and Hushyar thus disposed in Agra of the works which he had received, and sent them to his friends.

" During his last illness he was constantly engaged in reading the `Alhiyat Shifa' (Hymns of Recovery), and in translating the ` Asulujia Theologia.' He said : ' I believe in the divinity of the Most High Creator, the prophecy of intelligence, the Imamat (leadership) of the spirit, the heaven as a Qiblah* and the liberation of philosophy, and I detest the free-thinkers.' At the moment of death he pronounced the name of the self-existent Being, of -the intelligence and spirit, and of the' stars, and the bystanders also joined him in chorus, until he had cast aside his mortal garment. His life exceeded one hundred years, and he had preserved his strength and his faculties entire. He gave directions to Hushyar that after his death his body should be burnt ; but if the people prevented it, Hushyar should bury him with his face to the west, as all distinguished persons, such as Aristotle and his followers, repose in the same way. Hushyar carried out his wishes, and also, according to his direction, burnt at the head of his tomb during a whole week, every day and every night, a lamp to the honour of the star which at that time ruled over him, and distributed the food and raiment which are appropriate to that star among the Brahmins: After Kamran's death Hushyar saw him in a dream clothed in a fine garment and sitting by the side of the Lord Mushtari (the star Jupiter). Hushyar asked him : 'How camest thou to this place ?'

"He answered : 'The pure spirits, when they saw me free from worldly desires, drew me to them, and by the aid of their intercession I was made one of the angels.' "

---

* The point towards which Muhammadans pray.

17

BABISM AND BEHAISM

EVEN a brief sketch of Persian literature requires some notice to be taken of the two movements, Babism and Behaism, which have so profoundly affected modern Persian thought. All Muhammad the Bab, or " Gate," stands in the succession of the great heresiarchs of Islam, such as Mokanna, the Veiled Prophet, and Hassan Sabah, the founder of the Assassins. He was born at Shiraz, the native city of Hafiz and Sa'di, in a family belonging to a modest rank of life, his father being a cotton-merchant. His education was that of an ordinary Muhammadan boy, reading the Koran, writing, and arithmetic. He distinguished himself at an early age by a strong inclination to solitude ; he had a melancholy air, but was always ready to engage in conversation with strangers, especially travellers. At the age of scarcely fifteen he had been sent by his father to the port of Bushire in Southern Persia to learn commerce. There he seems to have come in contact with Sufis, whose mystical doctrines, especially their allegorical interpretation of the Koran, had a charm for his meditative nature. In common with other pious Shiahs, he made the pilgrimage to Kerbela and the tomb of the Imam Husain, held by the Persian in equal veneration with that of the Prophet himself. On his return from the pilgrimage he composed a commentary on the chapter of the Koran entitled " Joseph," which already showed his mystical tendencies. When he came back to Shiraz he gave himself up to preaching in the mosque and in the bazaar. Gifted with natural eloquence, he attracted the common people, while his dialectic powers enabled him to refute those who ventured to dispute with him. In a short time he became celebrated. Not long afterwards he assumed the title by which he was always subsequently known-that of the " Bab," or "Gate." In the language of the Persian mystics this phrase generally signified the means by which one enters into the knowledge of the true God, a very different Being, it may be remarked, to the God of orthodox Islam. The term had already been used by an heretical sect in Syria called the Nusairiyeh, and applied by them to those who expounded the mysteries of Deity.

About this time All Muhammad undertook the pilgrimage to Mecca, leaving behind as his representative at Shiraz a certain Mullah, Husain of Bushrawayh, who thenceforward played an important part in propagating the new doctrines. The disciples

Cf. for this chapter, Professor E. G. Browne, "The Episode of the Bab."

of the Bab increased in numbers daily, till the attentionof the political authorities was attracted to the matter. On his return from his pilgrimage, Ali Muhammad was arrested, confined to his house, and kept under strict surveillance. In the midst of the increasing excitement of which his new religion was the centre, he adopted a new title, that of the " Point" (Nuqta), or pivot of the world, which was in the eyes of Persians tantamount to claiming to be an incarnation of the Divine. His partisans thenceforward addressed him as " Hazrat Ala," or " Lofty Highness." The title " Bab " was relinquished to his representative, Mullah Husain.

Notwithstanding the close watch which was kept upon him at Shiraz, Ali Muhammad managed to escape and fly to Ispahan, where he put himself under the protection of Manuchihr Khan, the Governor. The latter had him placed in the house of the Imam of the principal mosque, whom he ordered to examine him tactfully regarding his new religion. Ali Muhammad's replies, however, were so adroit as to baffle all attempts to prove him a heretic. On the death of Manuchihr in 1847 the Government removed Ali Muhammad to Tabriz, in the province of Azerbijan. This was an ill-advised step on their part, as the reformer had numerous adherents in that province, and the population was friendly to him. One of the most remarkable of his new disciples was a woman named Qurrat-ul-Ayn, who was learned in Arabic, the science of the traditions, and the exegesis of the Koran: Besides her learning, she was endowed with brilliant eloquence and all the courage of an enthusiastic convert. She actually ventured to appear and speak in public without a veil, greatly to the horror of orthodox Muhammadans. Many fresh disciples were made by her preaching, and her bitterest enemies could find no fault with her moral character.

Meanwhile the Government had determined to put Ali Muhammad on his trial for heresy and teaching contrary to the Koran, a charge which, if established, would involve his destruction. In the year 1848 the Nasiruddin, the Governor of Azerbijan, convened a meeting of Mullahs and theologians to consider the matter. They pronounced a " fatwa " (decree) condemning the doctrines of Ali Muhammad, but did not venture to sentence him to death. He was relegated to close confinement at Maku, not far from the Russian frontier.

During the same year the reigning Sovereign, Muhammad Shah, died, and was succeeded by the above-mentioned Nasiruddin. The new Prime Minister, Mirza Taqi Khan, took energetic measures against the Babis, who had raised a revolt in Mazenderan, which was followed by several massacres. The Government resolved to get rid of Ali Muhammad, and had him brought to Tabriz in company with two of his disciples, one of whom, Syud Husain, was celebrated for his learning. After a protracted trial all three were sentenced to be shot, but by an extraordinary chance the bullets merely severed the cords by which Ali Muhammad was bound to a pillar, leaving him unhurt. Intense excitement ensued at the supposed miracle, but the soldiers kept cool, showing the crowd the cords which had been severed by the bullets. Ali Muhammad was seized, and this time the fusillade was successful.

After the death of their leader numerous risings took place among the Babis, which were suppressed by cruel massacres. In August, 18 52, an attempt was made on the life of the Shah Nasiruddin by three Babis, which was the signal for a general persecution. Seventy of them discovered at Teheran were put to death, among whom was the heroic Qurrat-ul-Ayn. The persecution extended throughout the whole empire. Those who were not arrested fled to foreign countries, many of them to Turkey.

As regards the religious teaching of Muhammad Ali, it differed at first very little from that of orthodox Islam. It seems to have resembled the doctrine of the Mutazilites,* who maintained that the ascription of attributes to God was unlawful and tended to polytheism. Besides this, the Babis held that no created thing was unclean in itself, and thus ignored the scruples of the Muhammadan's regarding swine's flesh, etc. The Bab himself, however, was strictly temperate, and eschewed the use of opium, tobacco, and coffee. He wished to accord women greater freedom than they usually possess in Muhammadan countries, and to put an end to arbitrary divorce.

The theological system of the Babis resembles that of the ancient Gnostics, such as Valentinus. According to them, God has created the world by means of seven words-Force, Power, Will, Action, Condescension, Glory, and Revelation -which words embrace the active plenitude of the virtues which they respectively represent. The Babist doctrine of revelation does not claim that the Bab has revealed the complete truth, but only, as his predecessors, the prophets before him, have done, that portion of truth necessary for the age.

The Babis declared their leader superior to Muhammad, as Muhammad was to Jesus. Nineteen is regarded by the Babis as a sacred number. All the prophets who have appeared are, like the world, manifestations of God; not God Himself, but emanations from Him. At the death of a prophet or saint his soul does not quit the earth, but joins itself to some soul still in the flesh, who then completes his work. Babism enjoins few prayers, and only upon fixed occasions ; and neither prescribes nor defends ablutions, which play so large a part in ordinary Muhammadanism.

In some of its aspects Babism seems to approximate to Christianity. In his "Book of Precepts" Ali Muhammad says: " Love your daughters, for they are more highly esteemed before God than your sons ; let there be no veil between husband and wife, even were it smaller than a leaf and finer than gossamer, in order that there may be no cause of affliction to the woman." These words show a delicacy of feeling rare among Orientals. As regards general kindness and humanity, he says : "It is forbidden to have recourse to blows , even when you are struck on the shoulder." Charity to the poor is inculcated, and gentleness of teachers towards their pupils is strictly enjoined. The Babis are also recommended to use chairs instead of sitting on the ground, and, what is a still more startling innovation, to shave. These prescriptions (the latter of which is extremely revolutionary, and was never before suggested by any Oriental lawgiver or prophet) were obviously designed to break up the routine of Eastern life by engrafting upon it European manners. Nevertheless, Ali Muhammad feared to open the gate too wide to foreign influences, as is seen in his strict prohibition of all books not in sympathy with, his sect, and in his disapproval of travelling in countries outside of Persia. He did not, however, regard his' own revelations as final, nor look upon his writings as ultimate, but foretold other prophets who would unfold still higher truths. Already in his lifetime Ali Muhammad had nominated as his successor an ardent young disciple named Mirza Yahya, who afterwards received the title Subh-i-Ezel (" Dawn of Eternity"). On the death of the Bab, Subh-i-Ezel continued to reside at Bagdad, where he was joined by his half-brother, Baha-ullah, who was

* *Cf.* Chapter II.

considerably senior to himself, and of a more ambitious character. Fearing disturbances from the proximity of the two brothers to Persian territory, the Persian authorities persuaded the Turkish Government to have them removed, first to Constantinople and then to Adrianople. Here the strife between the adherents of the two brothers became so bitter that both were banished—Mirza Yahya to Famagusta in Cyprus, and Baha-ullah to Acca in Syria. The followers of the latter generally call themselves Bahais, and show, as Professor Browne informs us, a tendency to ignore the Bab and his doctrines. Baha-ullah being of a more practical nature than Subh-i-Ezel, his party has grown considerably, while the adherents of the latter have dwindled to a mere fraction. Their doctrines have attracted attention in the West, especially in America, where several thousands have declared themselves Bahais. A few also exist in England.

In 1892 Baha-ullah died, and was succeeded by his son Abbas Effendi, though not without opposition from his younger brother, Muhammad Ali. Abbas Effendi is generally referred to by the Bahais as Abdul Baha (" The Servant of Baha "). The Bahais have been not inaptly termed " Persian Quakers," and Bahaism itself " Christianity and water." The following is an extract from a (message' from Abdul Baha) to his American disciples :

"O ye, the beloved of God and the children of God, the new heaven is already come, the new earth is already established, an the new Holy Jerusalem is already descended from Heaven, from the presence of the Almighty, in the form of a glorious virgin excellent in her beauty, an unequalled gem among the other virgins secluded in the tent. The angels of the Highest of the kingdom have called in the ears of the inhabitants of the earth and heaven with a loud and melodious voice, saying: 'This is the city of God, and His residence with the holy and sanctified souls of His servants. He shall live with them, for they are His people and He is their God.' He has wiped their tears, lighted their candles, given peace to their hearts, and widened their breasts ; therefore the roots of death were rooted out ; sorrow, wailing, and crying have ceased, and the lesser King of Majesty (Abbas Effendi) occupies the throne of the kingdom and renews the performance of untold actions. This is the absolute truth, and of a higher certainty than what was said in the Revelation by St. John: 'He is the Alpha and the Omega.' This is he who quenches the thirst from the spring of life. This is he who heals the sick with the antidote of safety, and confirms with a flood of grace from this kingdom. He is of the greatest heirs to the apostles and saints; the Lord is his God, and he is His dearest son.

" Good tidings to you, O beloved of God, His people, His children, and His party. Raise your voices in praising and glorifying the glorious Lord, for the lights have shone, the traces appeared, the seas moved, and gave out every precious gem."*

Bahaism, like many other mystical systems, is syncretic, and derives from many sources. Many of Beha's reported utterances seem to be mere echoes of the Gospels—*e.g.*, " Ye are the leaves of one tree, the fruit of one tree. Be ye kind to one another." ; and utterances of the early Muhammadan mystics are constantly recurring. "At every turn," says Professor Browne,** "we are face to face with some familiar echo of a past more or less remote-now of the Manichæans, now of the Ismaili propagandists,

* Dr. Isaac Adams, "Persia by a Persian," p. 477.

** Introduction to "Life and Teachings of Abbas Effendi," by M.H. Phelps, p. xvii.

now of the early Sufis. Here we are reminded of a line of Sadi, there of Jalaluddin Rumi, there of Farid-uddin-Attar, there of Shams-i-Tabriz, there of Hafiz." In the matter of beliefs the Bahais are tolerant to the verge of indifferentism, some holding the doctrine of individual immortality, and others that of absorption into God. For the personality of Abdul Beha it is impossible not to feel great respect.

Competent observers, such as Professor Browne and Mr. Myron Phelps, have described the magnetic power he exercises on those around him, and the earnestness with which the devotes himself to a life of self-denial, charity, and the promotion of peace. The spread of such a religion in materialistic America is certainly striking, and for those who cannot be content with old paths, it is probably preferable to the curde incoherences of Christain Science." At the same times, as a writer in the *Quarterly Review** has rightly observed, "In turning to the East, as though our vital problems might there find a solution, we shall be exchanging the philosophy of ripe age for the passions of youth and the enervating dreams of sensuous fancy.'

* January, 1892.